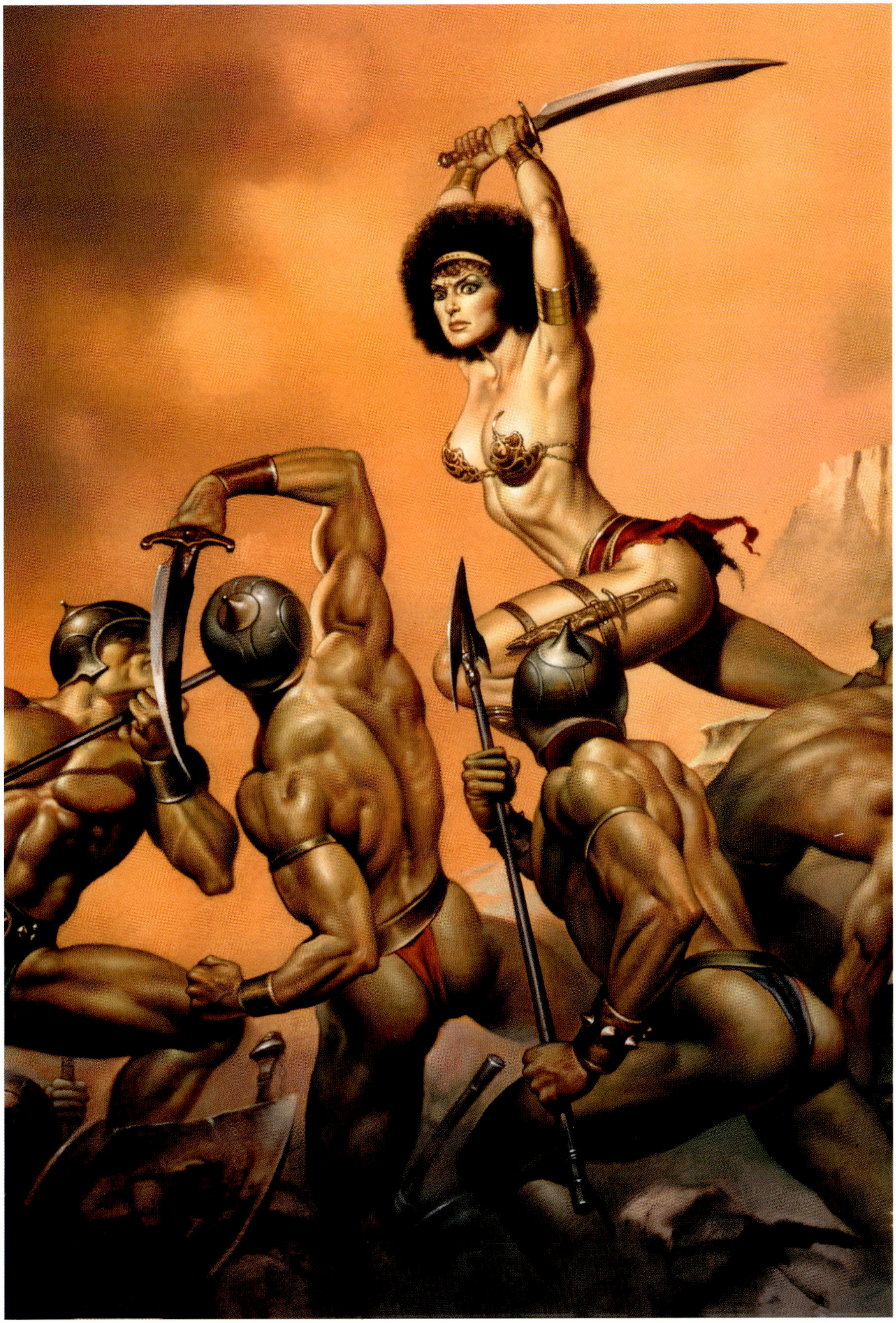

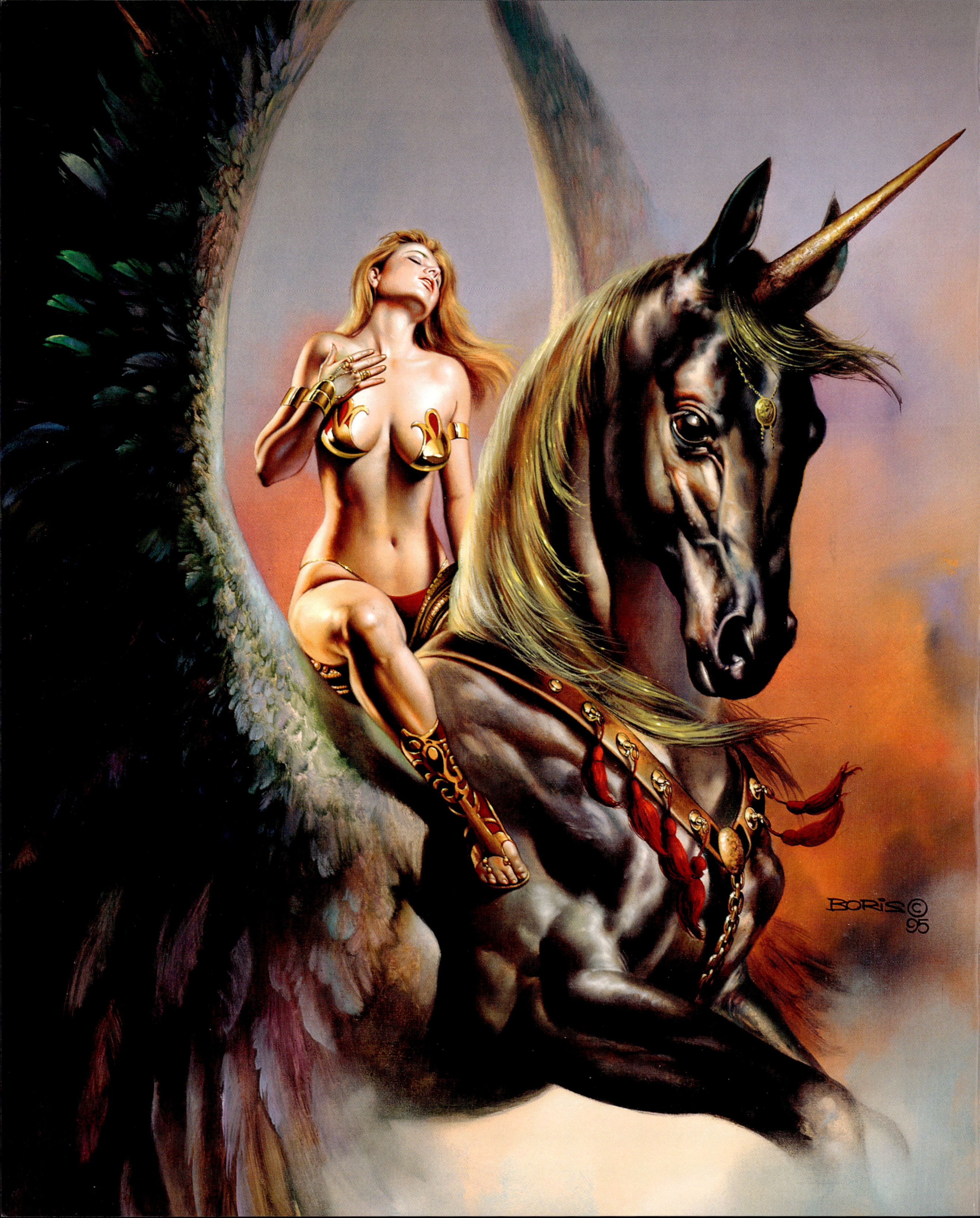
BORIS ©
95

FABULOUS FANTASY WOMEN

BORIS VALLEJO
JULIE BELL

TEXT BY ANTHONY AND DAVID PALUMBO

COLLINS & BROWN

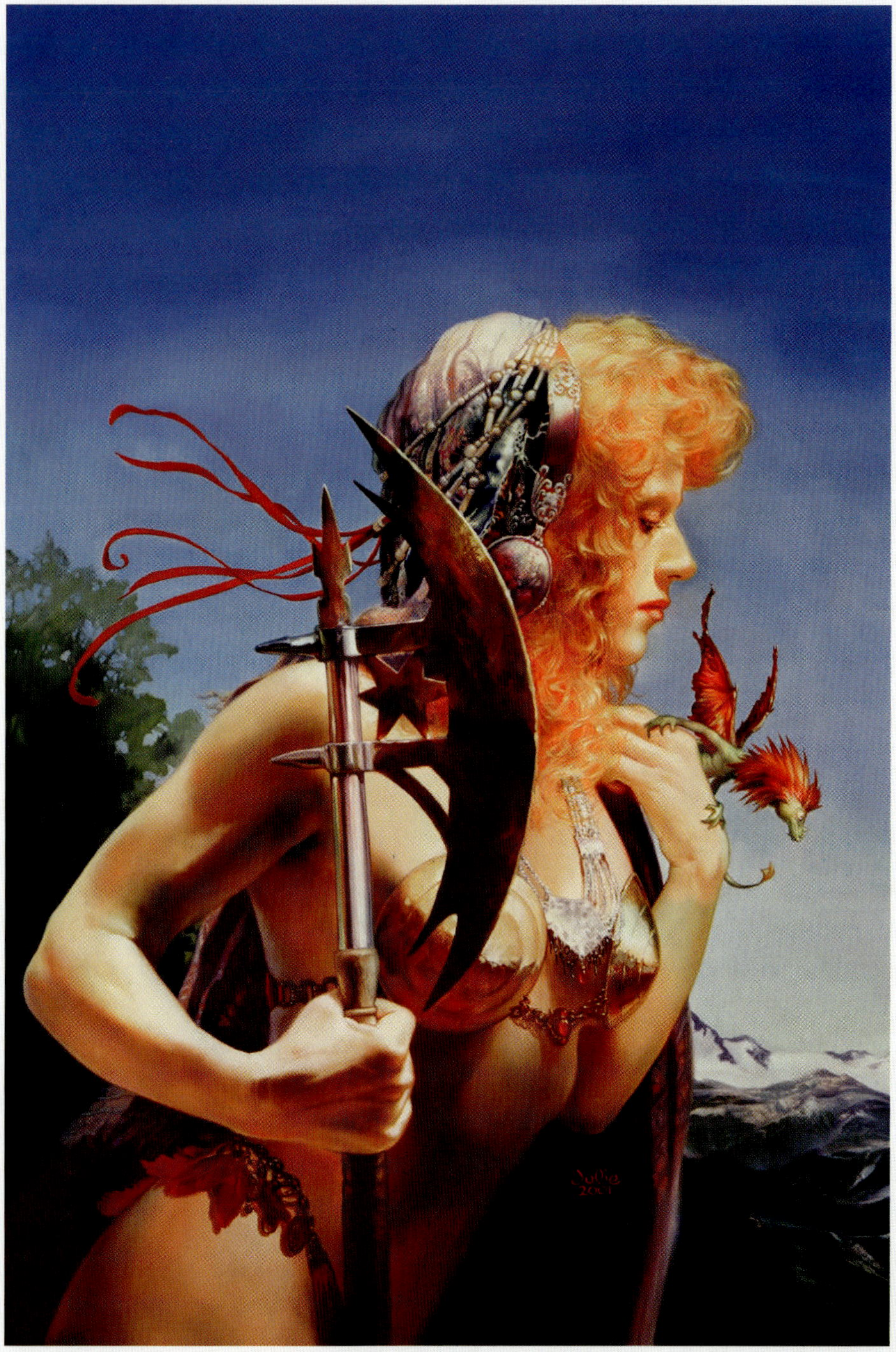

First published in the United Kingdom in 2006
by Collins & Brown
151 Freston Road
London
W10 6TH

An imprint of Anova Books Company Ltd

Commissioning Editor: Chris Stone
Design Manager: Gemma Wilson
Senior Production Controller: Morna McPherson
Designer: Philip Clucas MSIAD
Text: David and Anthony Palumbo

ISBN 1 84340 379 X

A CIP catalogue record for this book is available from the British Library.

10 9 8 7 6 5 4 3 2 1

Reproduction by Anorax, UK
Printed by Craftprint, Singapore

This book can be ordered direct from the publisher. Contact the marketing department, but try your bookshop first.

www.anovabooks.com

Page 1: **Lilith,** Boris Vallejo, *1988, calendar*

Page 2: **Black Unicorn,** Boris Vallejo, *1995, calendar*

Journey, Julie Bell, *2001, calendar*

Gryphon Keeper, Boris Vallejo, *1989, calendar*

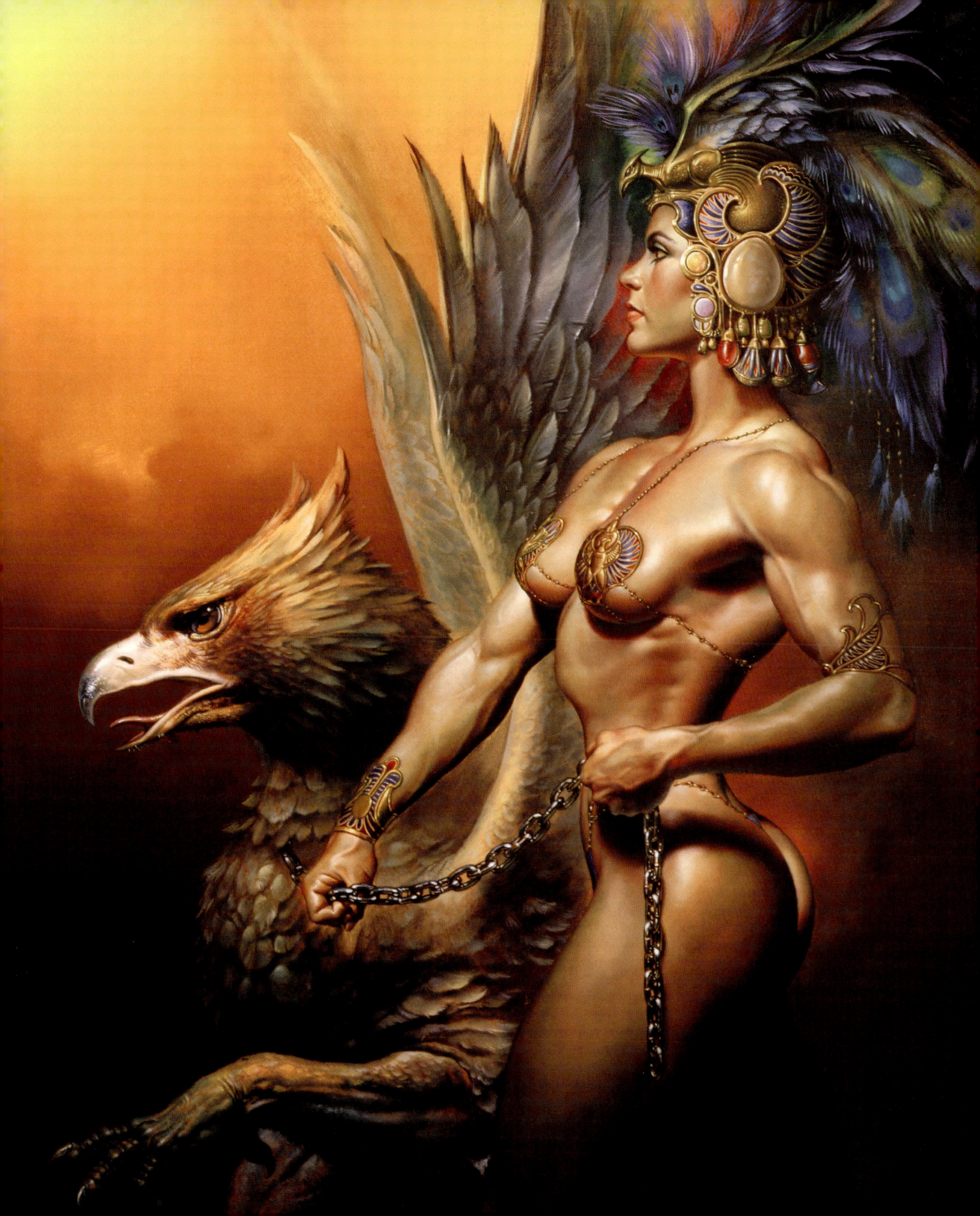

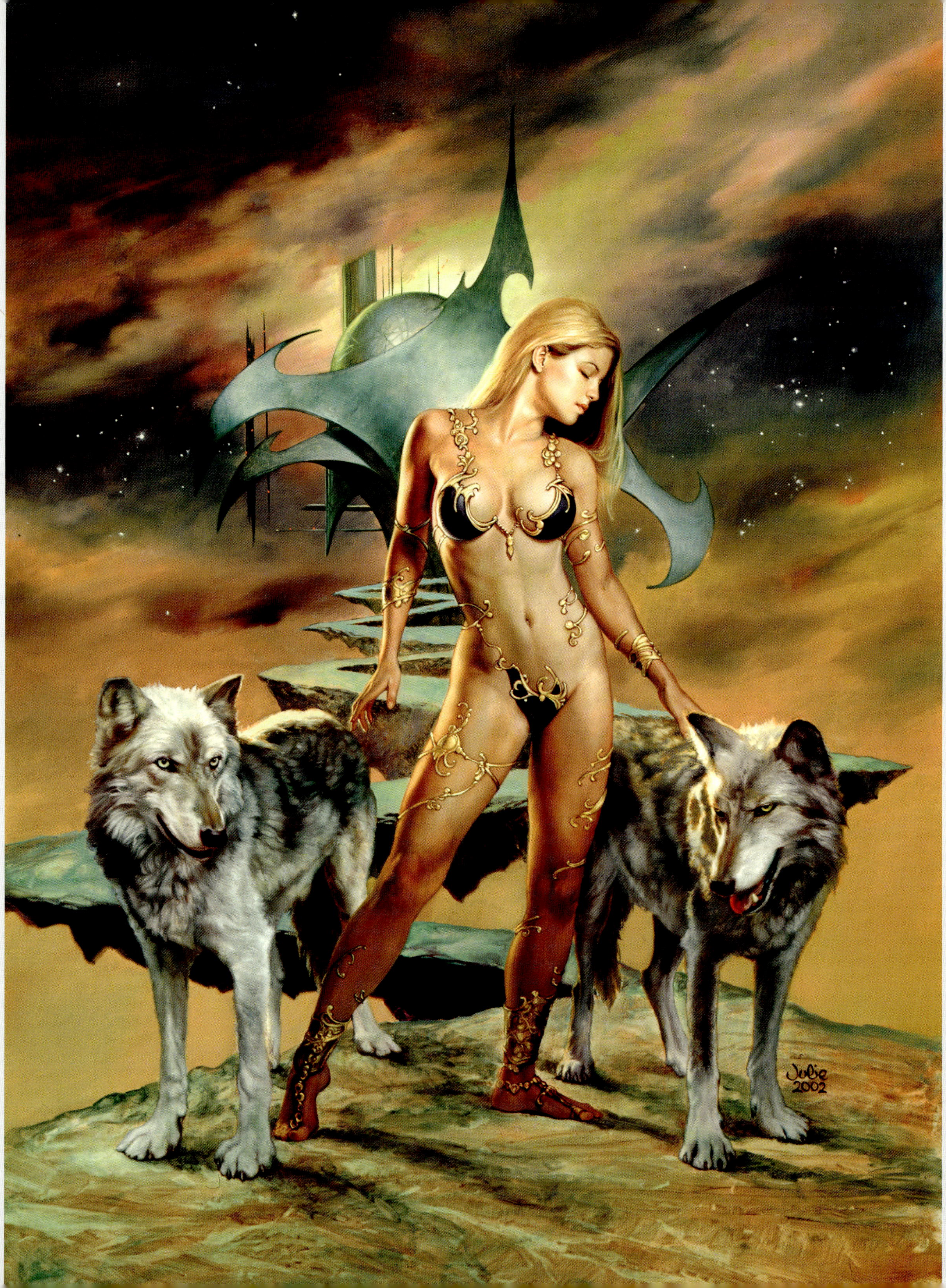
Julie
2002

INTRODUCTION

In 1989, our mom wanted us to meet a man named Boris. We were small-town kids aged seven and nine, and until then, totally unaware of Boris Vallejo and his art. This big man with a strange accent came to our door, and we dutifully stuck out our hands for a polite, manly shake, as our mother made us practice. Boris slapped us five. We were impressed. We'd never met anyone like Boris, and this grown-up who spent all day painting monsters, dragons, and mysterious women, this man with long silver hair who shared his Peruvian street-fighting tactics with us for dealing with school-yard bullies, well... he seemed like a pretty cool guy. Boris was our introduction to fantasy art. Before we knew it, we were family.

Julie had been drawing and painting for years, but had yet to fully develop her abilities as an artist. Boris shared his techniques and knowledge with her, for which she proved to be a shockingly quick study. It wasn't long before Julie was illustrating professionally, pupil keeping pace with the master. They set up a pair of easels next to one another in the family room, and painted side-by-side all day long, listening to classical music on the stereo and resting their brushes only for meals and daily excursions to the gym. Having suddenly found ourselves with professional fantasy artists for parents was a great thrill. We'd come home from school to discover that Mom was bringing our favourite superheroes to life more vividly than anyone ever had before, or that Boris was painting the artwork for a video-game that hadn't yet been released. Getting the red carpet treatment at science fiction conventions was also a nice treat for a couple of young, geeky boys. Receiving hordes of free comics, coming face to face with the likes of Darth Vader or The Misfits, watching our parents sign autographs, they were memorable experiences. All the while, they painted and painted. Boris helped Julie hone her skills, and she in turn made an unexpected, dramatic impact on his work. It is their meeting which marks a meaningful turning point for Boris. He found his feminine ideal in Julie, and from then on it was strong women who would be the star subjects of his paintings. They are the female embodiment of power and beauty, a vision to behold.

Today, more than fifteen years later, we find Boris and Julie still painting alongside one another. They are closer every day, and have recently begun collaborating on occasional projects: painting the elements separately and combining them digitally, or simply passing the board back and forth between their easels as they take turns with the figures. They go to the gym only three days a week now, and the stereo is as likely to be playing one of Julie's rock CDs as it is a selection from Boris' vast collection of classical music, but the art continues to be as enrapturing as ever. Monsters, dragons, and mysterious women. Power and beauty, a vision to behold.

Anthony and David Palumbo, June 2006

◂◂ **Alfa,** Julie Bell, *2002, calendar*

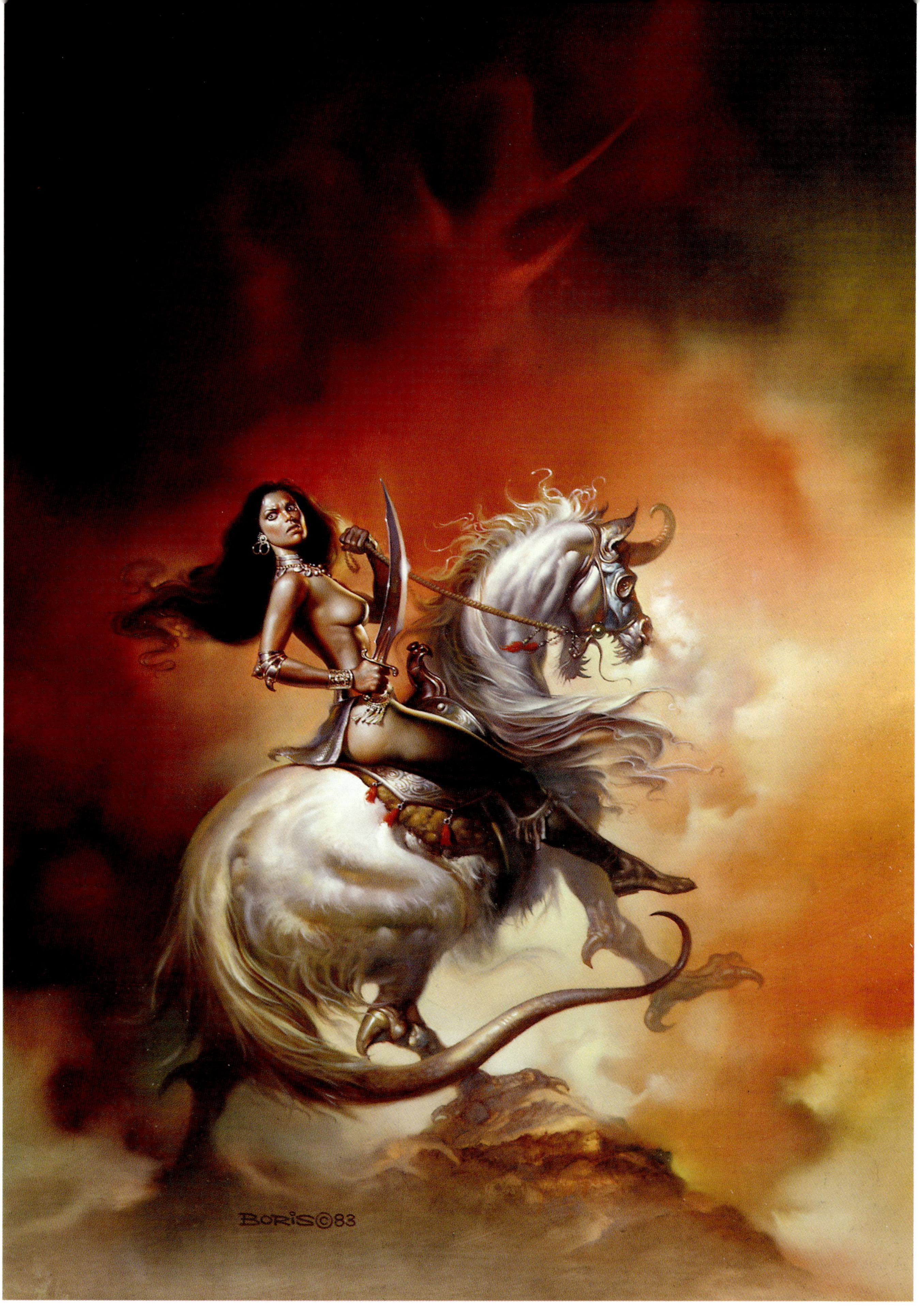
BORIS©83

Amazon Rider, Boris Valllejo, *1983, book cover*

Boris painted more than 400 book jackets over a period of 20 years. In this cover from the early Eighties, we see how Boris's vision of powerful females has evolved over time. Julie says, "She looks like she is powerful in temperament, but her body isn't as powerful as those of the women Boris paints now. That animal is insane, look at the feet!" Boris laughs, "It's a wild, crazy unicorn."

Russian Fairy, Julie Bell, *2002, calendar*

"There was a certain person who was questioning whether or not I was really doing my own work. This person was suggesting that Boris was hiding income by having me take credit for his paintings. When I did this for the calendar, I video taped myself doing every step of the painting and explaining what I was doing. I never had to show anyone the video though. I've never even watched it." – Julie

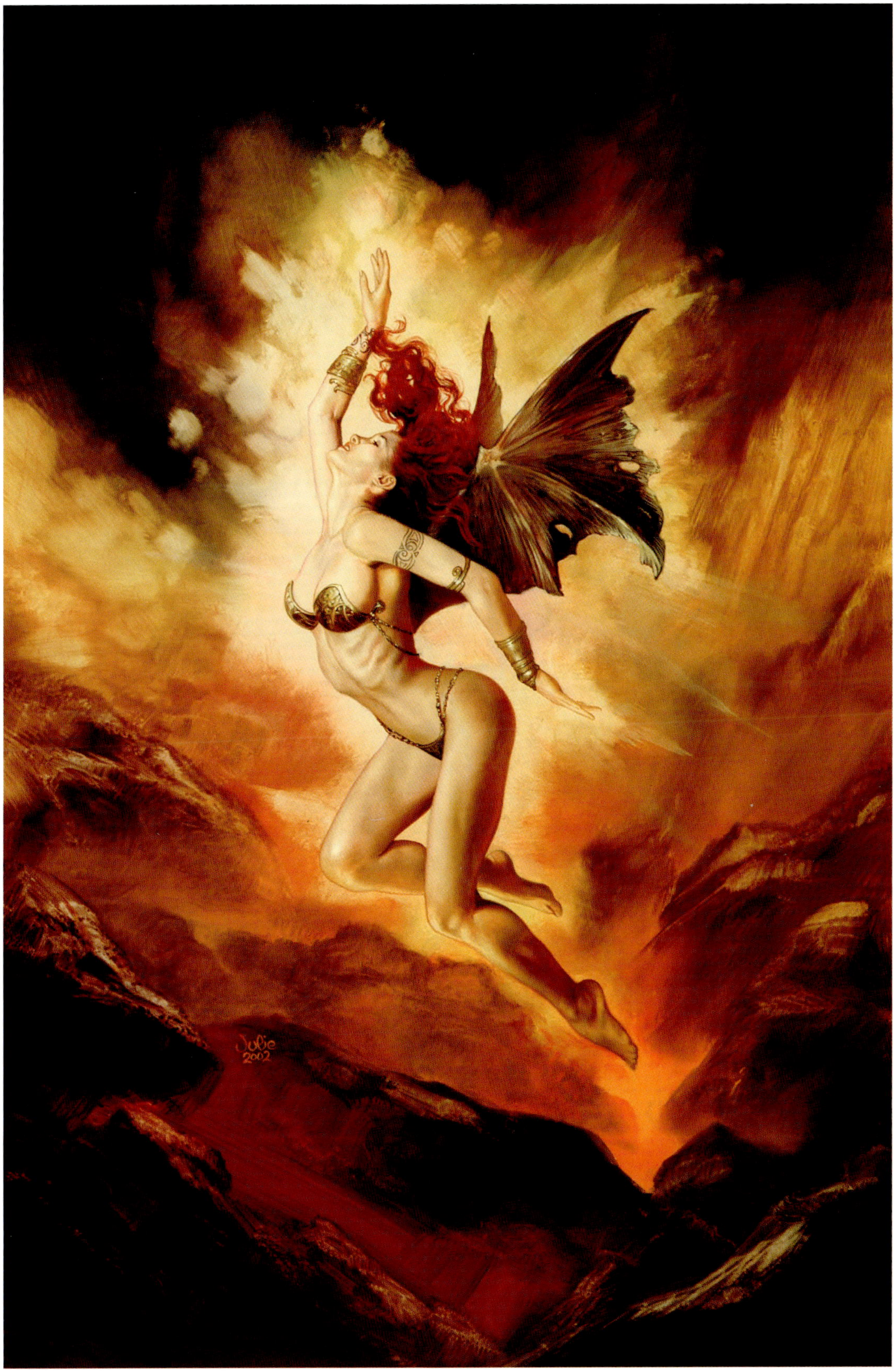

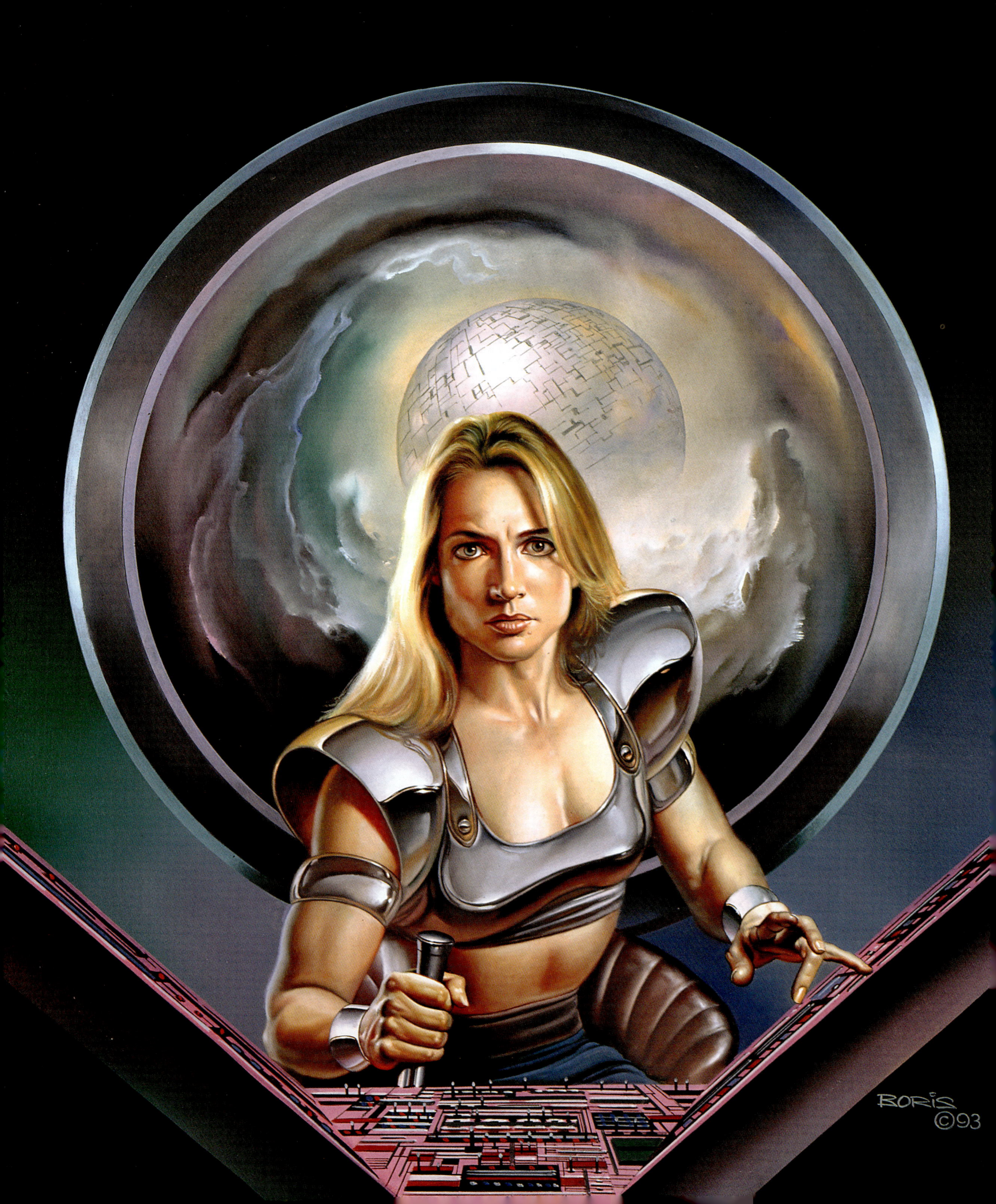
BORIS
©93

Commander,
Boris Vallejo, *1993, book cover*

Something of a departure from Boris' typical illustration, this painting focuses less on the body and more on the intensity of the woman's face. The sense of danger, drama, and action, are described though the character's tense expression in an otherwise static composition.

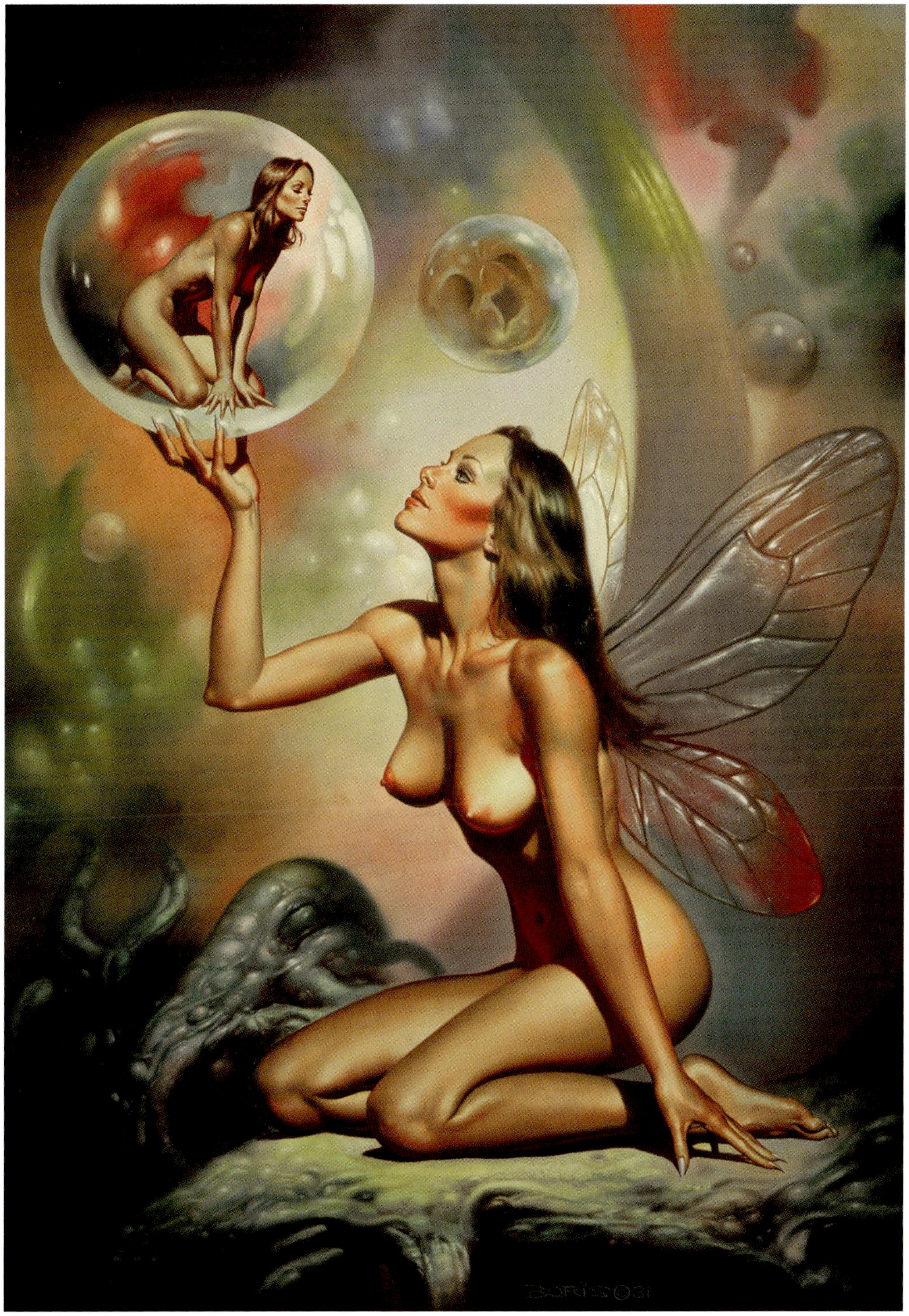

"THE MESSAGE OF THIS PIECE IS THAT THE FIRST ONE WE SHOULD LOVE IS OURSELVES."

BORIS

First Love, Boris Vallejo, *1981,* Mirage *interior art*

Boris spent three years preparing work for *Mirage*, during which he was under no art direction, thus creating some of his most personal pieces. "The message of this piece is that the first one we should love is ourselves."

"ILLUSTRATIONS HAVE TO TELL A STORY USING ONLY PICTURES, AND WHEN I ADD SOMETHING UNEXPECTED TO IT, I FEEL IT'S LIKE I'M CREATING A PLOT TWIST. BORIS

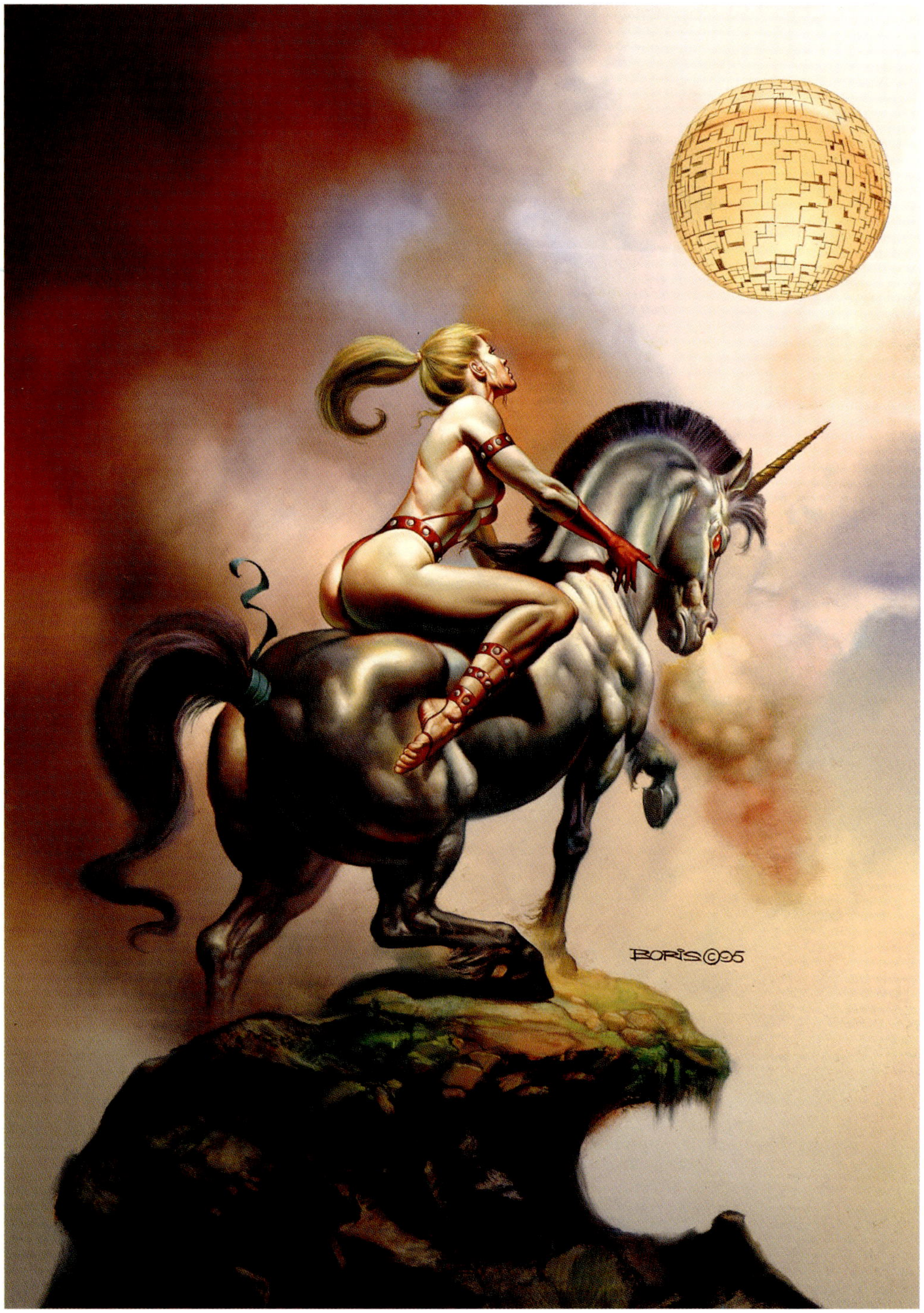

Blessed are the Stars, Boris Vallejo, *1995, calendar*

A common ingredient in Boris' fantasy paintings is unexpected imagery from other genres. "Illustrations have to tell a story using only pictures, and when I add something unexpected to it, I feel it's like I'm creating a plot twist."

Dangerous Kiss, Julie Bell, *1994, calendar*

Both Boris and Julie were fans of the old Zorro movies as youngsters. They got the chance to live out a childhood fantasy by taking on the roles in this painting. Says Julie, "I liked Zorro's accent, which is also something I like about Boris!"

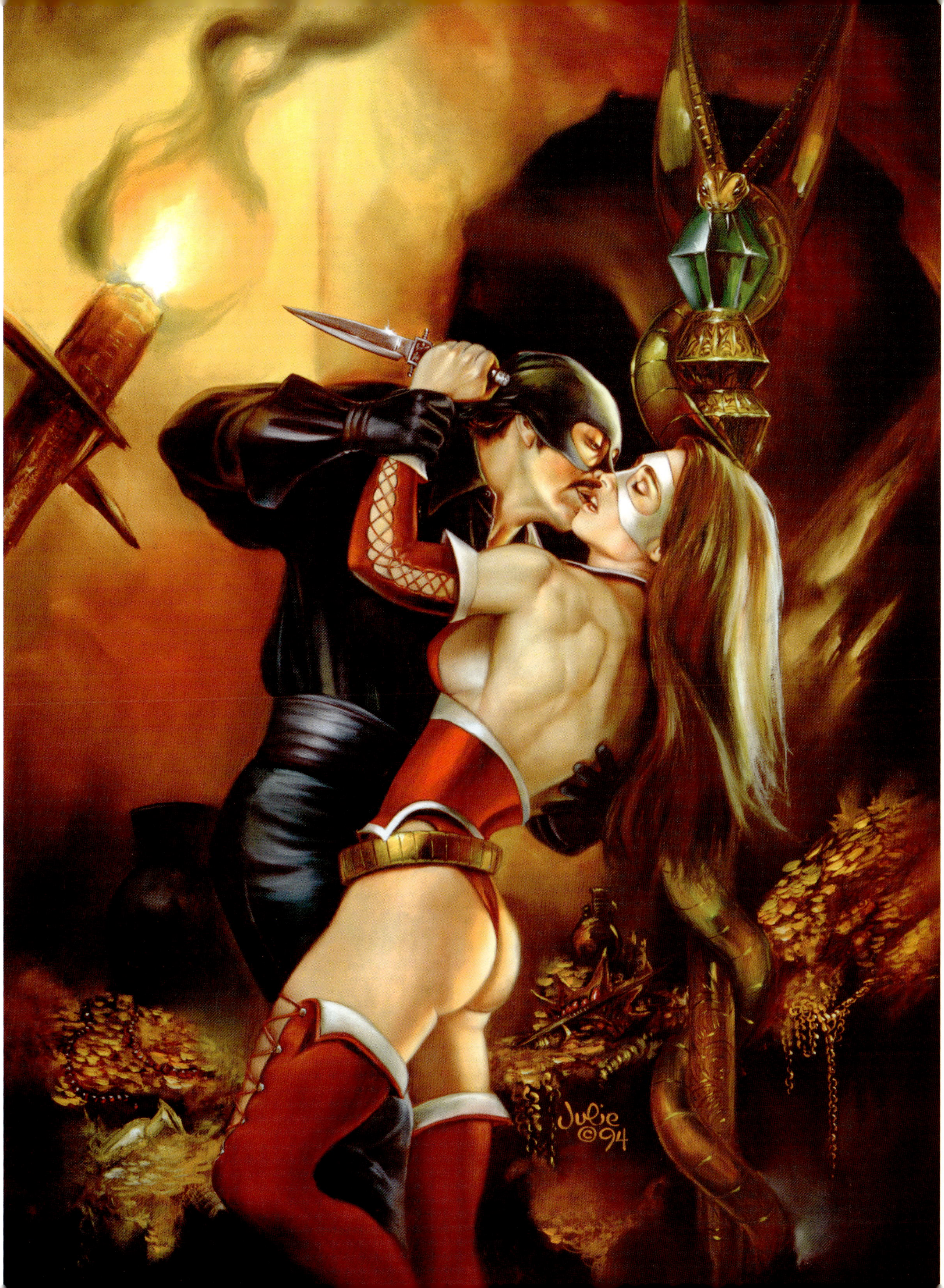
Julie
©94

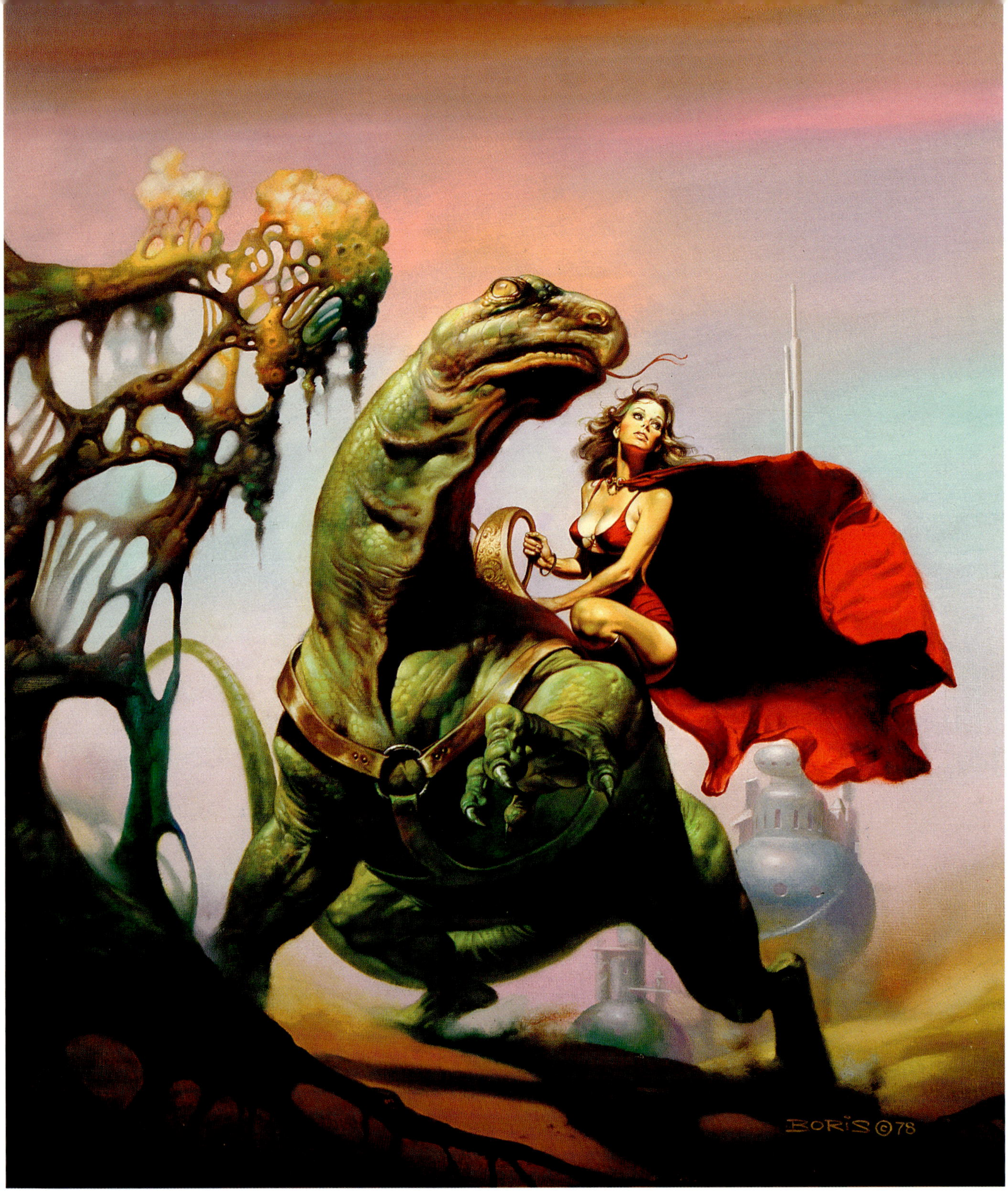

Space Guardian,
Boris Vallejo, *1978, book cover*

In this painting, we can see the influence of Esteban Maroto, a Spanish fantasy artist whom Boris has long held in high regard.

End of the Day, Julie Bell, *2003, calendar*

Julie was very inspired by her model, Lana, while working on this piece. “Her poses are always very sensuous. She immediately got into this character, making me think she was part dragon. When I started this, I saw the dragons as her lovers, but as I painted, I began to see that she is their child and will become a dragon. She’s got little fins and she’s gonna become her mother some day. That sucks!” she laughs.

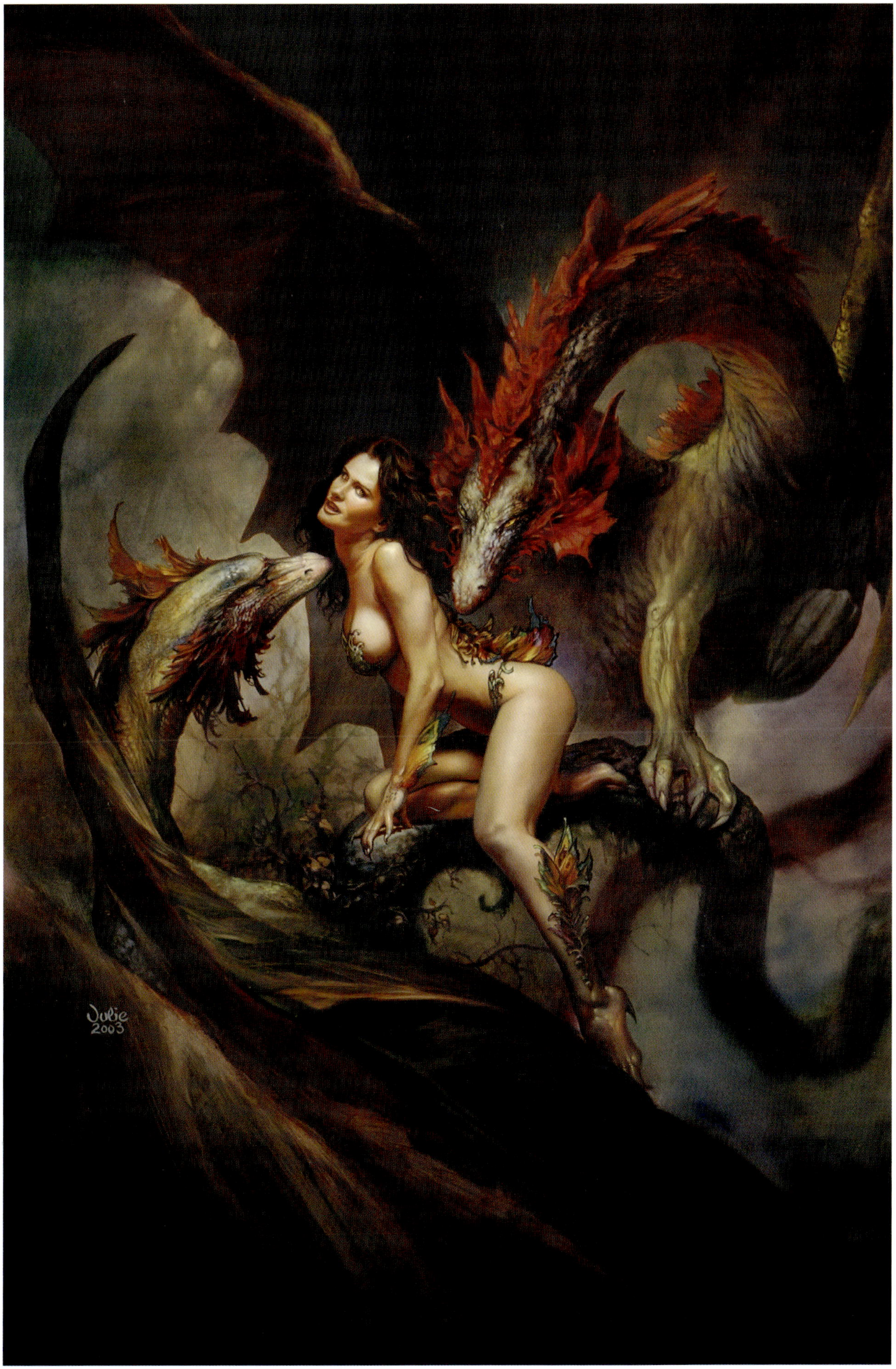
Julie
2003

"IT'S A FUNNY STORY ON THIS ONE. ORIGINALLY IT WAS A PAINTING OF A CABLE REPAIR GUY PARTING THE SEAS LIKE MOSES. AFTERWARDS, BORIS TOOK OUT THE GUY AND PUT THE GIRL IN."

JULIE

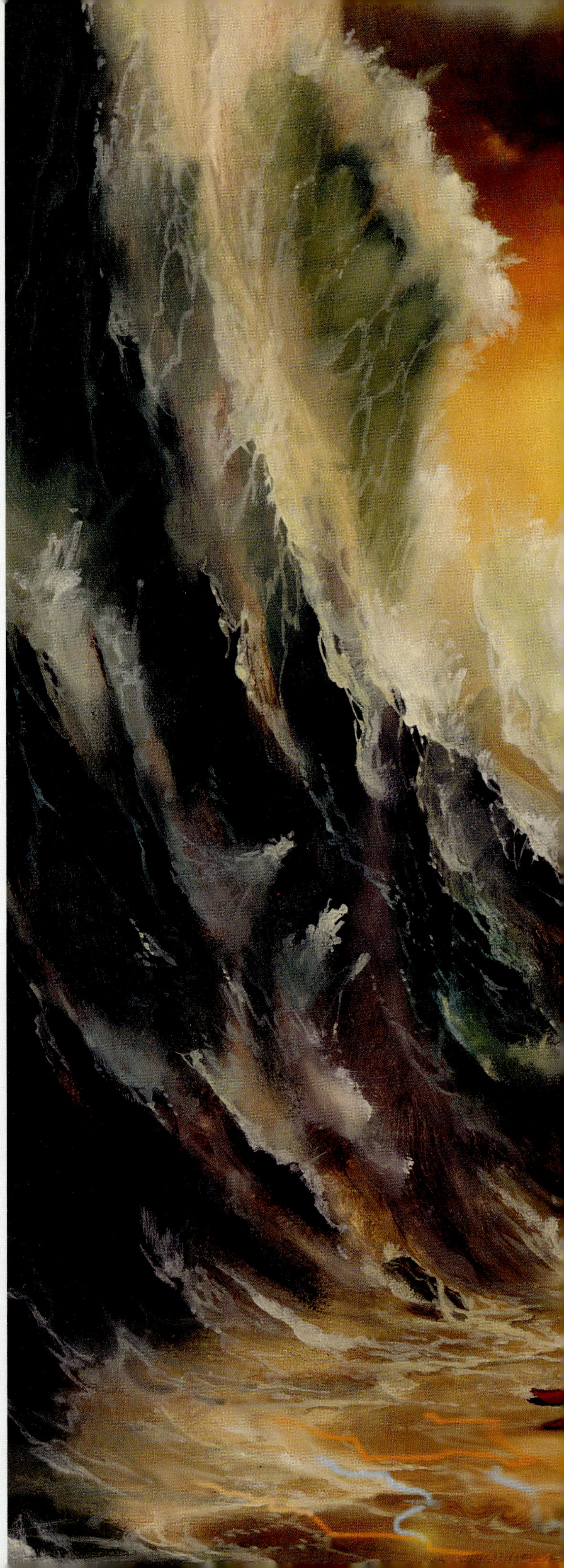

Parting the Seas, Boris Vallejo, *1999, calendar*

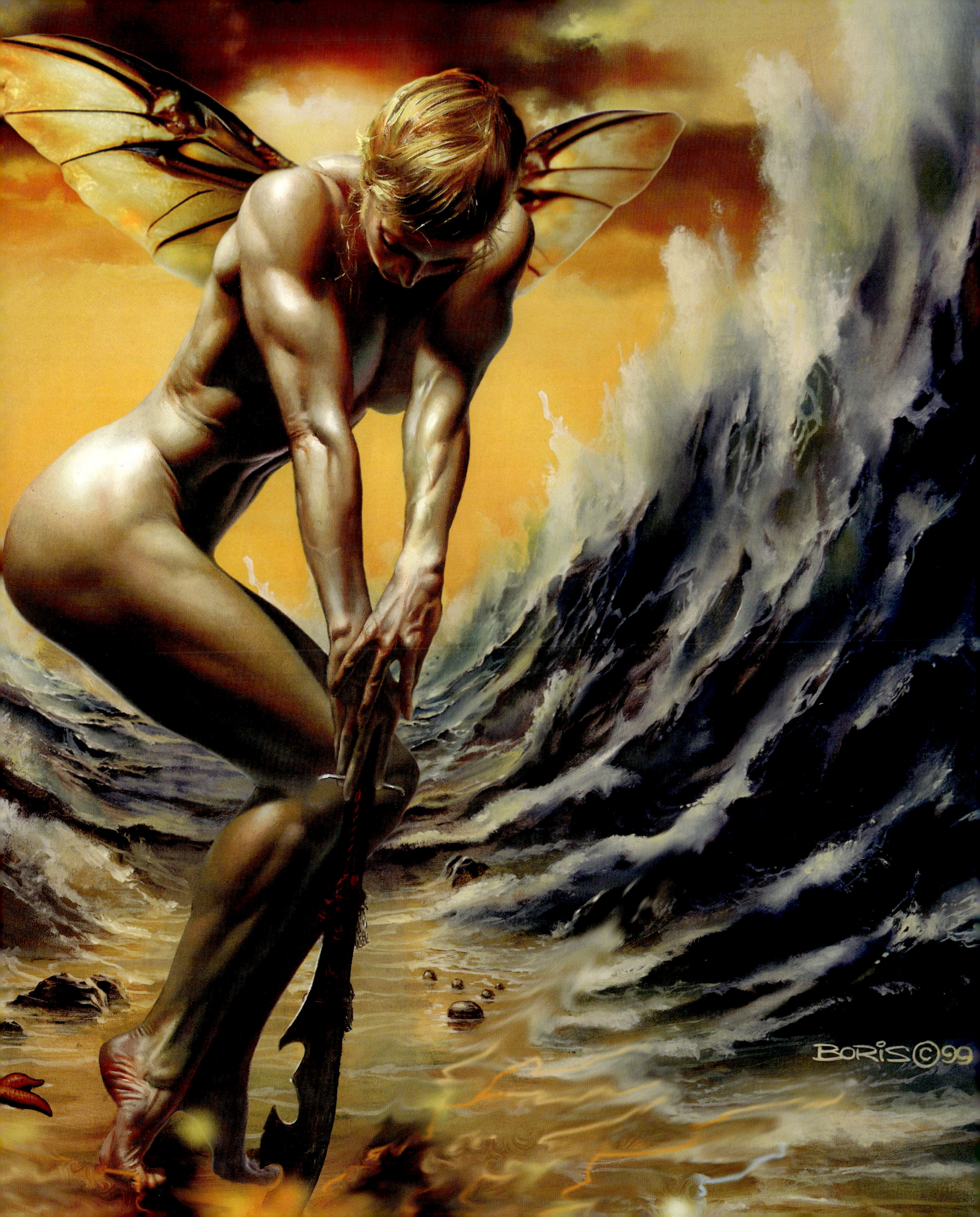
BORIS©99

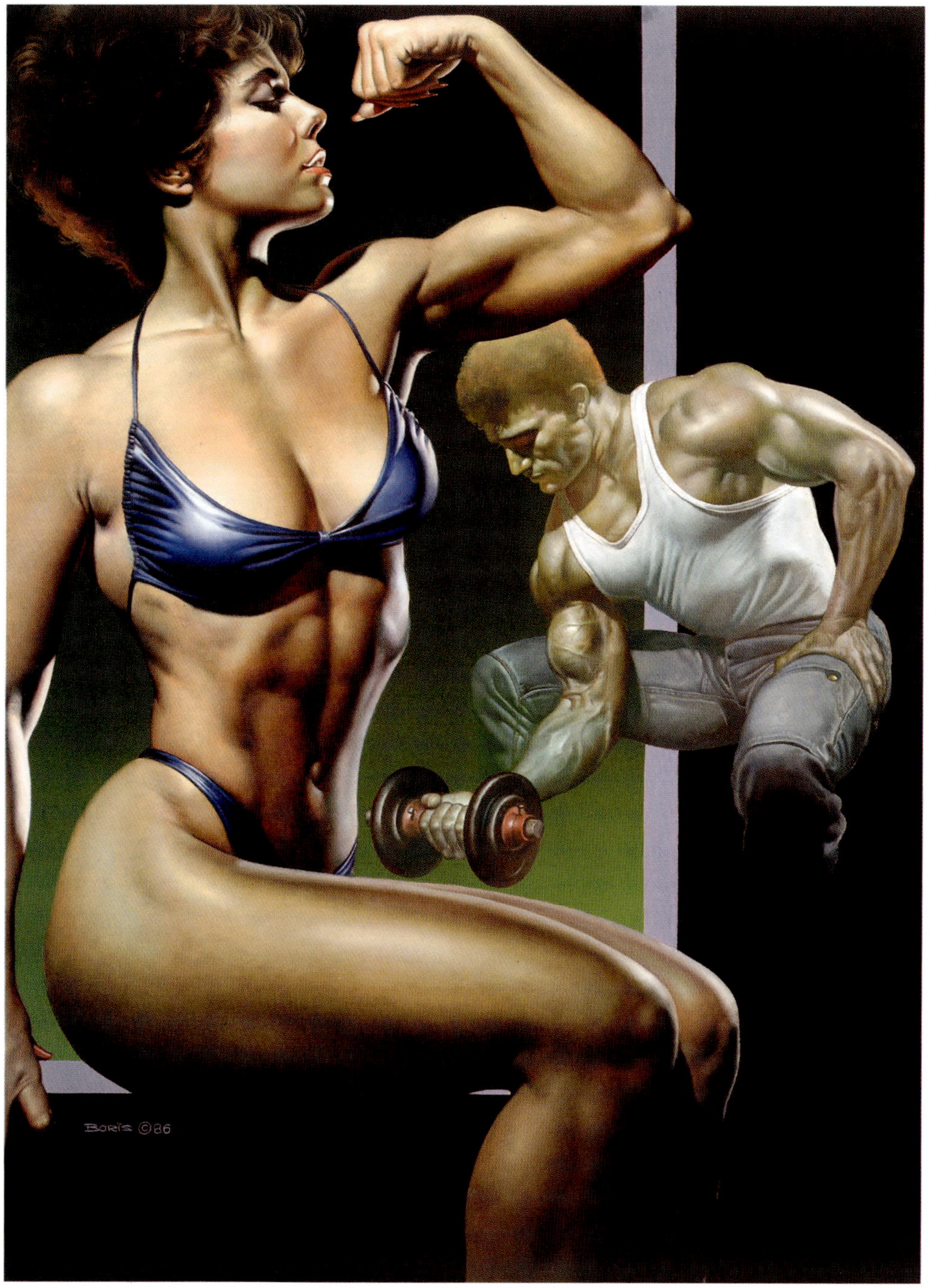

Sun Princess, Boris Vallejo, ▸▸
1978, book cover

This painting shows Boris' early experimentation with blending graphic art nouveau patterns and highly rendered figures. This is an idea he would further develop in his first book, *Mirage*.

"I DIDN'T LIKE IT [WORKING IN OILS]. I FELT IT MADE EVERYTHING LOOK TOO MECHANICAL."

BORIS

Bodybuilding, Boris Vallejo, *1986, promotional poster* ▴

Boris has always worked primarily in oils, but with this painting he experimentally incorporated the use of an airbrush. "I didn't like it. I felt it made everything look too mechanical."

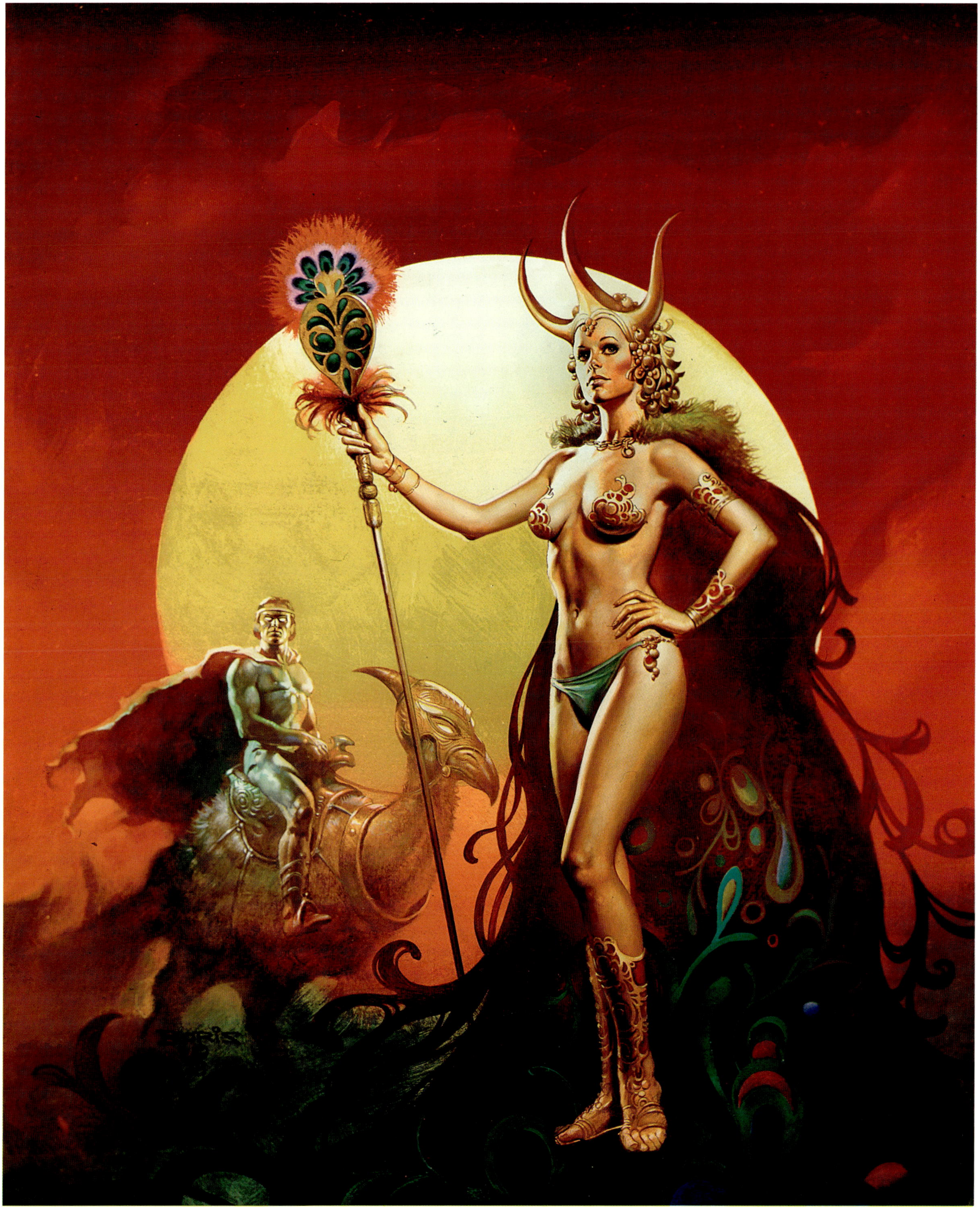

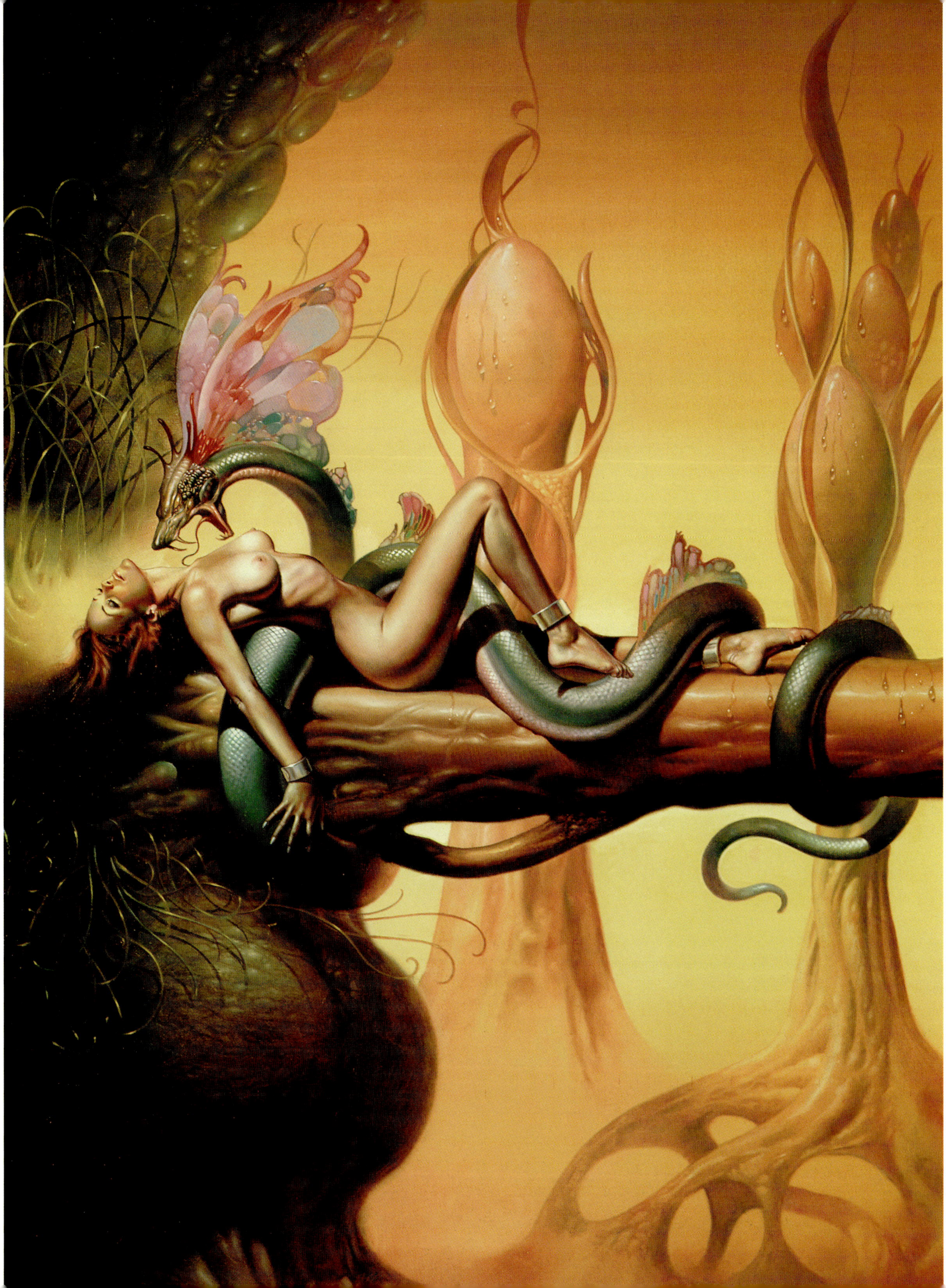

Instants, Boris Vallejo,
1979, Mirage *interior art*

"I generally don't like to spell things out in my paintings, though the symbolism in this one is pretty obvious. It's all very aggressive and blatant, which I tried to offset with the delicate butterfly wings."

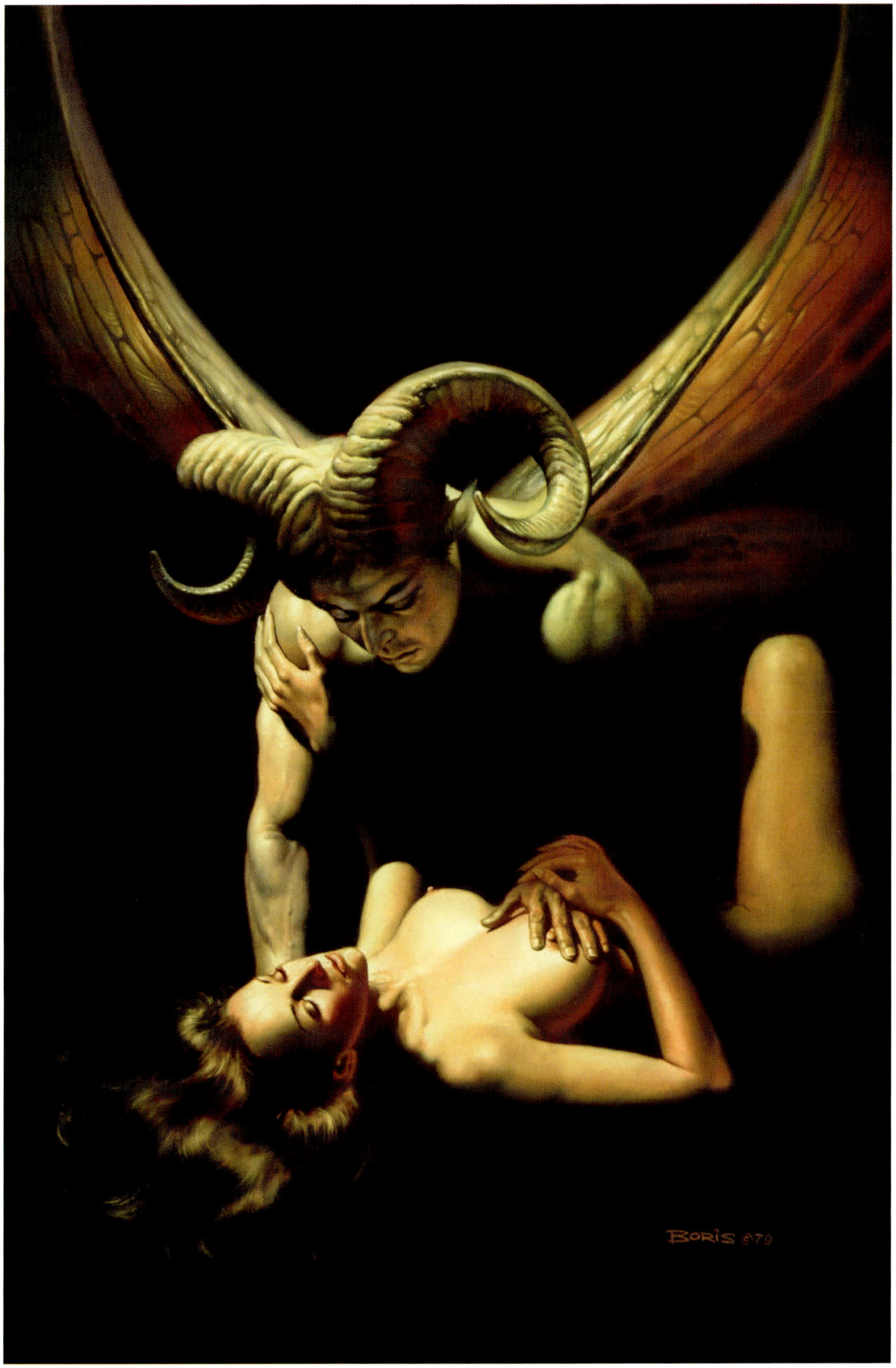

Touches, Boris Vallejo, ▸▸
1979, Mirage *interior artwork*

Boris was surprised to spot a scene in the film *The Cell* very similar to the one shown here. "If you've seen the movie, you'll recognize this painting." Boris was very influenced by Caravaggio while working on this piece.

"WHEN JULIE PAINTS THE WOLVES, SHE DOES THIS VERY BELIEVABLE FUR. IT LOOKS LIKE YOU COULD TOUCH IT. I WISH I COULD DO IT AS WELL."

BORIS

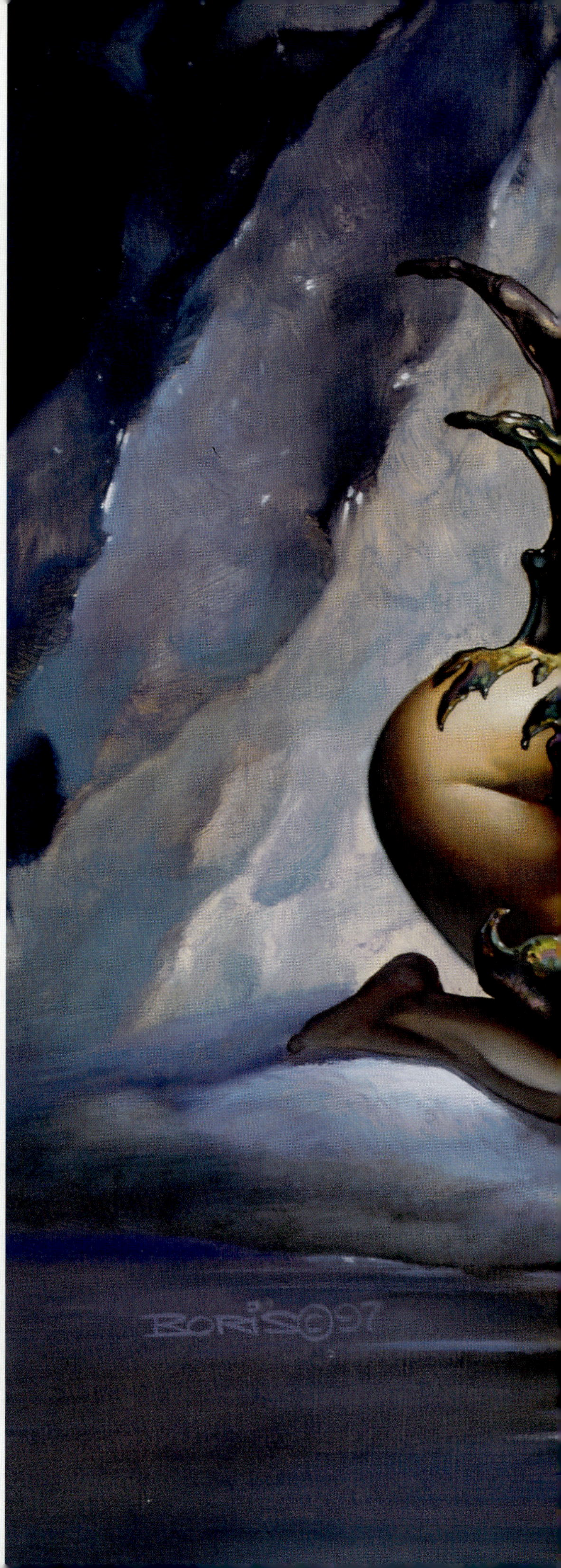

Wolf Girl, Boris Vallejo, *1997, calendar*

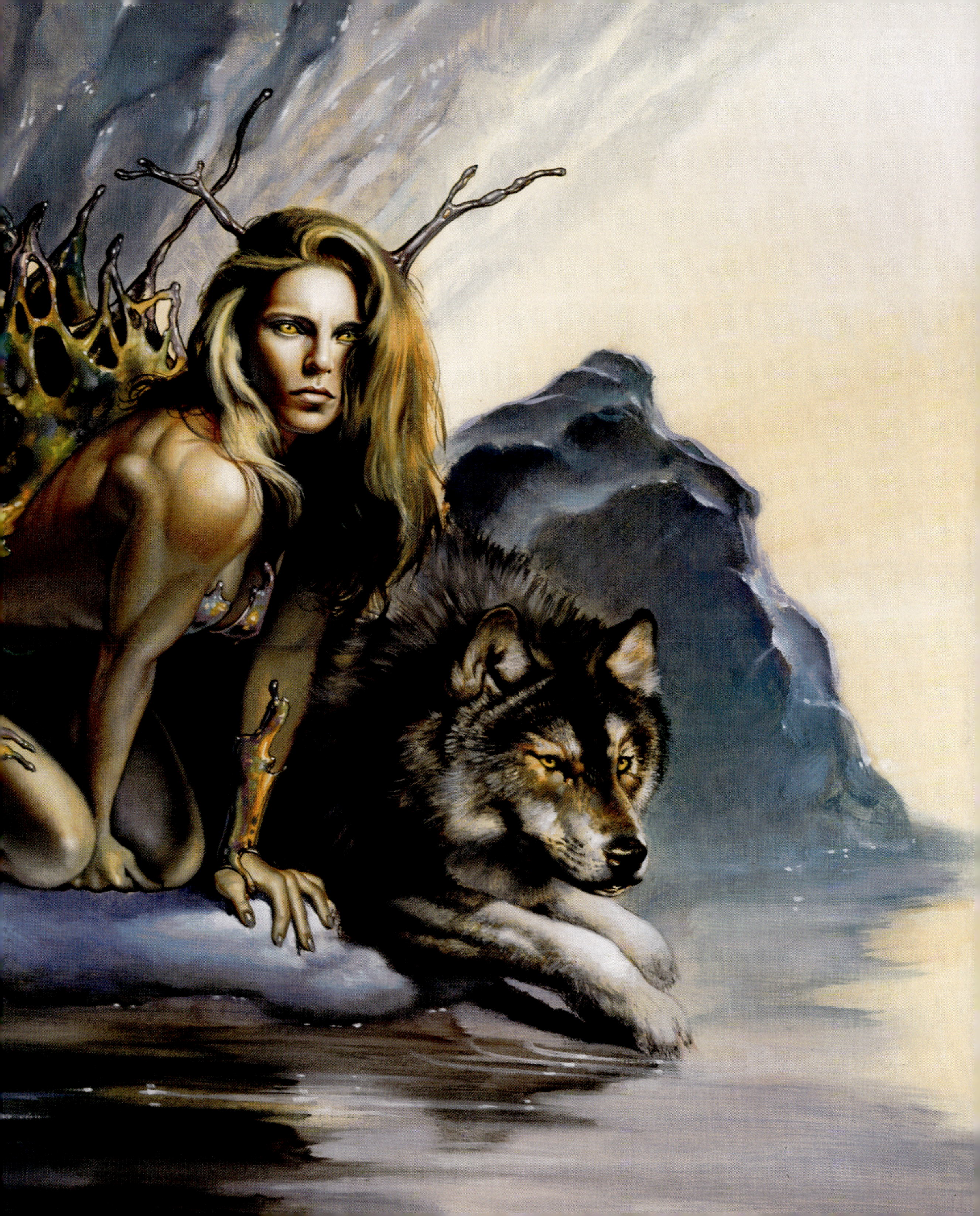

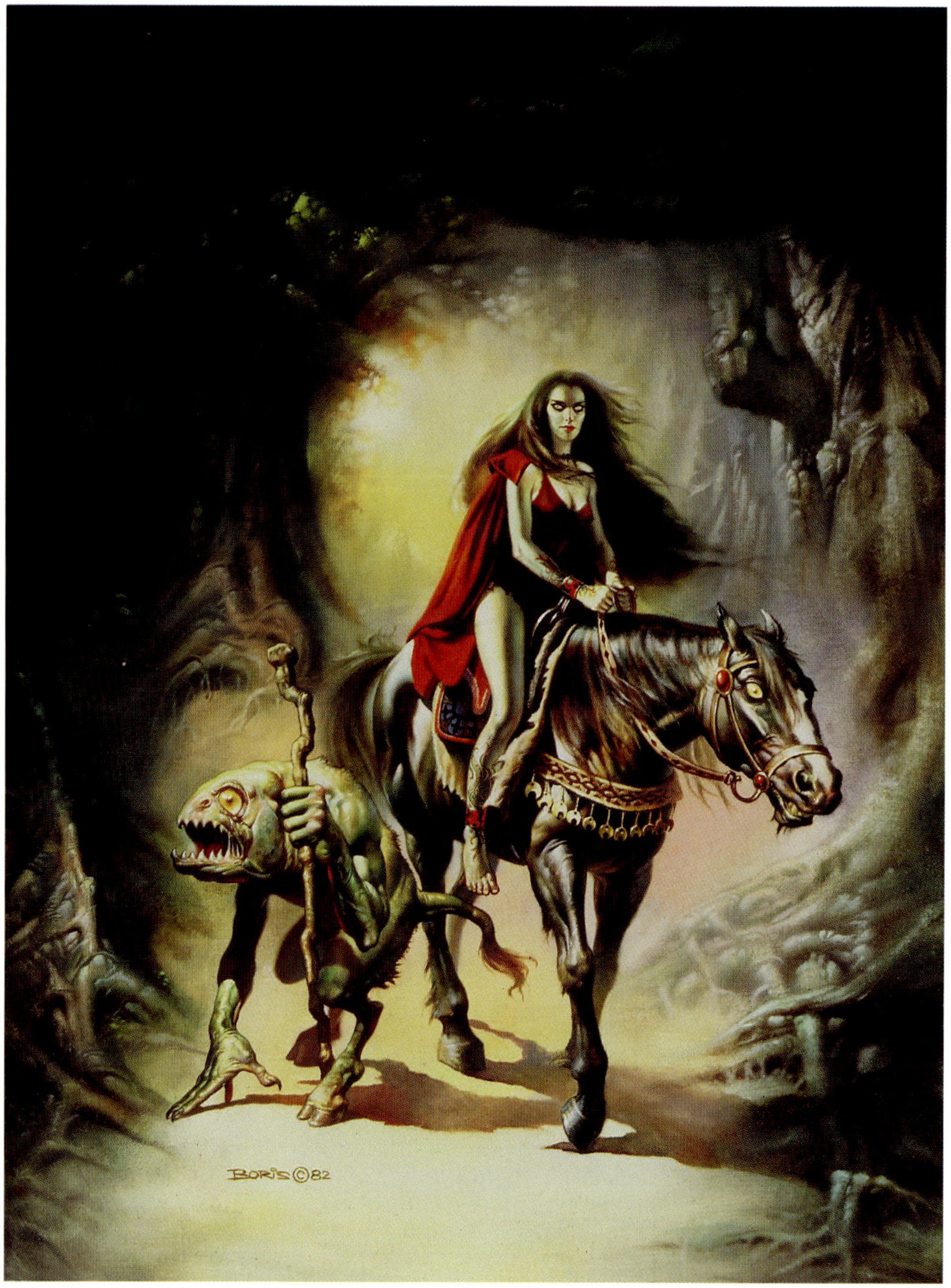

"SOMETIMES IT'S FUN TO IGNORE THE RULES. IT'S ONE OF THE THINGS I LOVE ABOUT FANTASY ART."

JULIE

Witch and her Familiar, Boris Vallejo, *1982, calendar*

"Boris always liked horror movies and this reminds me of a horror movie. He used to sit up at night as a kid and hope that ghosts would come to him. That's something I would never do 'cause I was really scared of ghosts and witches when I was a kid!" – Julie

Suzanne, Boris Vallejo, *1993, calendar*

Boris: "This painting was a sort of exercise for me. I forced myself to leave out the lower body, which is an area I enjoy painting. I wanted to challenge myself, to be as outrageous as possible, so I tried to include as many fantasy clichés as I could."

Julie: "Sometimes it's fun to ignore the rules. It's one of the things I love about fantasy art."

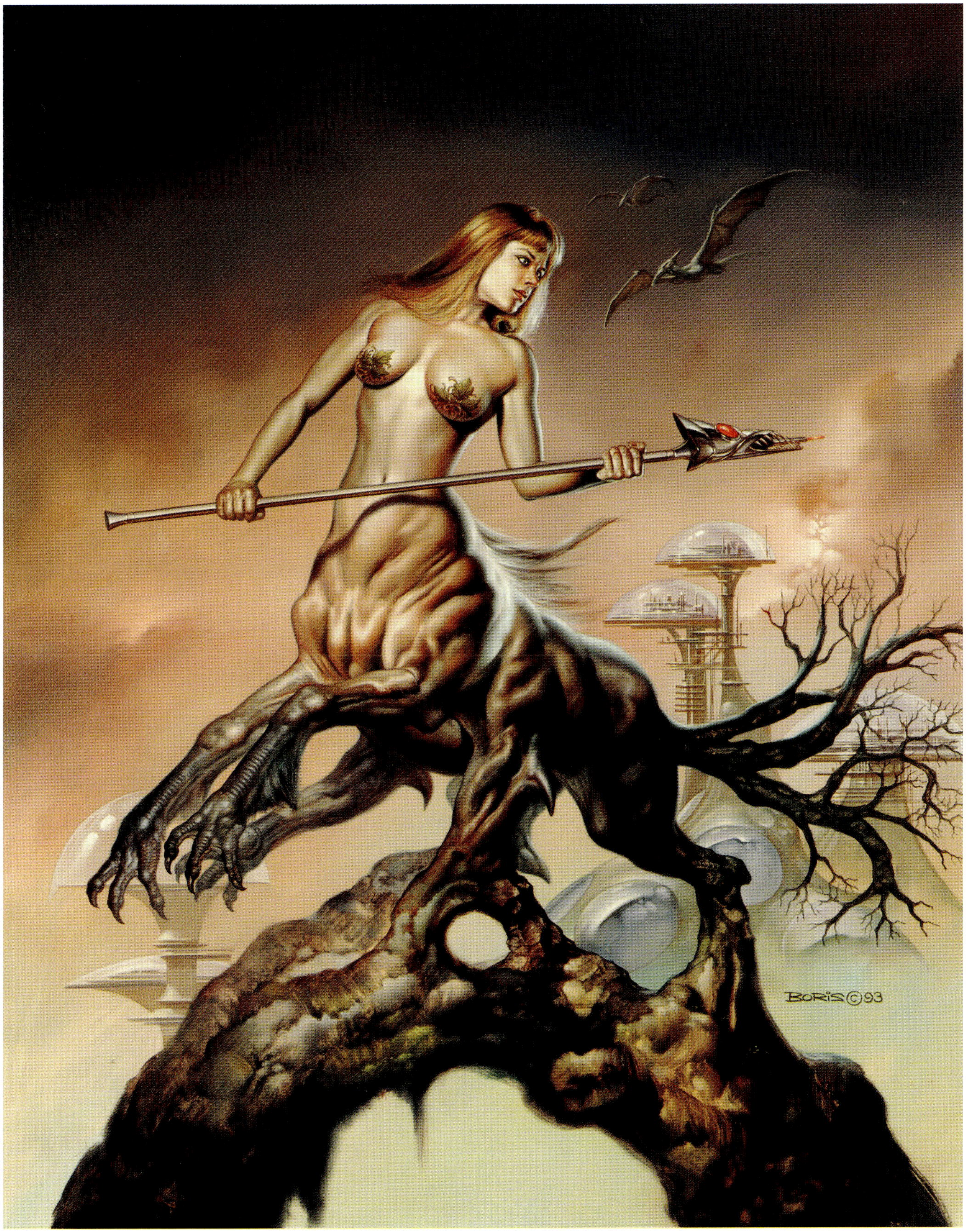
BORIS©93

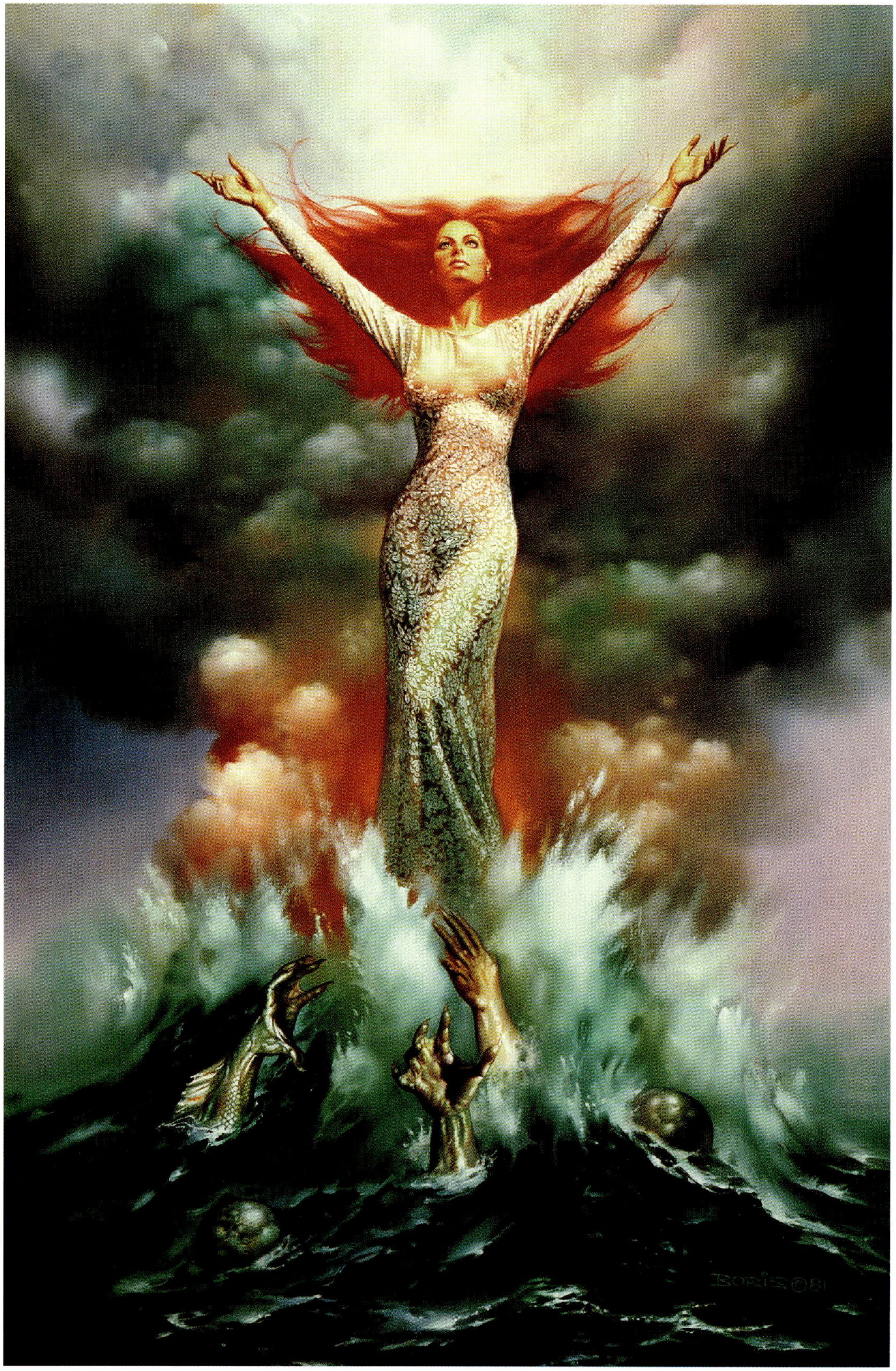

Bride, Boris Vallejo,
1981, book cover

This is the original cover of *Mirage*, of which several variations have been printed. Boris says, "It was probably used as the cover because it didn't show nudity. Looking at this painting after so many years, I see that I never get tired of painting water. One of the reasons why I think I love the sea so much is that I grew up at the shore. My house was about two blocks from the ocean. If I woke up at night, I would hear the waves." Boris was raised in La Punta, Peru, outside of Lima. He has yet to learn how to swim.

Gemini, Boris Vallejo,
1987, calendar

"The image of Gemini being twins. I wanted to create a butterfly out of the two women, which was exactly what I saw when I shot the pictures of my model."

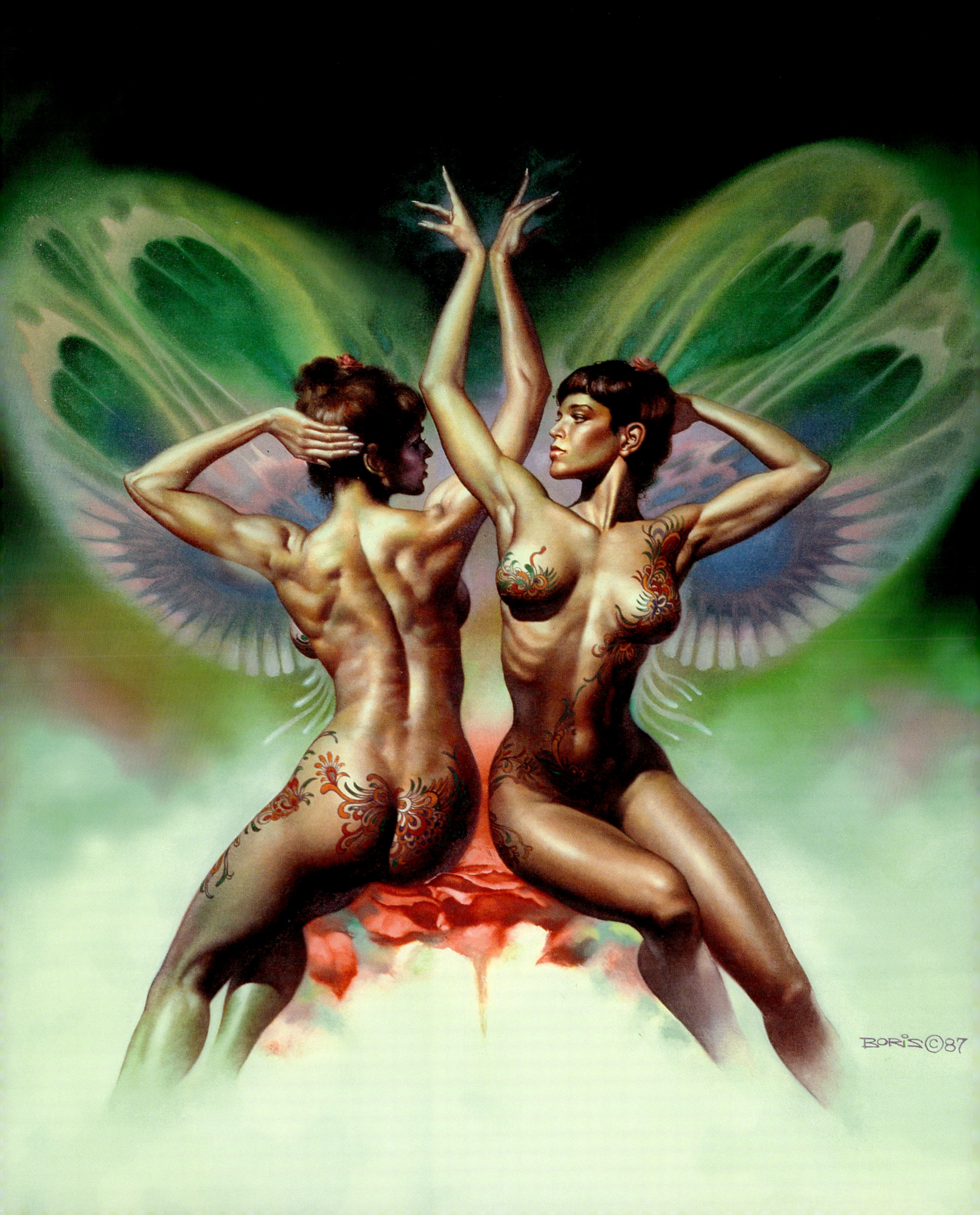
BORIS©87

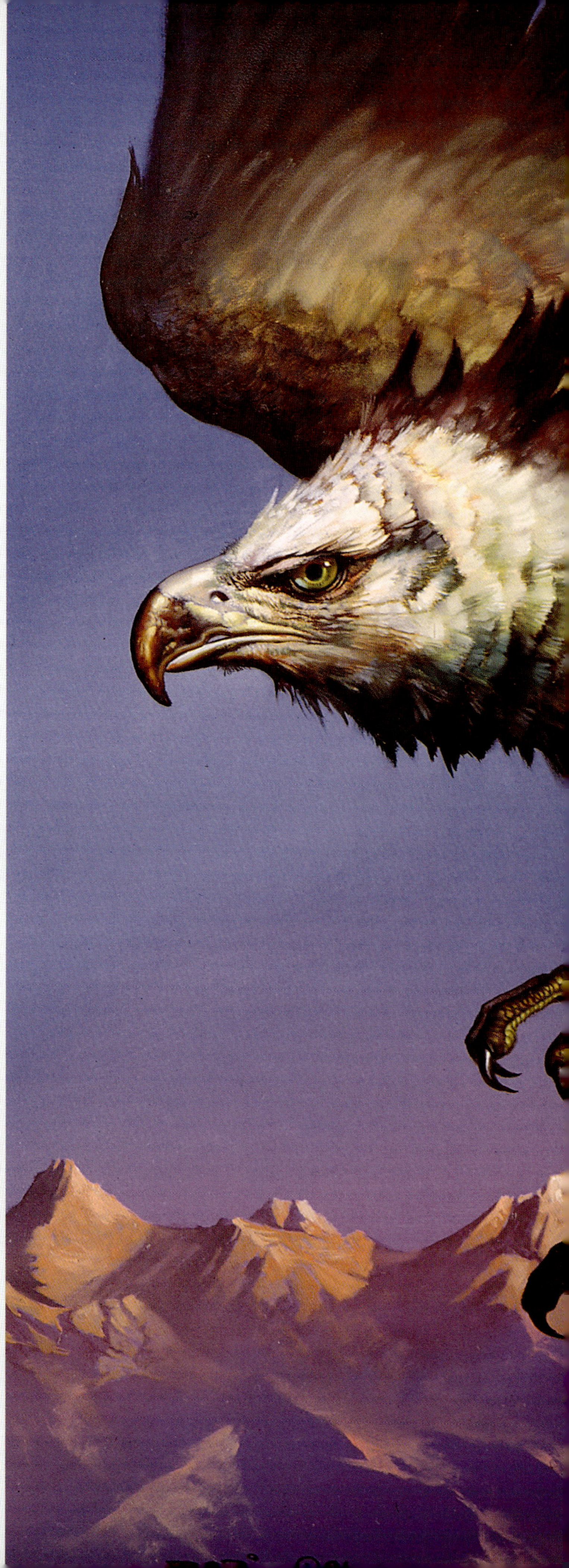

Gryphon Keeper, Boris Vallejo, *1991, calendar* ▸▸

The model in this piece is Janice Ragain, a top female bodybuilder of her time. One reason that Boris enjoys working with bodybuilders is because they know their physiques very well, and they know what kind of poses will show them off.

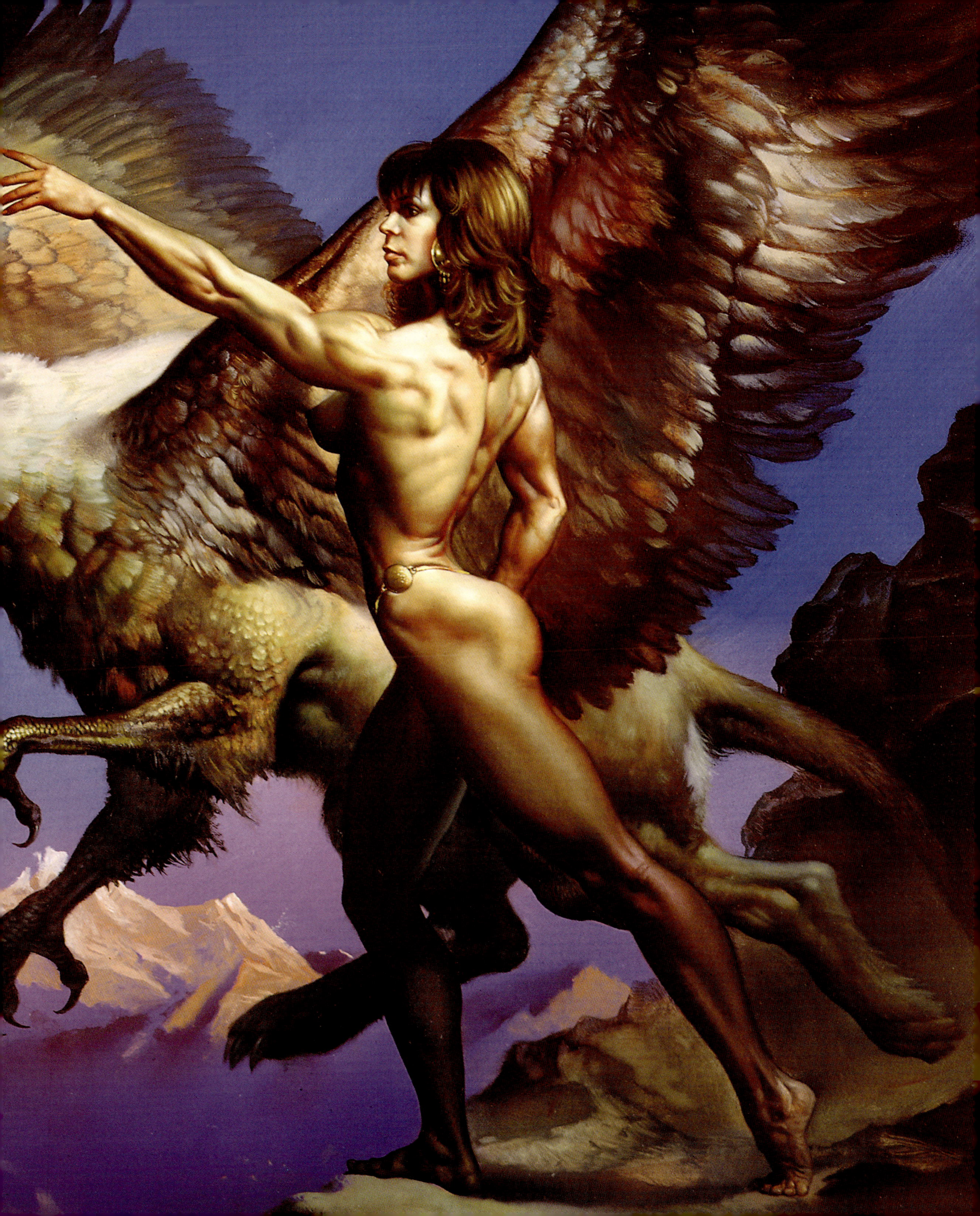

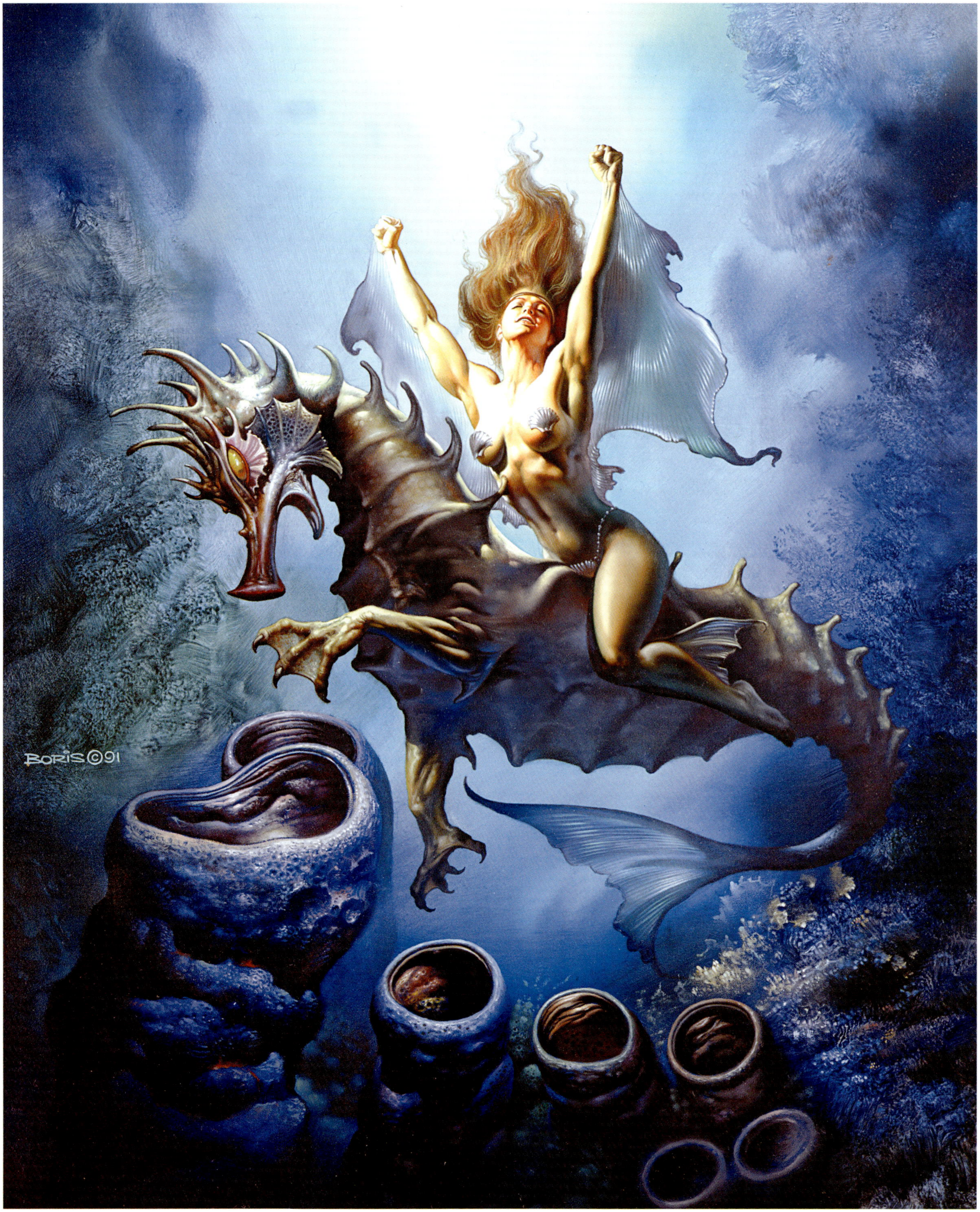
BORIS©91

The Hippocampus,
Boris Vallejo, *1991*

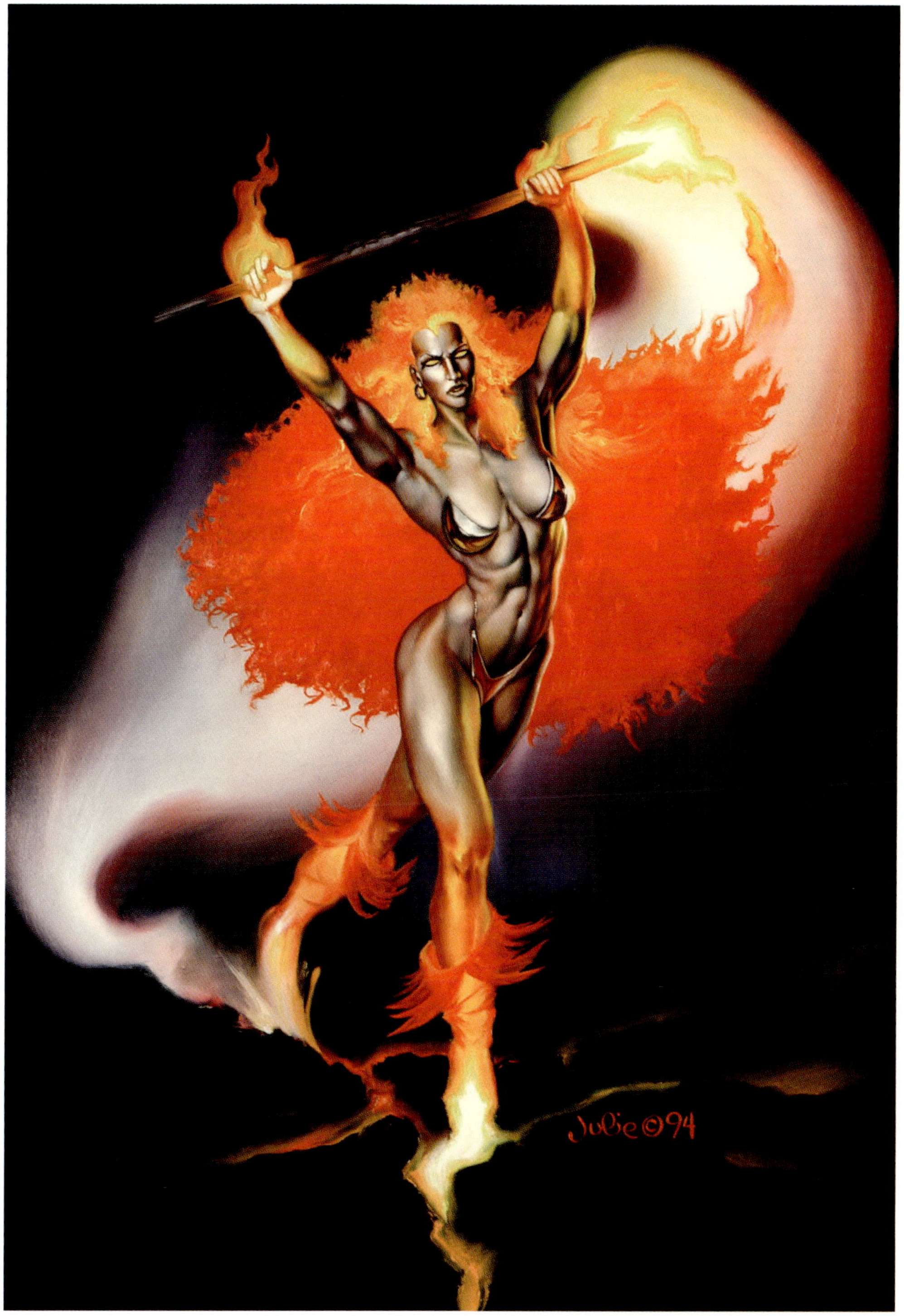

Ash, Julie Bell, *1994, trading card*

This painting appeared in the Creators' Edition Master Series trading cards, in which the participating artists presented their own original characters. Here we see Julie's Ash, the element of fire on her planet.

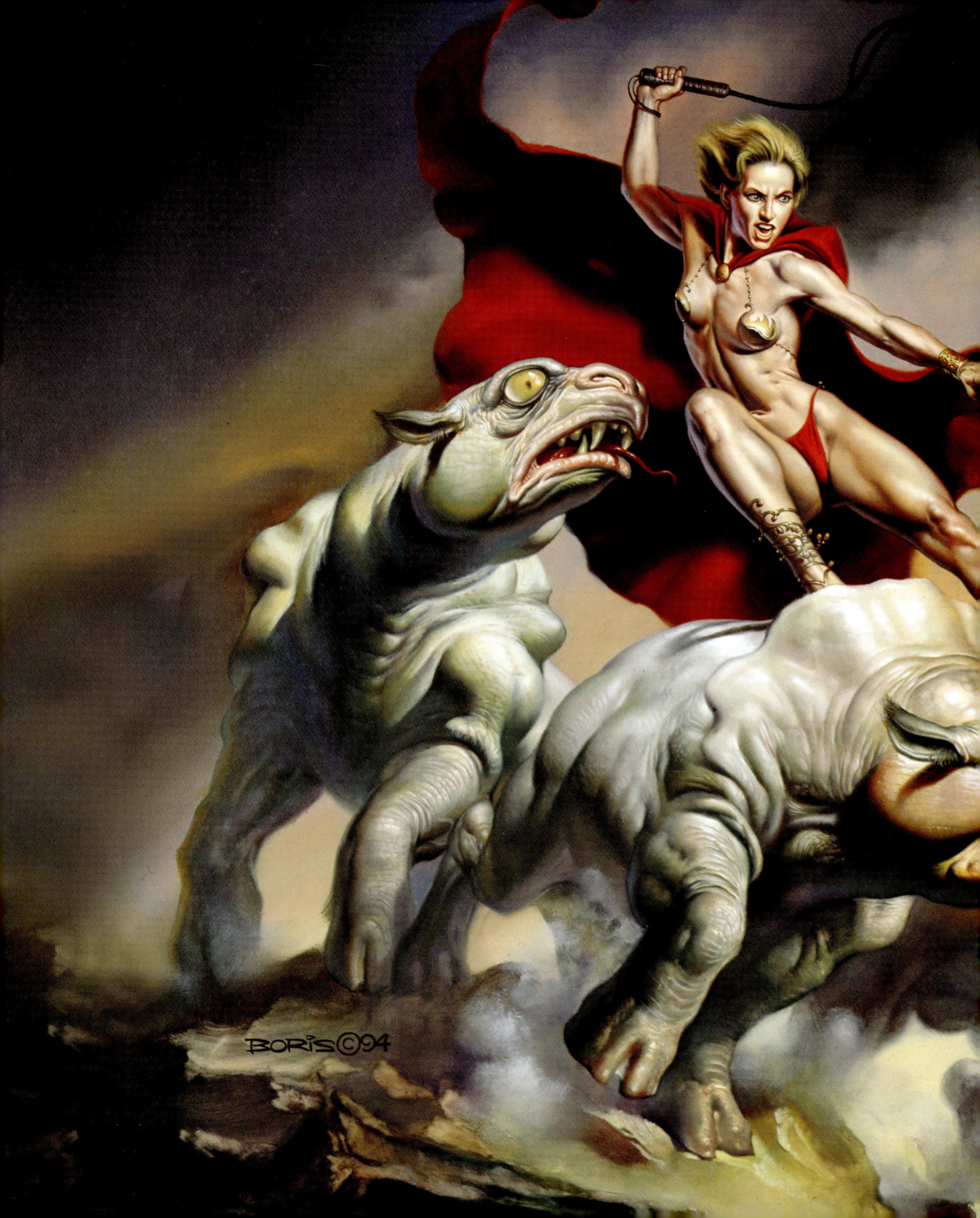
BORIS©94

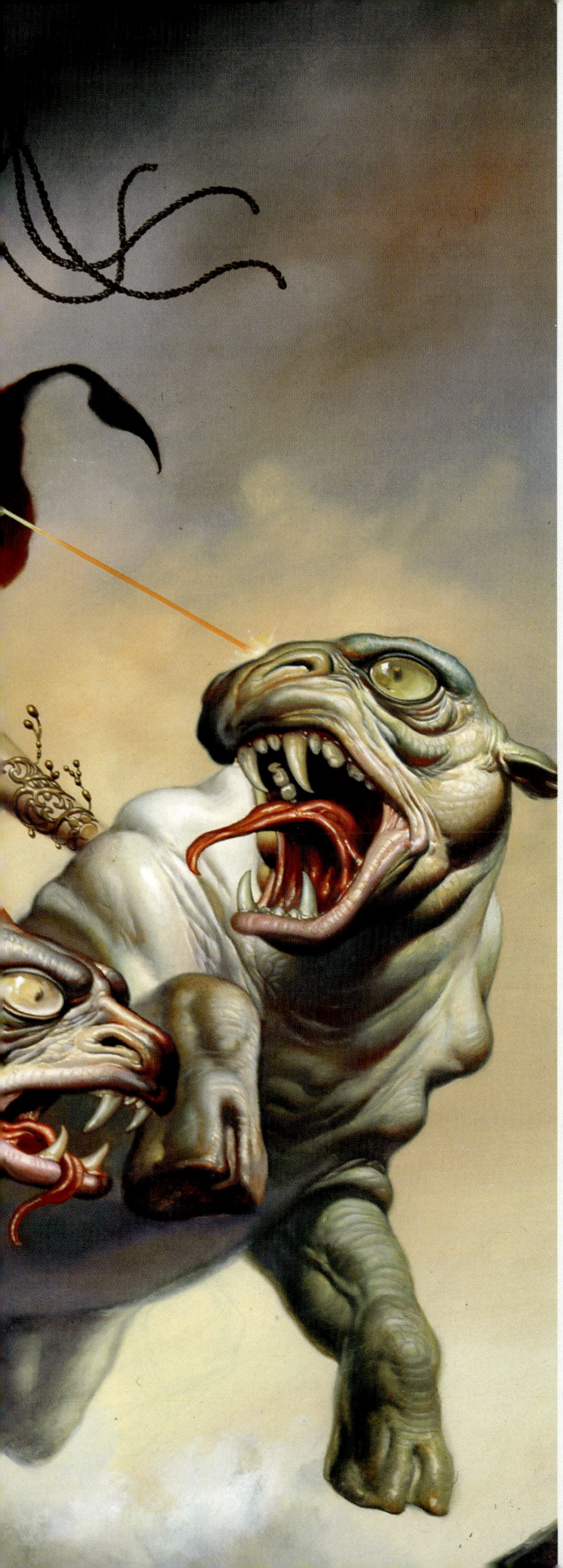

Berserk, Boris Vallejo, *1994, calendar*

A recurring theme in Boris' paintings is that of Beauty and the Beast, with Beauty typically being a woman in control of the Beast.

"IT SHOWS HER POWER, THAT SHE IS IN COMMAND OF THESE MONSTERS THAT ARE ALL FIGHTING WITH EACH OTHER."

BORIS

"MOST OF MY FEMALE MODELS WANT TO BE MERMAIDS... I PREFER MERMAIDS WITHOUT THE FISH TAILS." BORIS

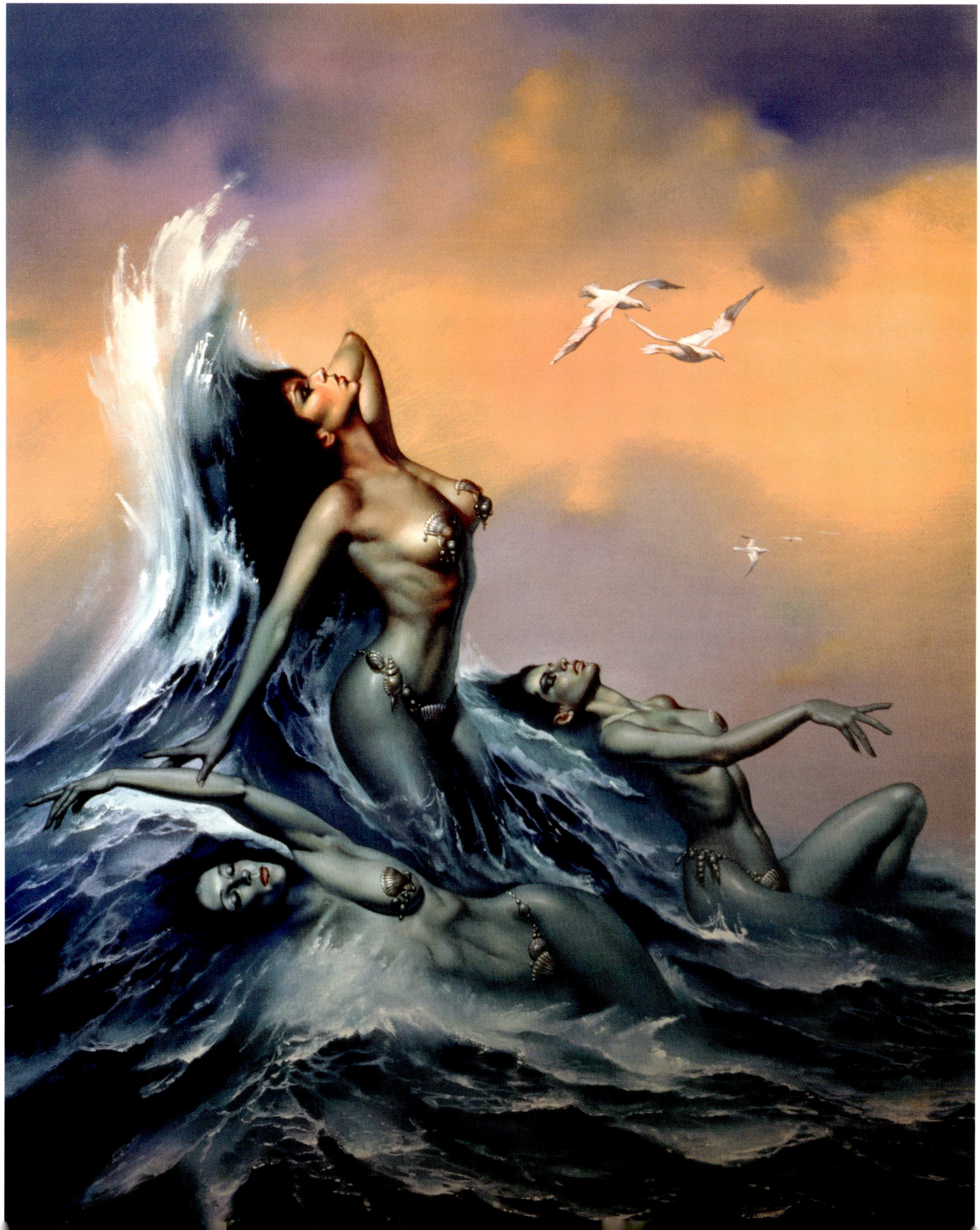

Nyads, Boris Vallejo, *1989, calendar*

"Most of my female models want to be mermaids. I have to say I prefer mermaids without the fish tails. The Nyads are creatures of Greek mythology, and fish tails are never mentioned in any of the descriptions I've seen."

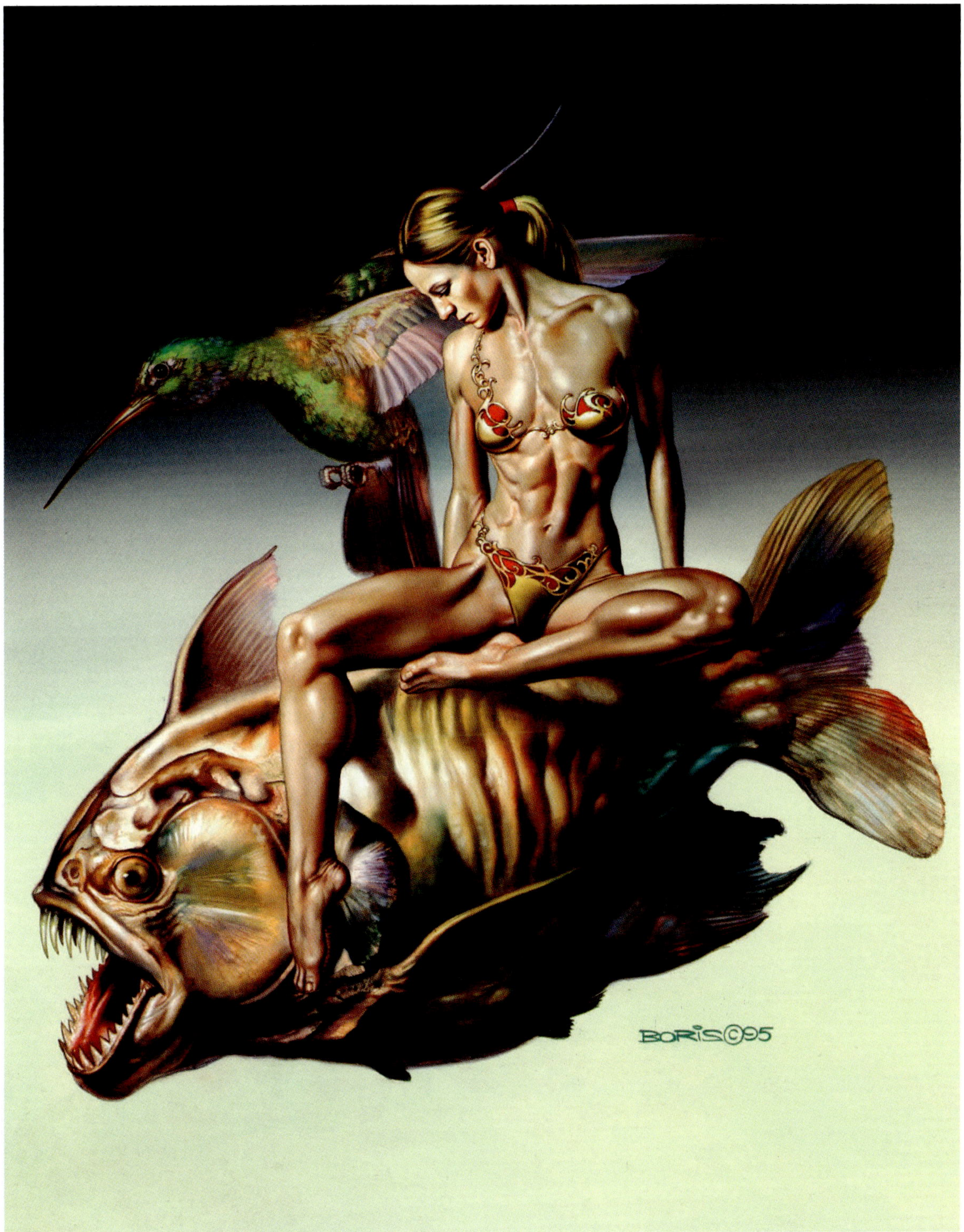

Piranha, Boris Vallejo, *1995, calendar*

"I like the simplicity of a high-tech gradient background to enhance the details in the main subject."

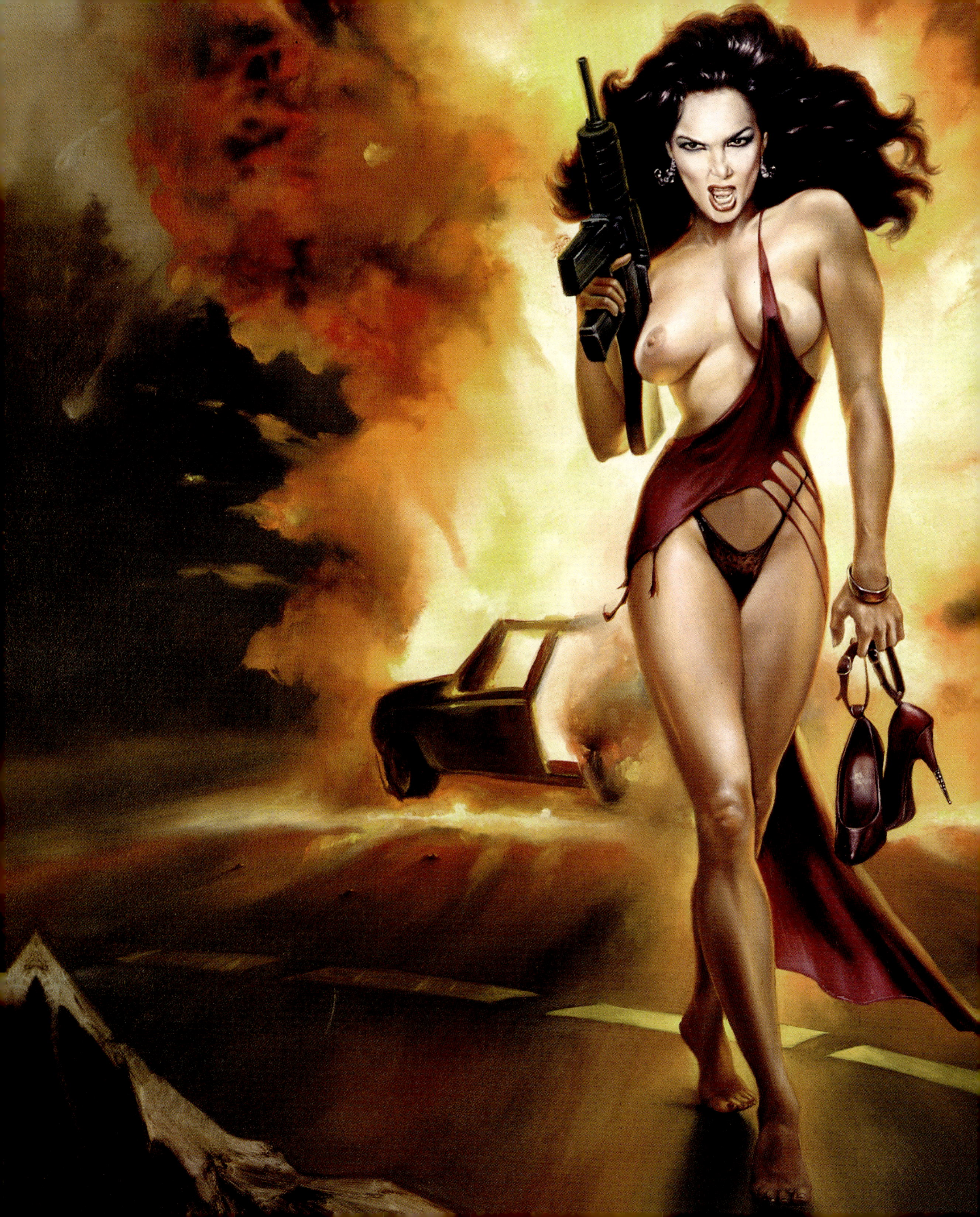

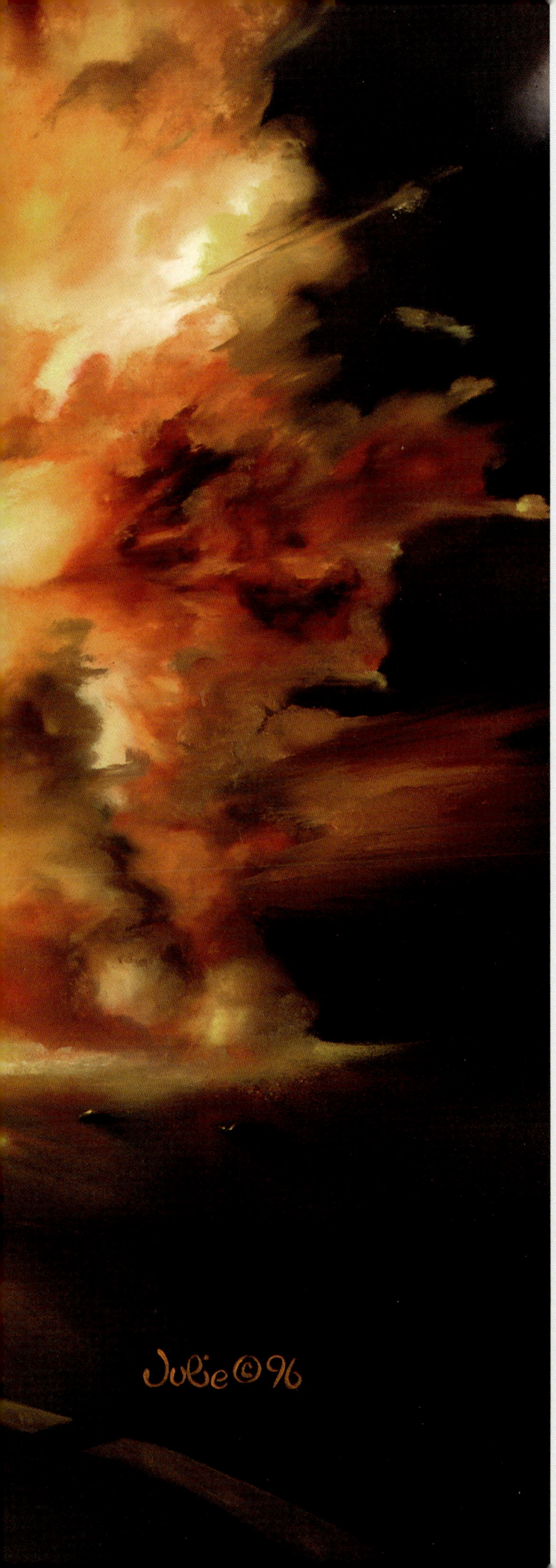

"I LIKE TO REALLY EXAGGERATE THE FIGURE SOMETIMES. IN THIS PORTRAYAL OF JULIE STRAIN, I EMPHASIZED HER JESSICA RABBIT FIGURE AND THEN PUSHED IT EVEN MORE BY FRAMING IT WITH AN EXPLOSION."

JULIE

Bitch, Julie Bell, *1996, calendar*

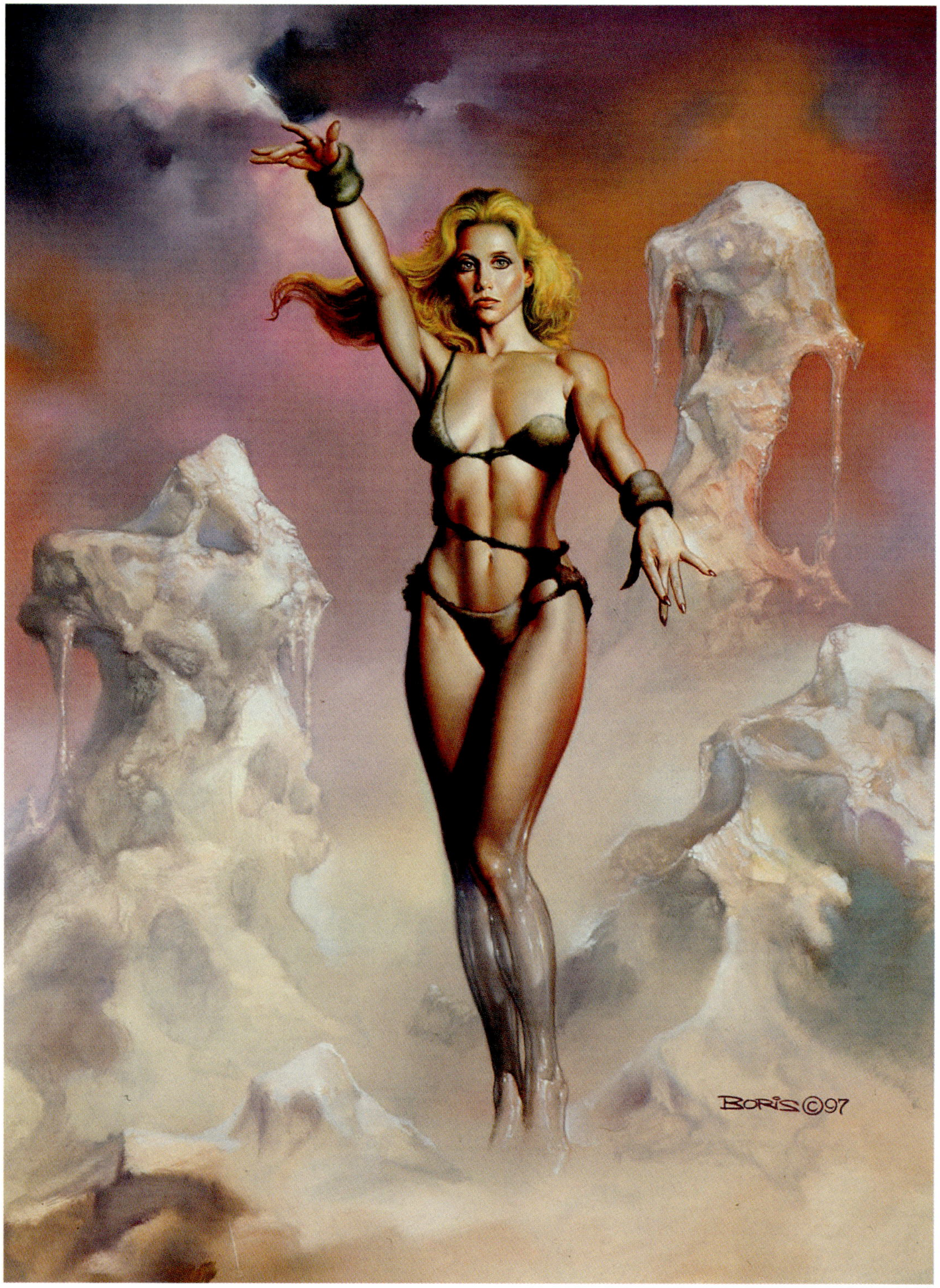

Ice Queen,
Boris Vallejo, *1997, calendar*

"We ran into this girl at the gym. We get a lot of our models there. I often wonder what this girl is doing in the ice without any clothes, but heck, she is the Ice Queen, so who am I to question?"

The Angel Rides,
Julie Bell, *2000, calendar*

"This girl is a total bad-ass." says Julie. "She just goes all over the place, wherever she wants, not afraid or restricted, totally free." The piece was born from her design of a fantastic motorcycle figurine for the Franklin Mint. She was taken with the idea and elaborated on it, eventually developing the concept into a painting. "...I used to wear this bathing suit as a teenager."

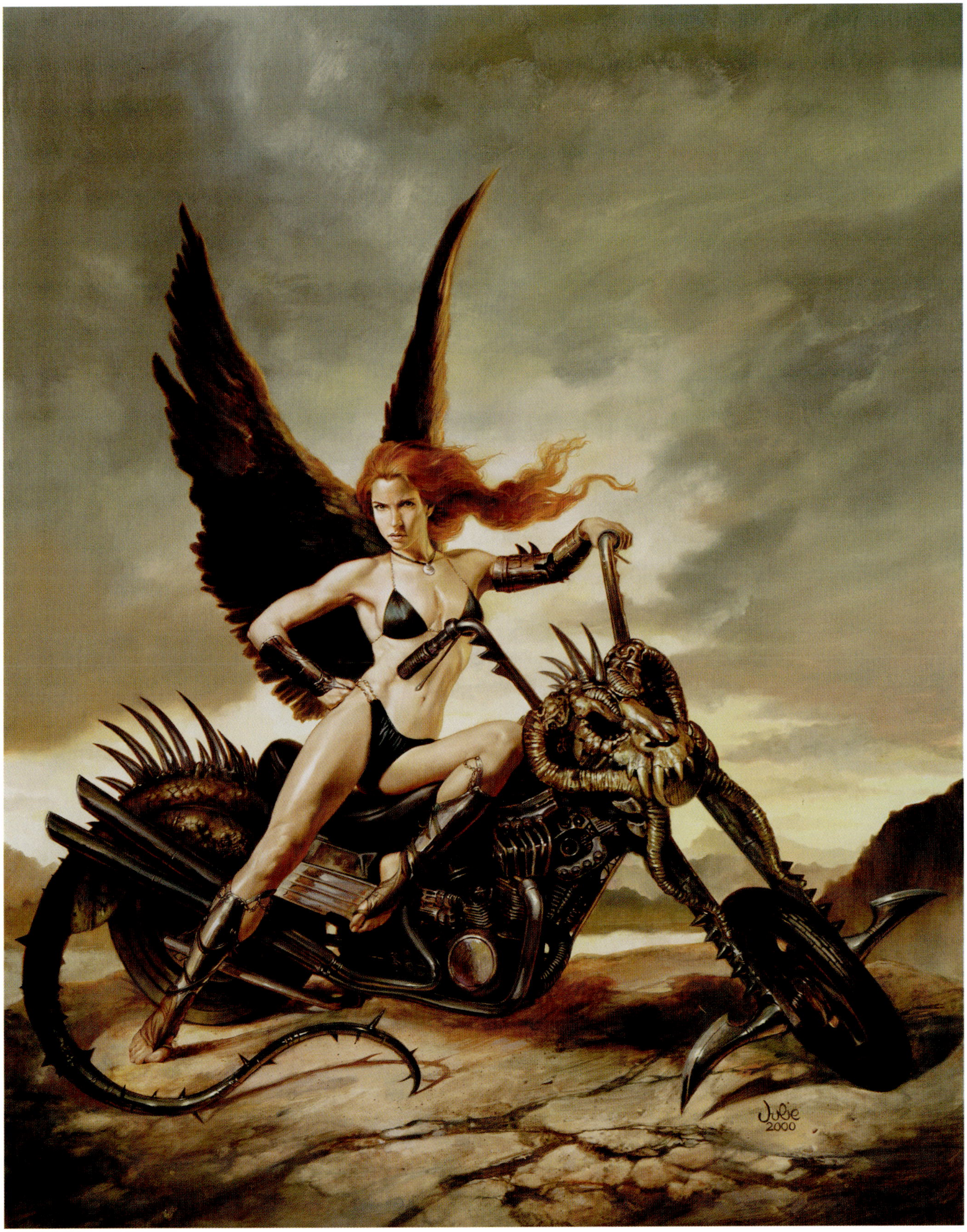
Julie
2000

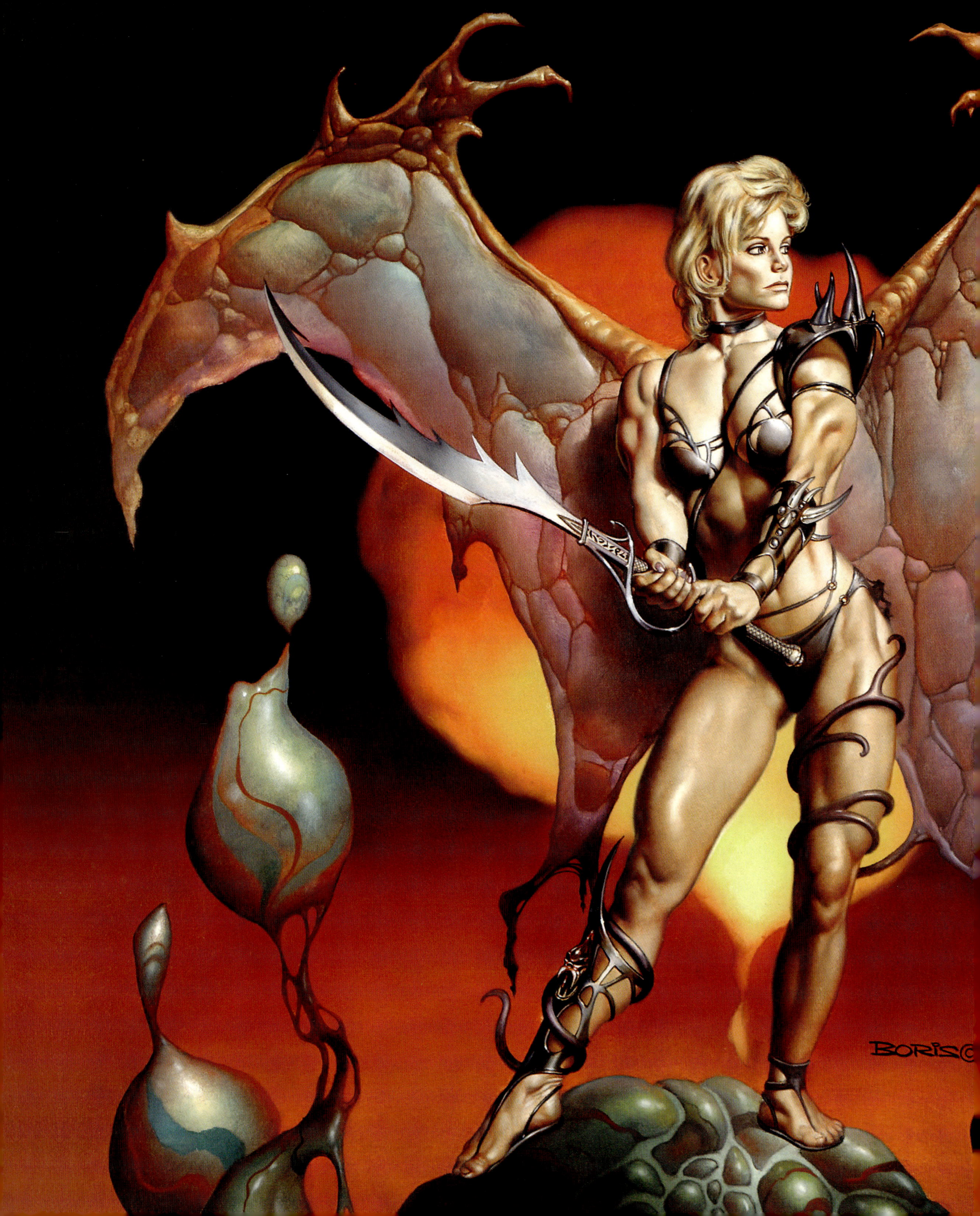
BORIS©

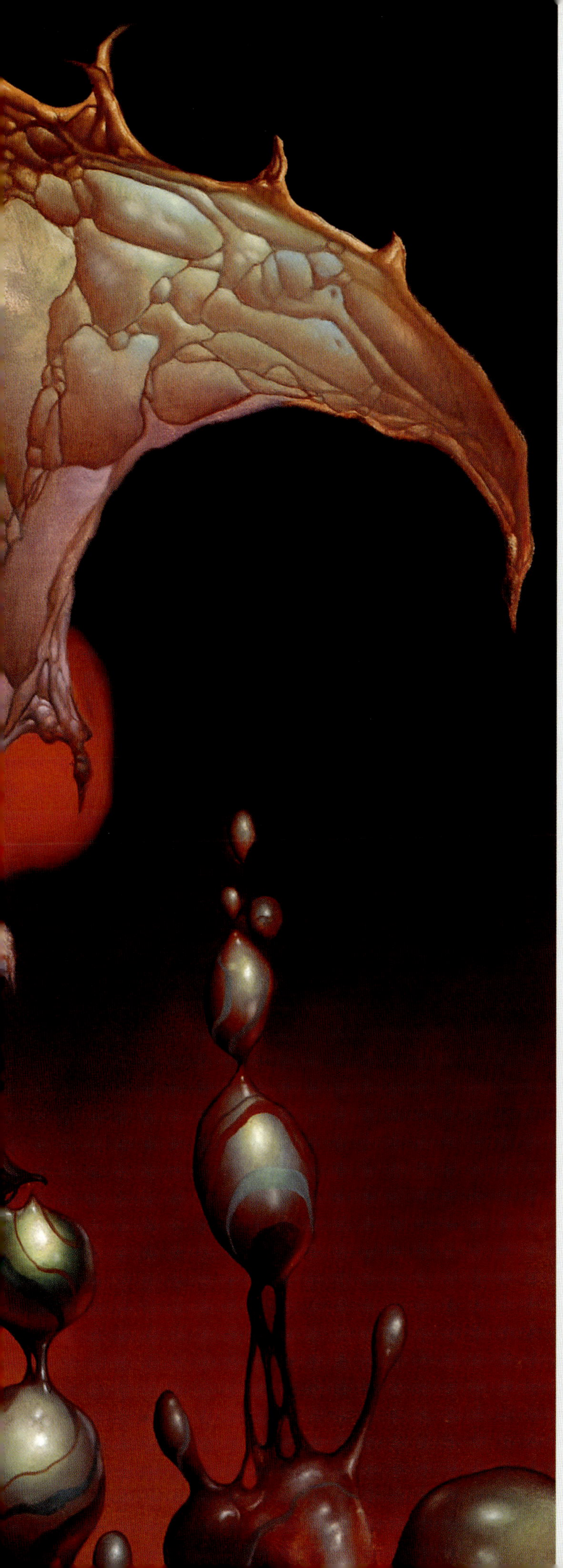

Winged Warrior, Boris Vallejo, *1997, calendar*

Boris hired Dinah Anderson, one of Julie's bodybuilding heroes, to model for this painting.

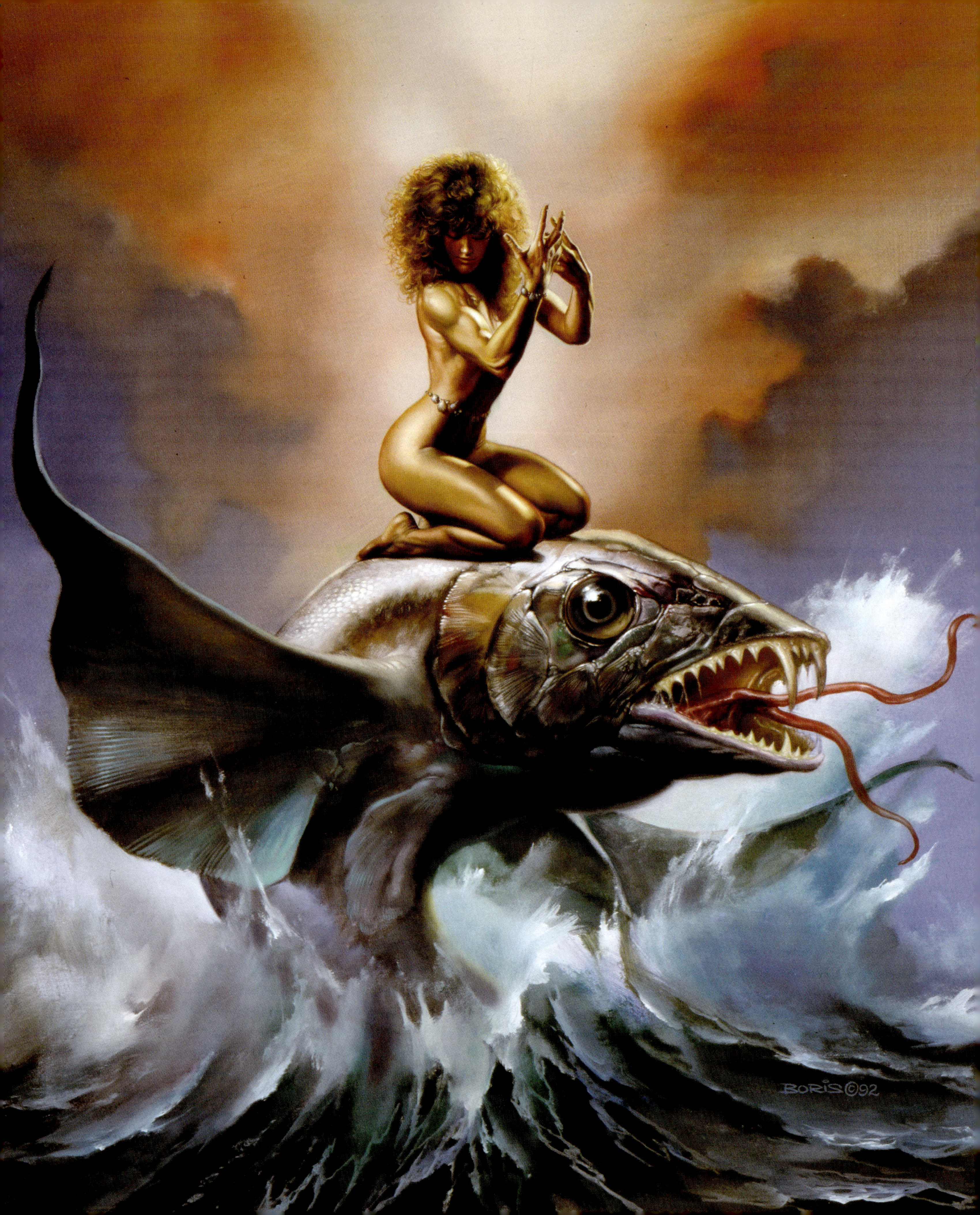
BORIS©92

Fish Queen,
Boris Vallejo, *1992, calendar*

"This girl was from New Jersey and she had the hair to prove it," says Boris with a smile. "Seriously though, the creature in the piece is very dominant, more important even than the girl. That's very unusual for my paintings."

"AS I GET OLDER, I TEND TO FOCUS ON THE BEAUTY, COMPLEXITY, AND STRENGTH OF MY SUBJECT'S CHARACTER AS WELL AS THEIR PHYSICAL BEAUTY"

JULIE

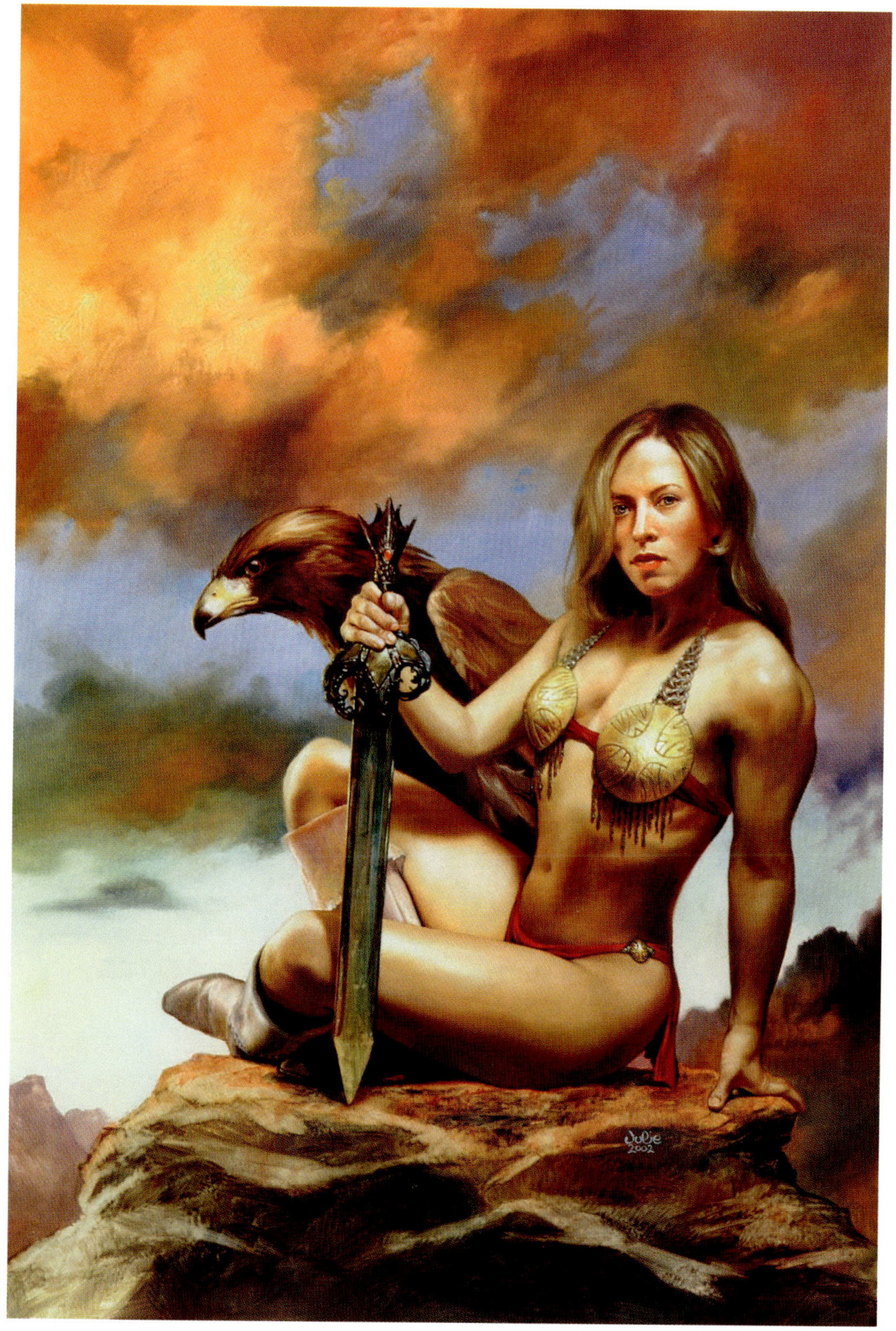

Jesse, Julie Bell, *2002, calendar*

"It's a portrait of a friend of mine." says Julie. "I didn't glamorize her, and that approach led to other jobs with new art directors. As I get older, I tend to focus on the beauty, complexity, and strength of my subject's character as well as their physical beauty."

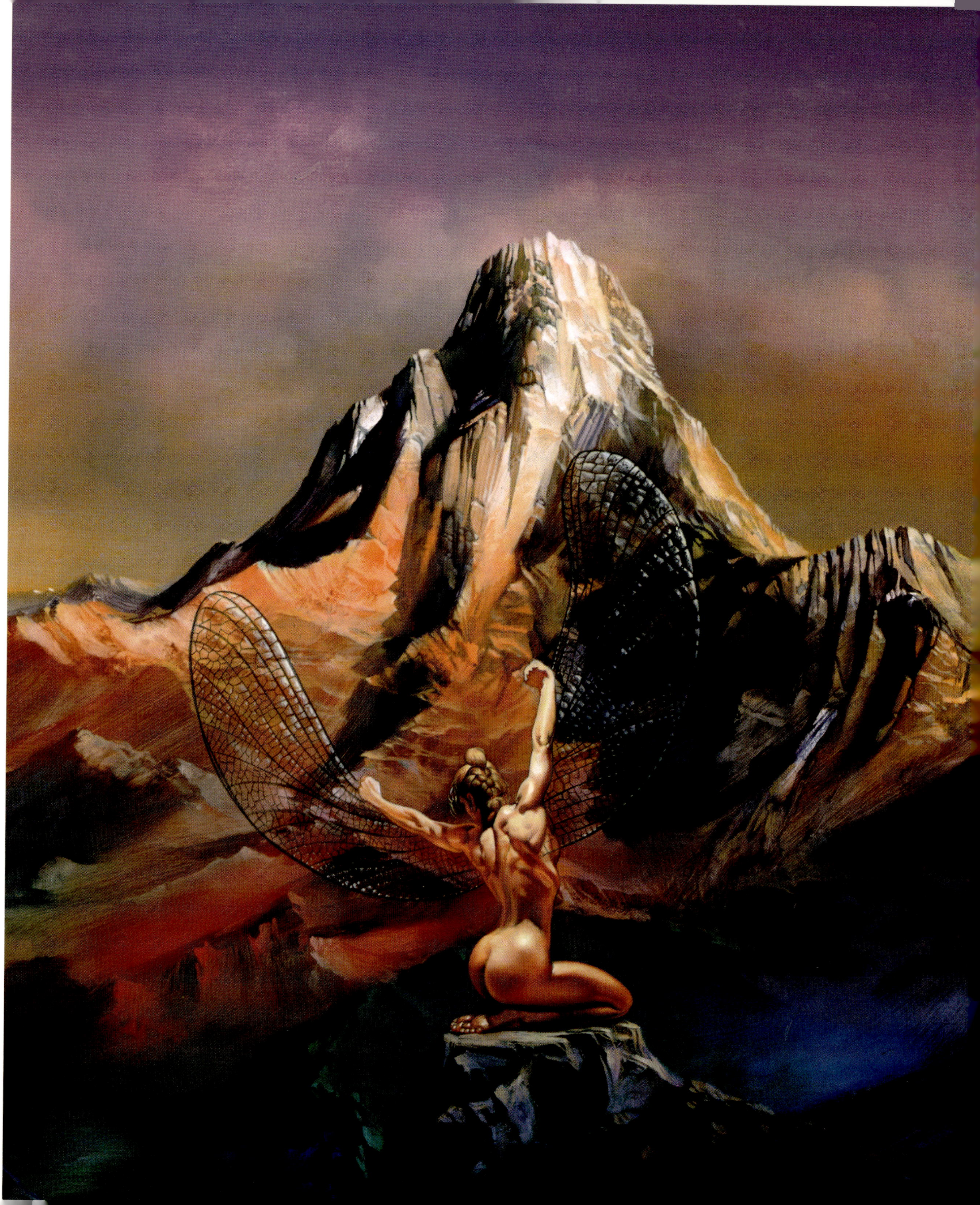

Summit, Boris Vallejo,
1994, book cover/calendar

Originally a landscape, Boris reworked this painting to add the kneeling figure.

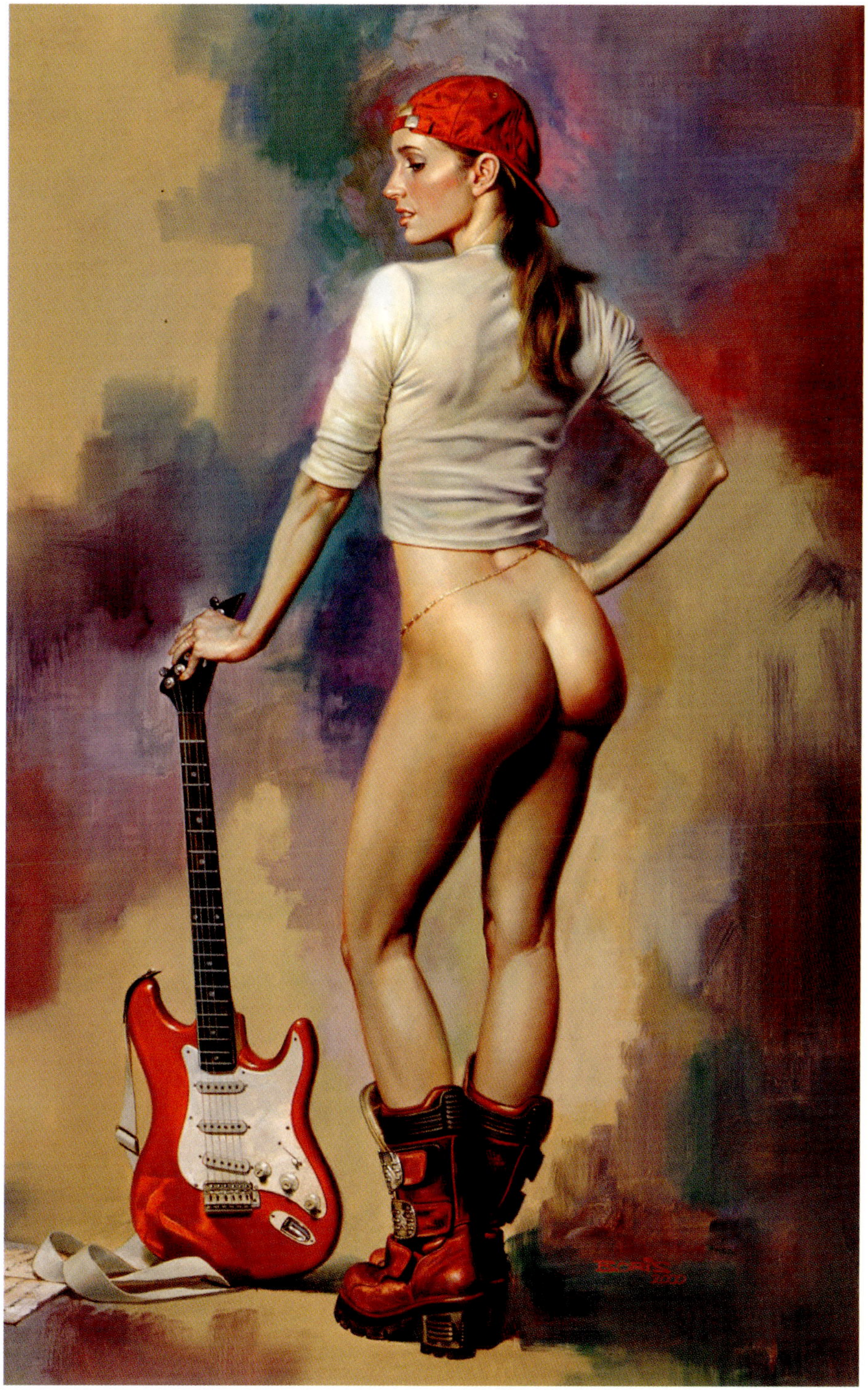

Music Lesson, Boris Vallejo, *2000*

This painting was done for an exhibition of pin-up art at Meisel Gallery in New York. Often Boris and Julie sell their original paintings to collectors, but they very rarely exhibit them in galleries.

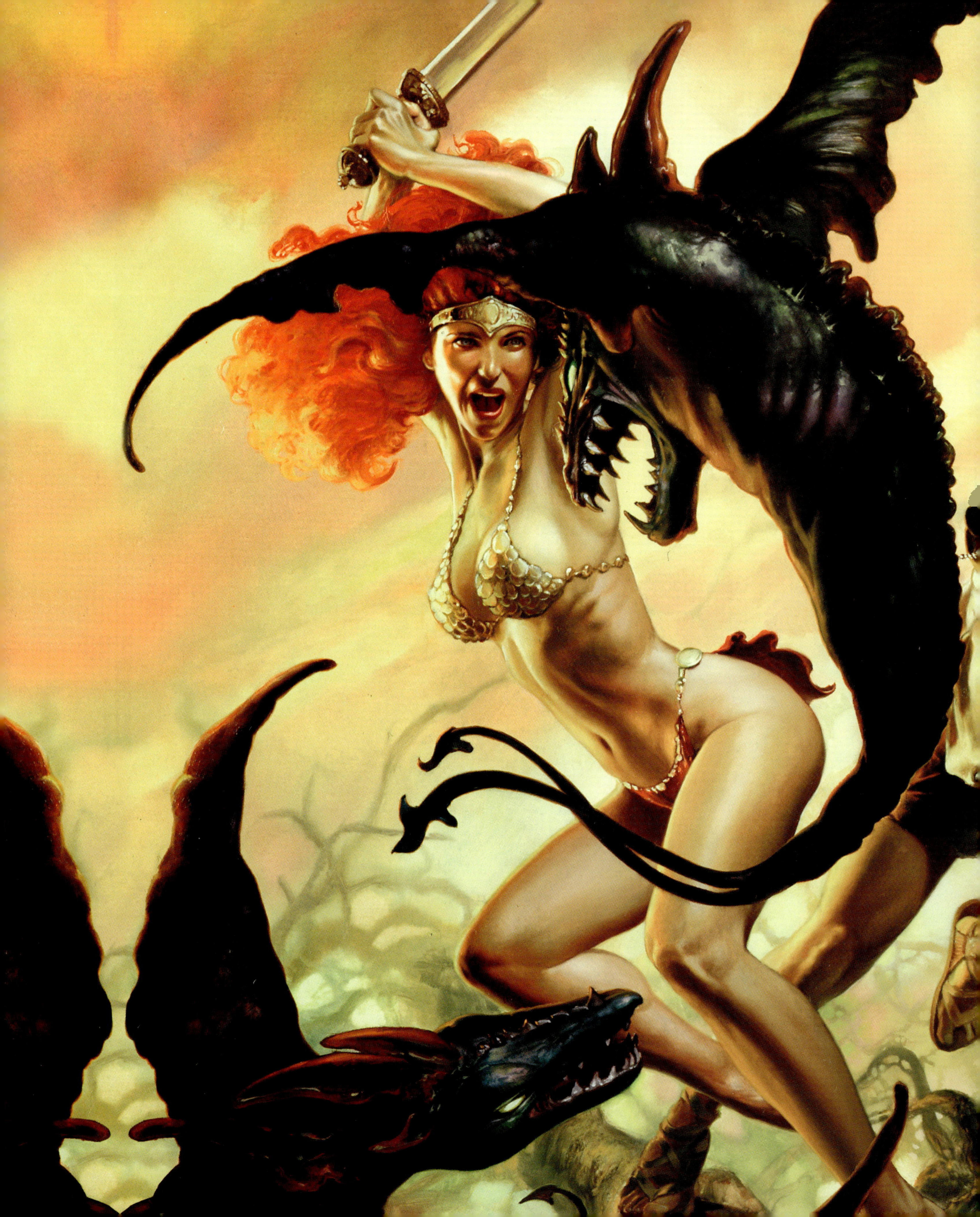

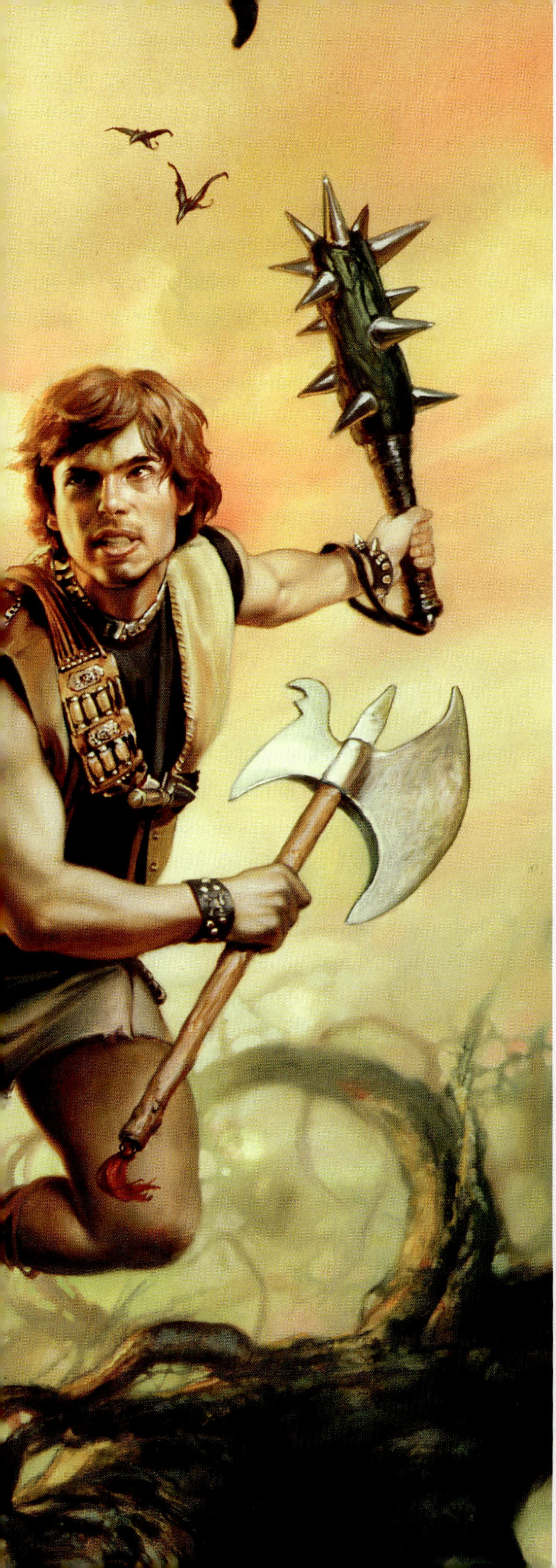

"I WAS ASKED TO DO SOMETHING FOR THE CALENDAR WITH SOME REAL ACTION. THEY WANTED A BATTLE SCENE. HER HAIR WAS INSPIRED BY BORIS' PAINTING, THE BRIDE."

JULIE

Monster Bash, Julie Bell, *2001, calendar*

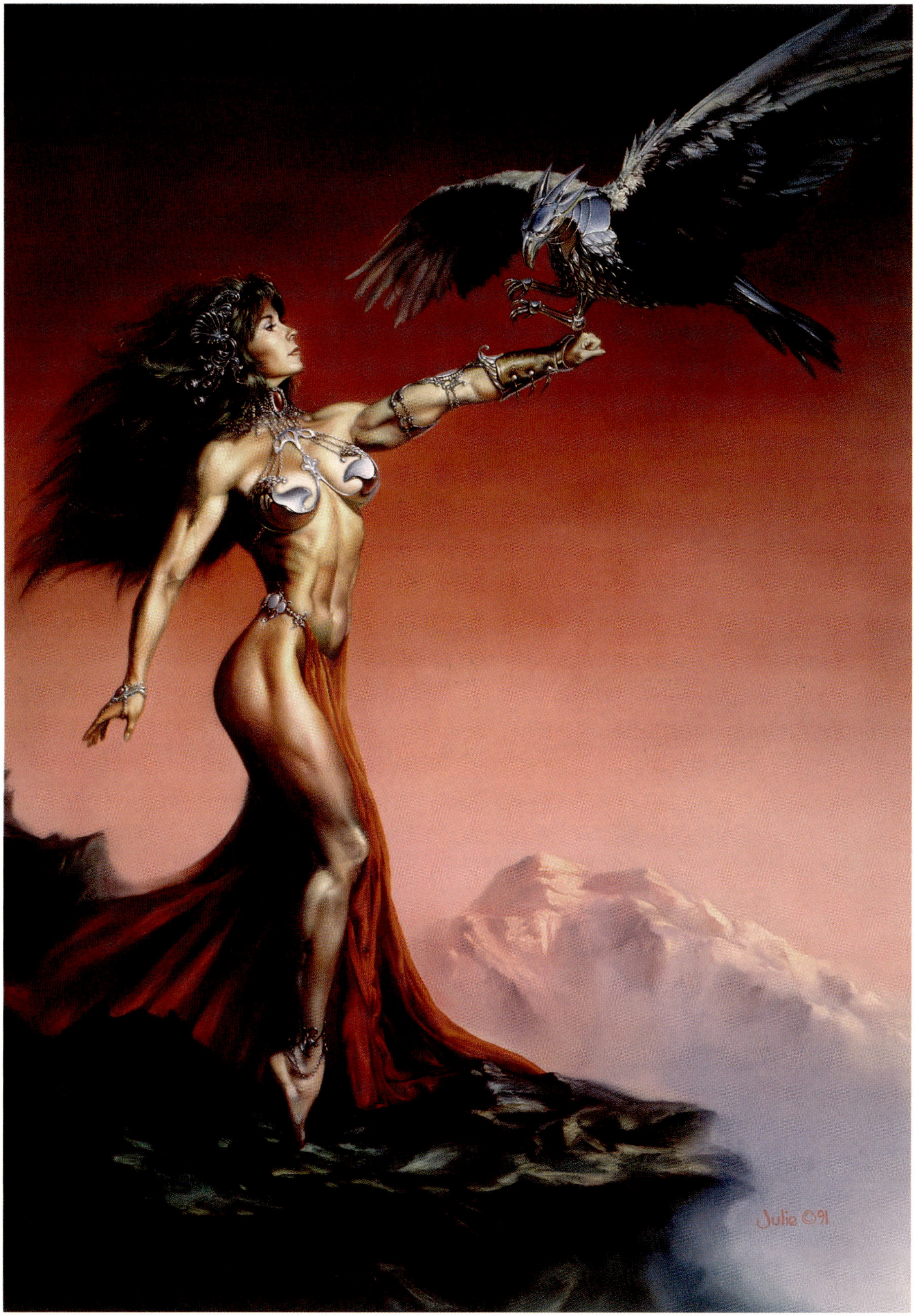

◂◂ **Robobird,** Julie Bell, *1991*

Obstacle Course, ▸▸
Julie Bell, *1998,*
book cover

"I loved making my own obstacle courses as a kid. I'd test my physical reactions, setting it up so I'd have to jump over stuff or get sprayed by the hose. I'd run or ride my bike through them."

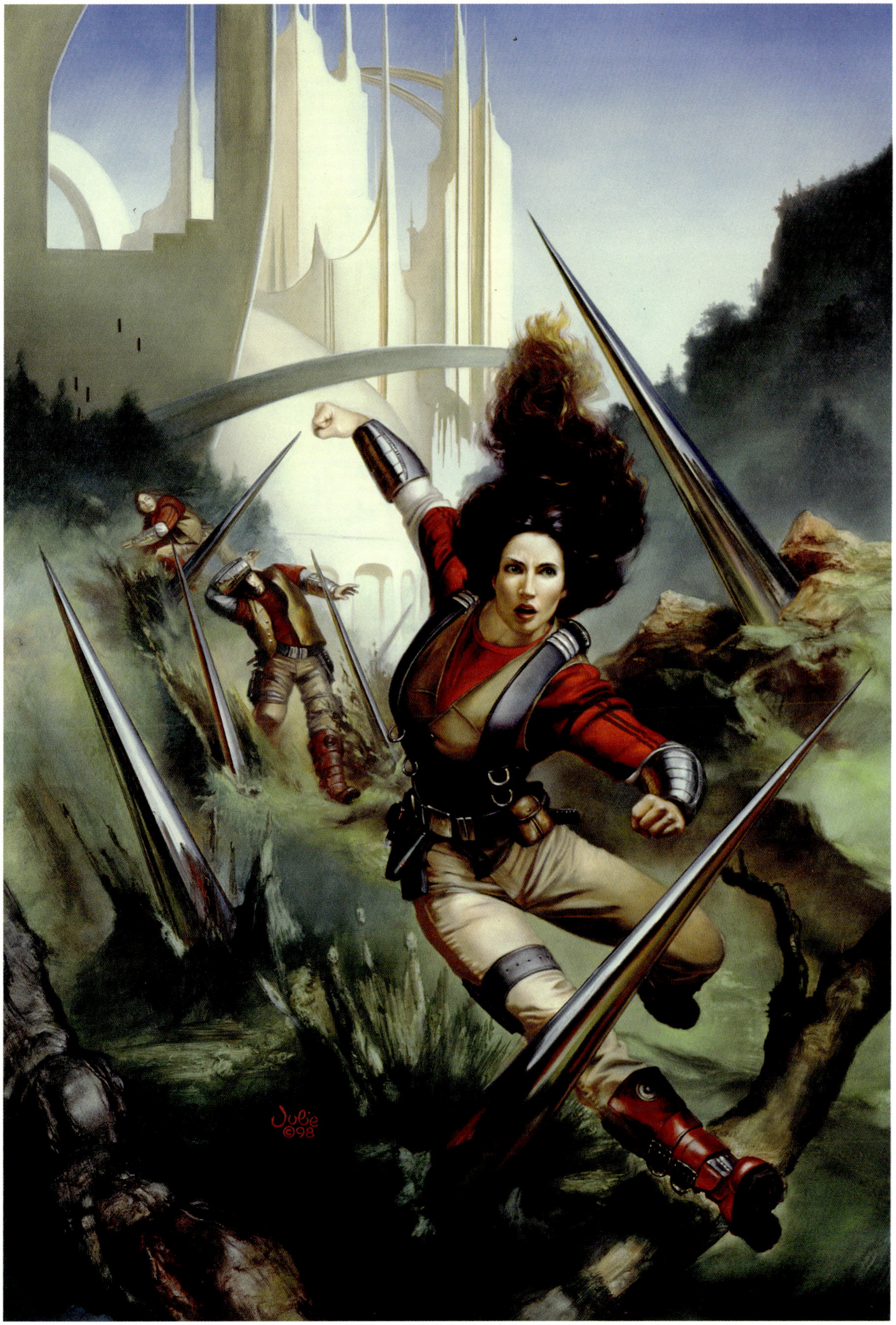
Julie
©98

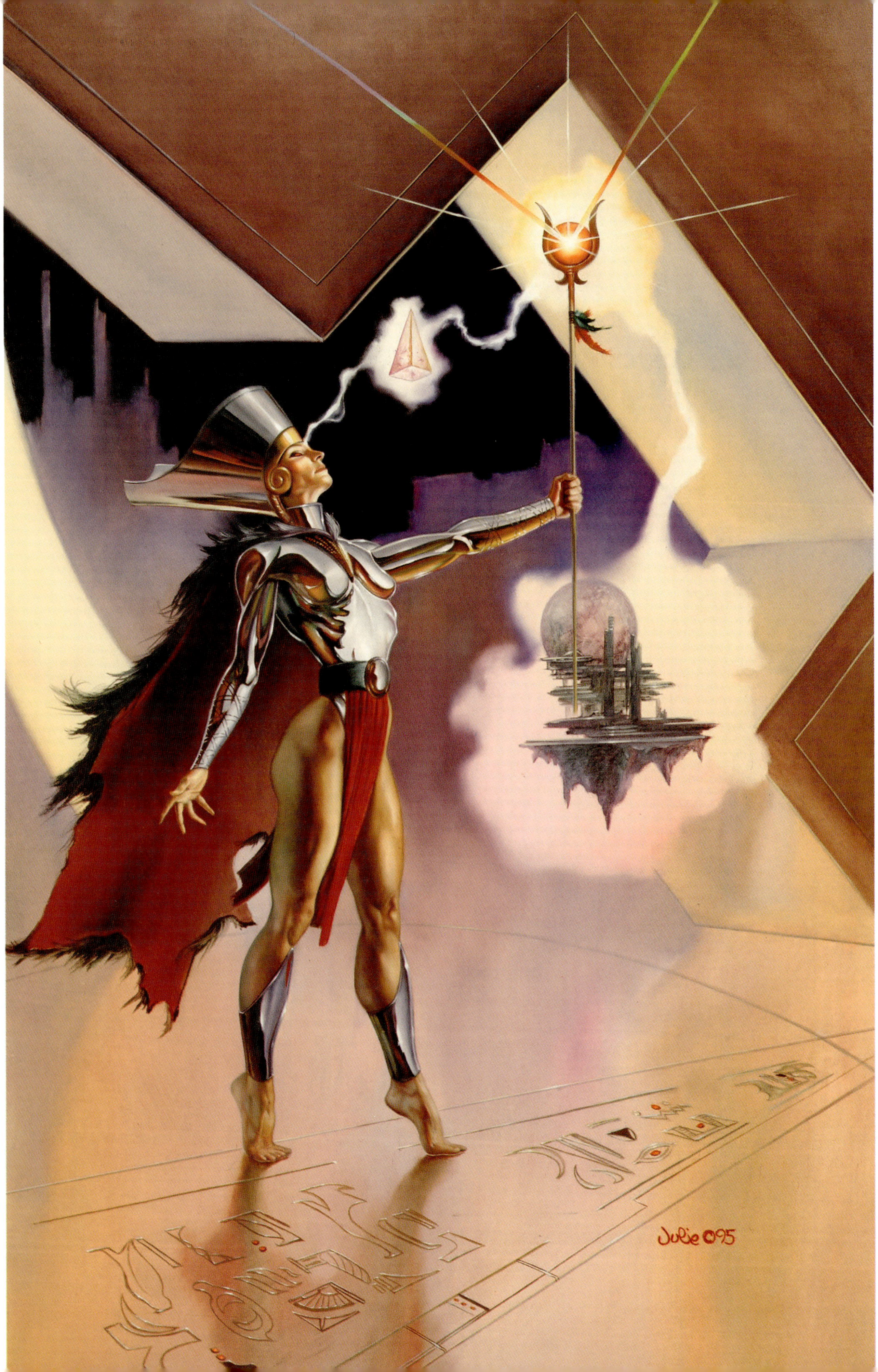
Julie ©95

Pompeii, Boris Vallejo, ▸▸
1986, film poster

"I was asked by the producers to not include the actual lead actress in this poster, despite a great deal of pressure on me from her agent. When the painting was finished and she wasn't included, he called me up. I answered the phone and the first thing he said was 'You son-of-a-bitch.' What could I do? The producers write the checks!"

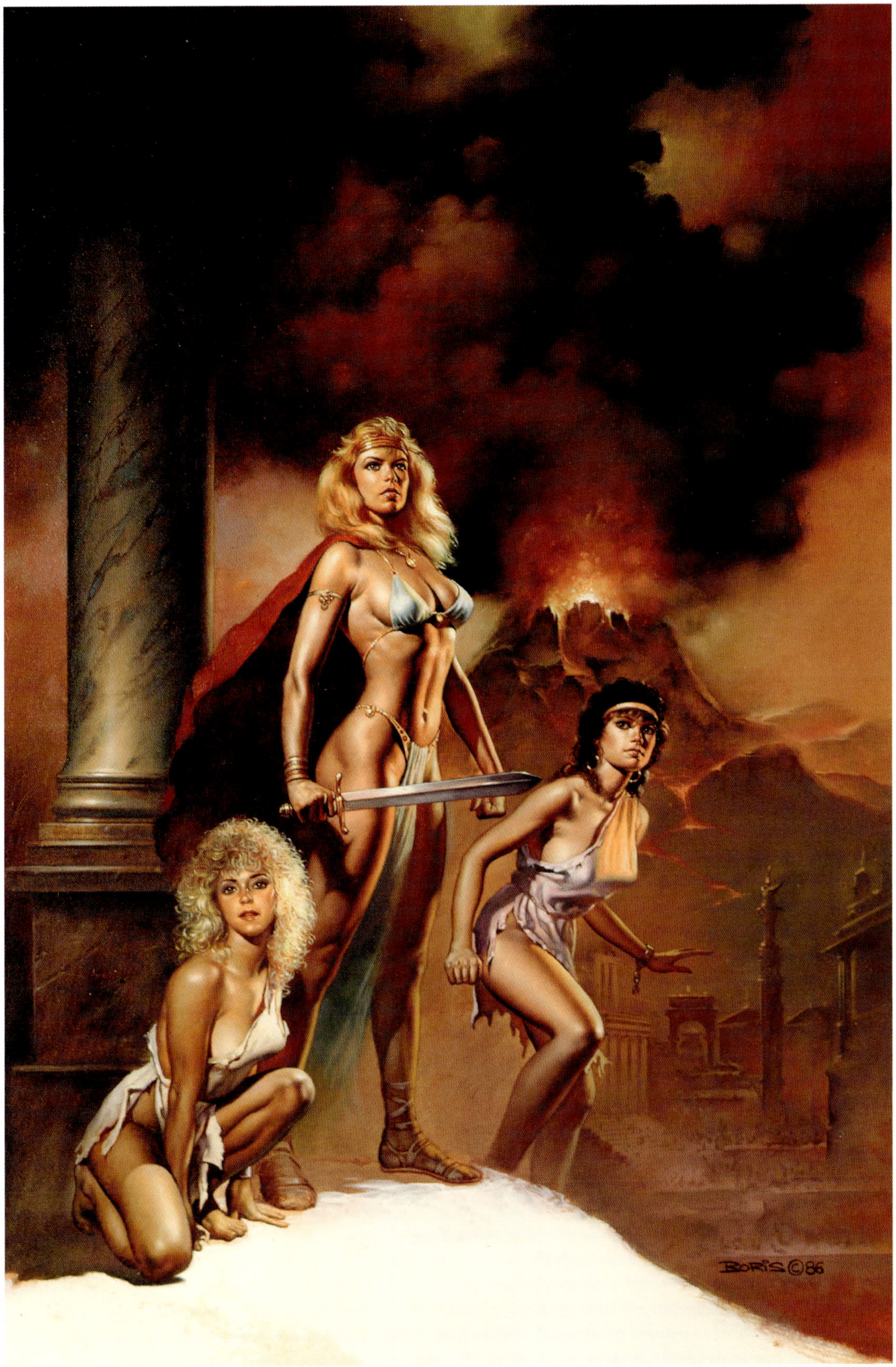

◂◂ **Empress of a New World,**
Julie Bell, *1995, trading card*

"I was influenced by the movie *Stargate* when I painted this. I liked the idea of a high-tech Egyptian priestess."

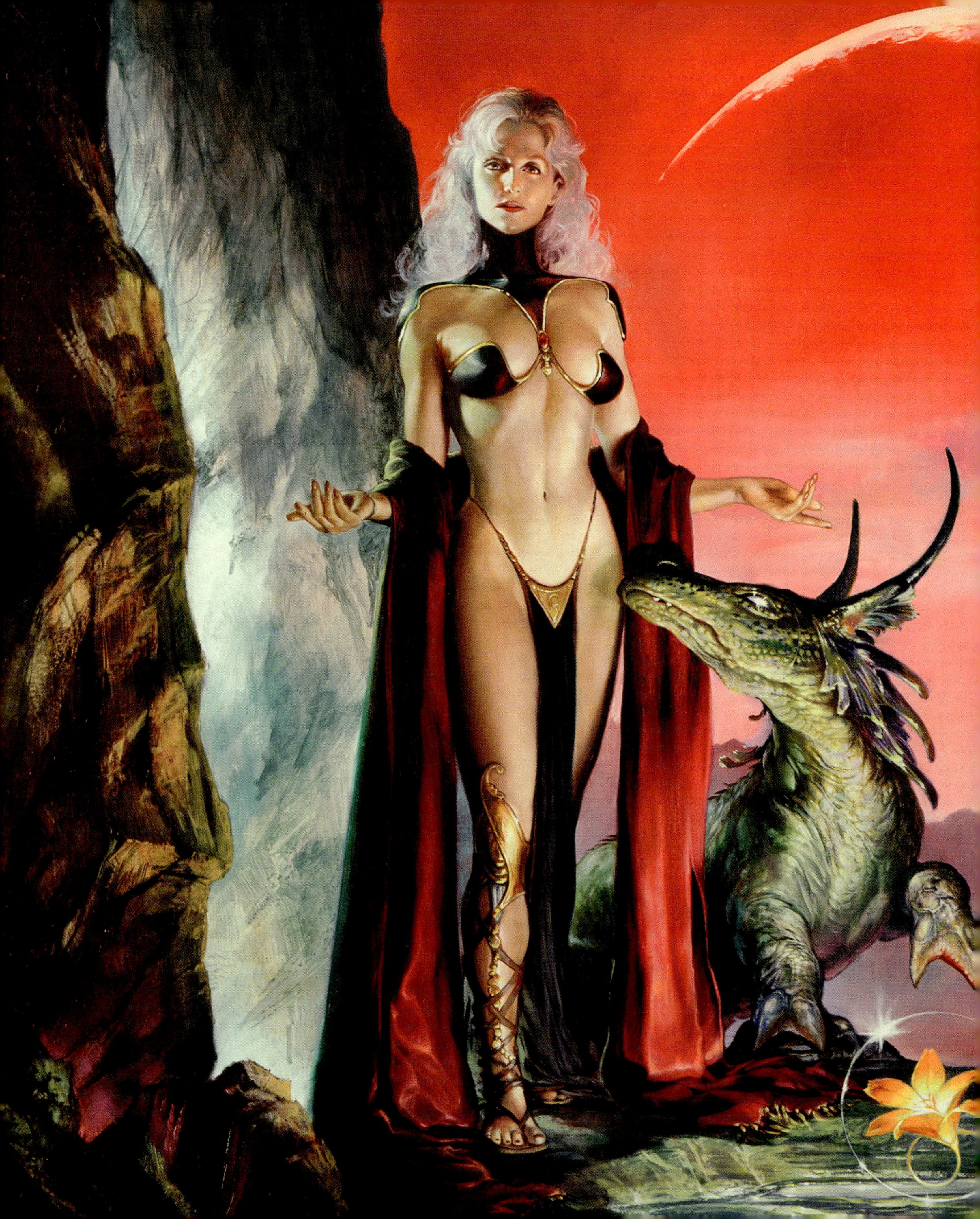

Dragon's Mentor, Julie Bell, *2000, calendar*

Exuding a graceful feminine power, this sorceress instructs her dragon in the ways of her mysterious art.

"IT IS INTERESTING, A CONTRAST BETWEEN MY WORK AND JULIE'S. I AM MOSTLY CONCERNED WITH PAINTING THE FEMALE FORM, WHILE FOR JULIE, THE CHARACTER'S COSTUME IS OFTEN OF EQUAL IMPORTANCE TO THE FIGURE. FOR ME IT IS JUST AN ACCESSORY."

BORIS

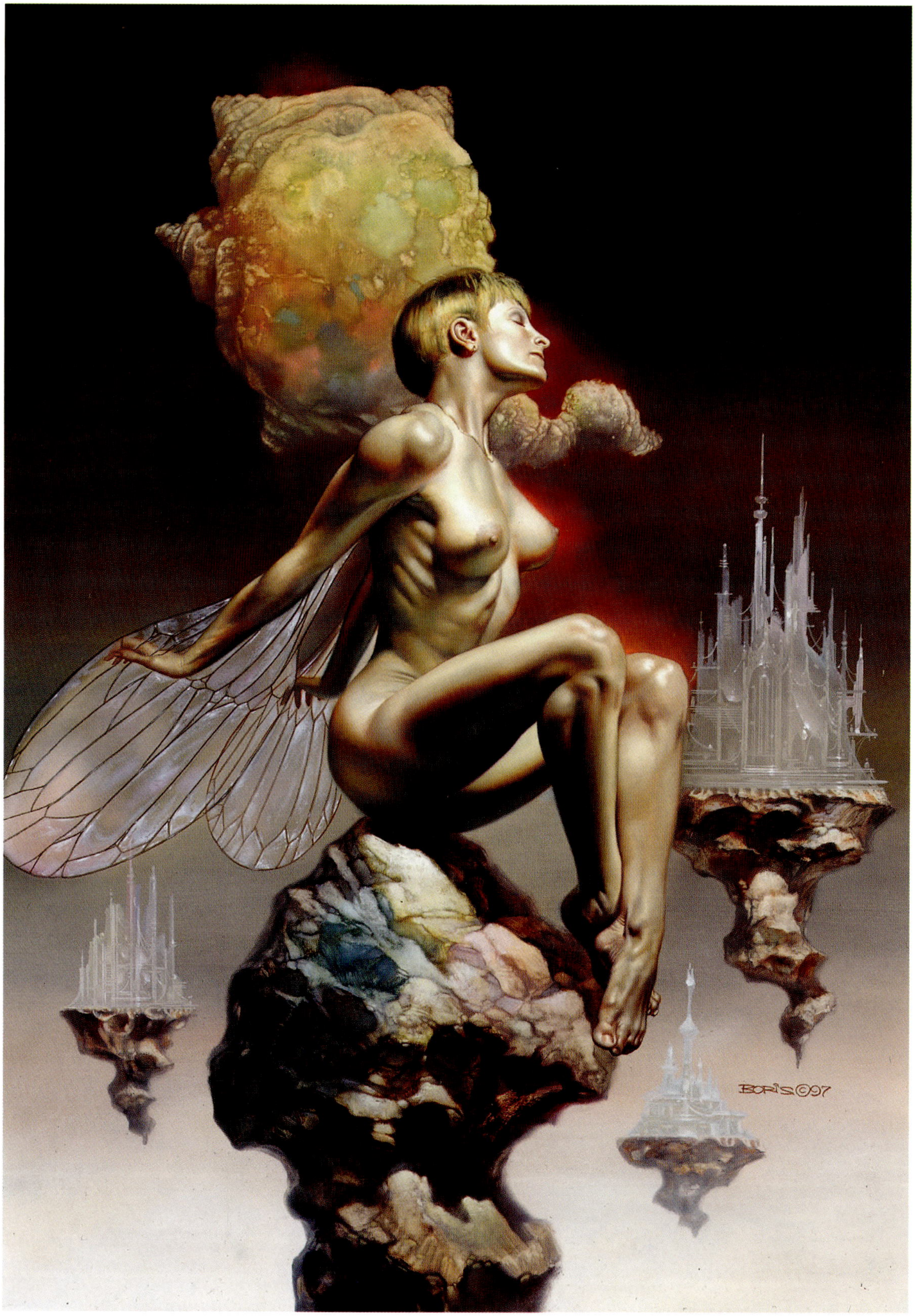

Cindy, Boris Vallejo,
1997, portrait commission

Boris and Julie do portrait commissions on occasion, though always with their own fantastical twist on the conventions of portraiture. This painting was eventually featured in their calendar.

Tara, Boris Vallejo,
1997, calendar

Boris recalls Julie's painting, "Possibilities Bound", as the inspiration for this piece. "The creature is like time, moving slowly and deliberately. The girl is the present moment, contemplating."

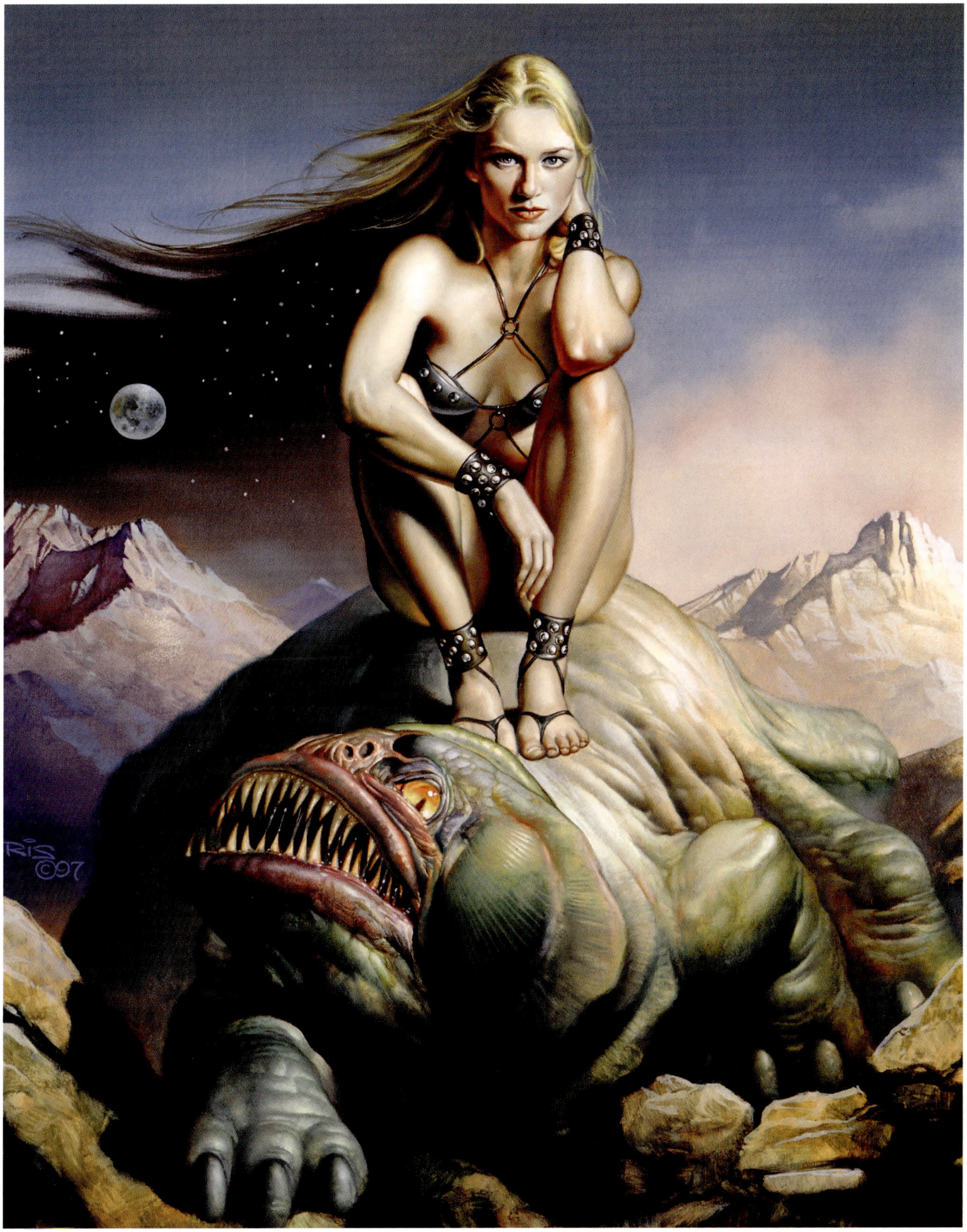
RIS
©97

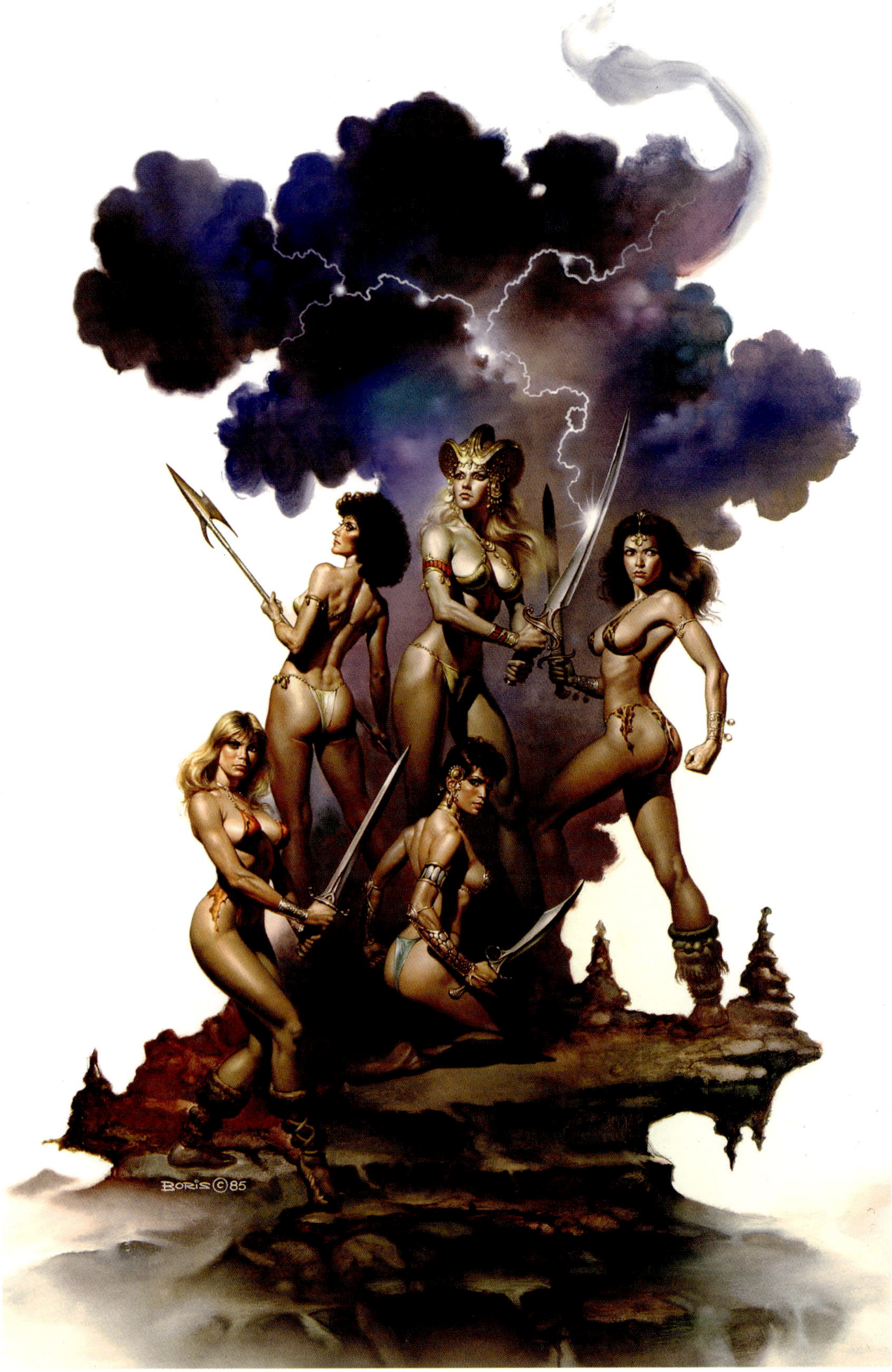

Amazon Queen,
Boris Vallejo, *1985, film poster*

Boris says of this movie poster, “There was a series of Roger Corman fantasy movies featuring female warriors. They are cult classics. These movies were not much in the way of substance, but visually they were appealing. Roger Corman is a great guy. I had a long working relationship with him. There is precious little traditional illustration in movie posters these days. Most of what you see is digital. Things shift all the time and move around, so you move with the times.”

Hallucin, Julie Bell, *1994, trading card*

"This is the painting Meat Loaf saw that made him want to hire me to paint the cover of his new album. The colors and the girl's pose appealed to him."

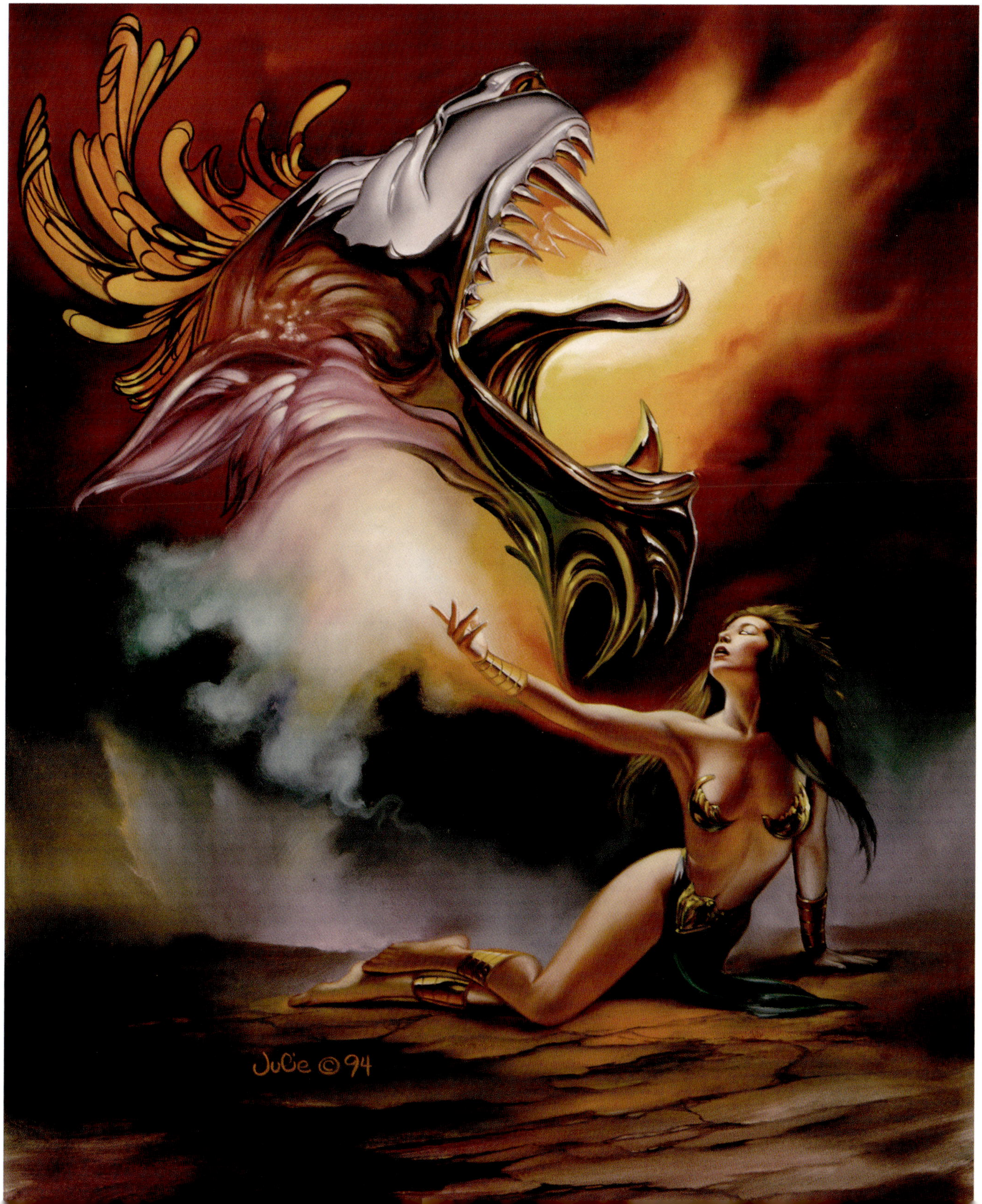

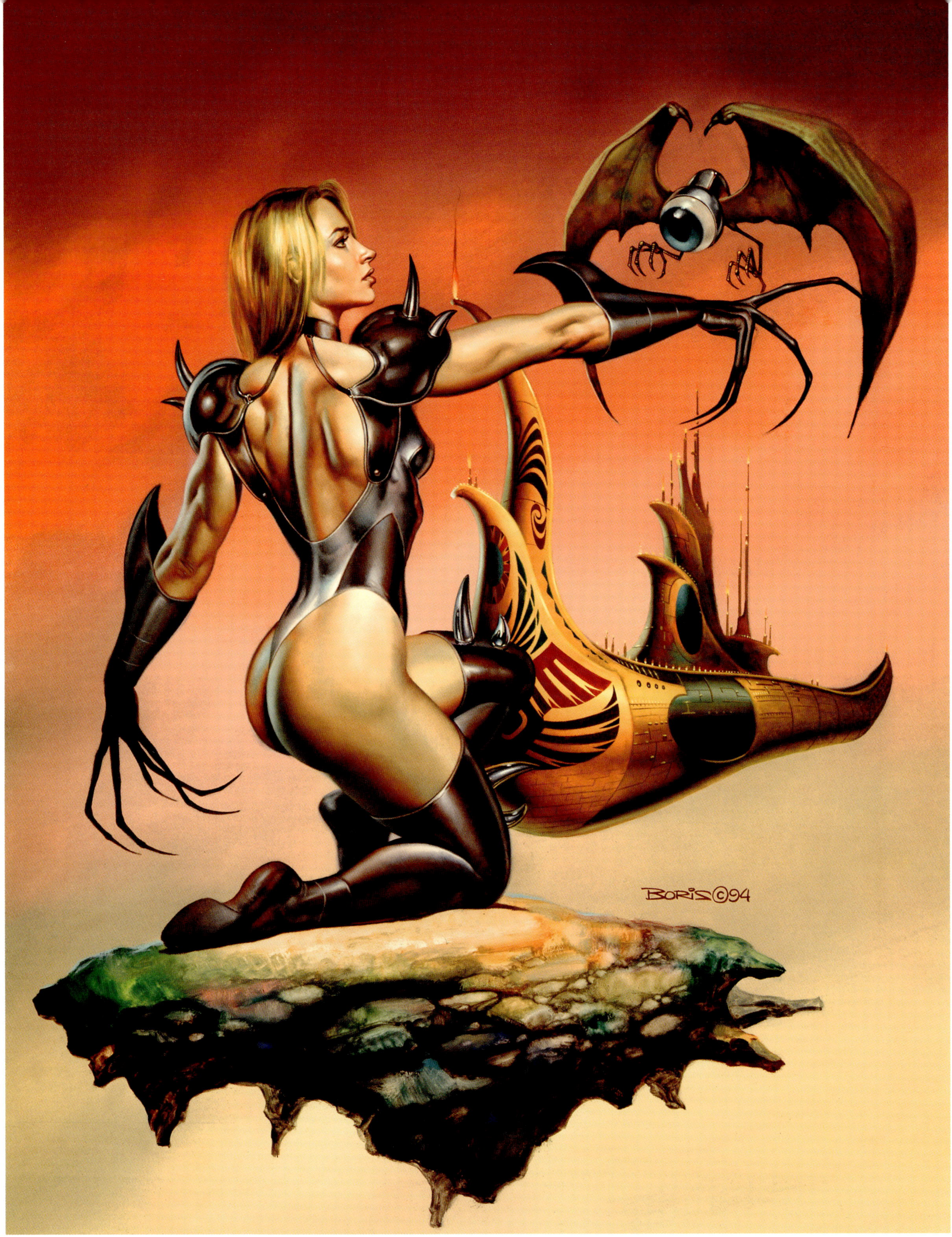
BORIS©94

"WHEN I DO A PAINTING, I SEE IT HAPPENING IN MY HEAD, LIKE A MOVIE. WHEN I SEE A FRAME THAT I LIKE, I FREEZE IT. THERE IS NO STORY, JUST AN IMAGE."

BORIS

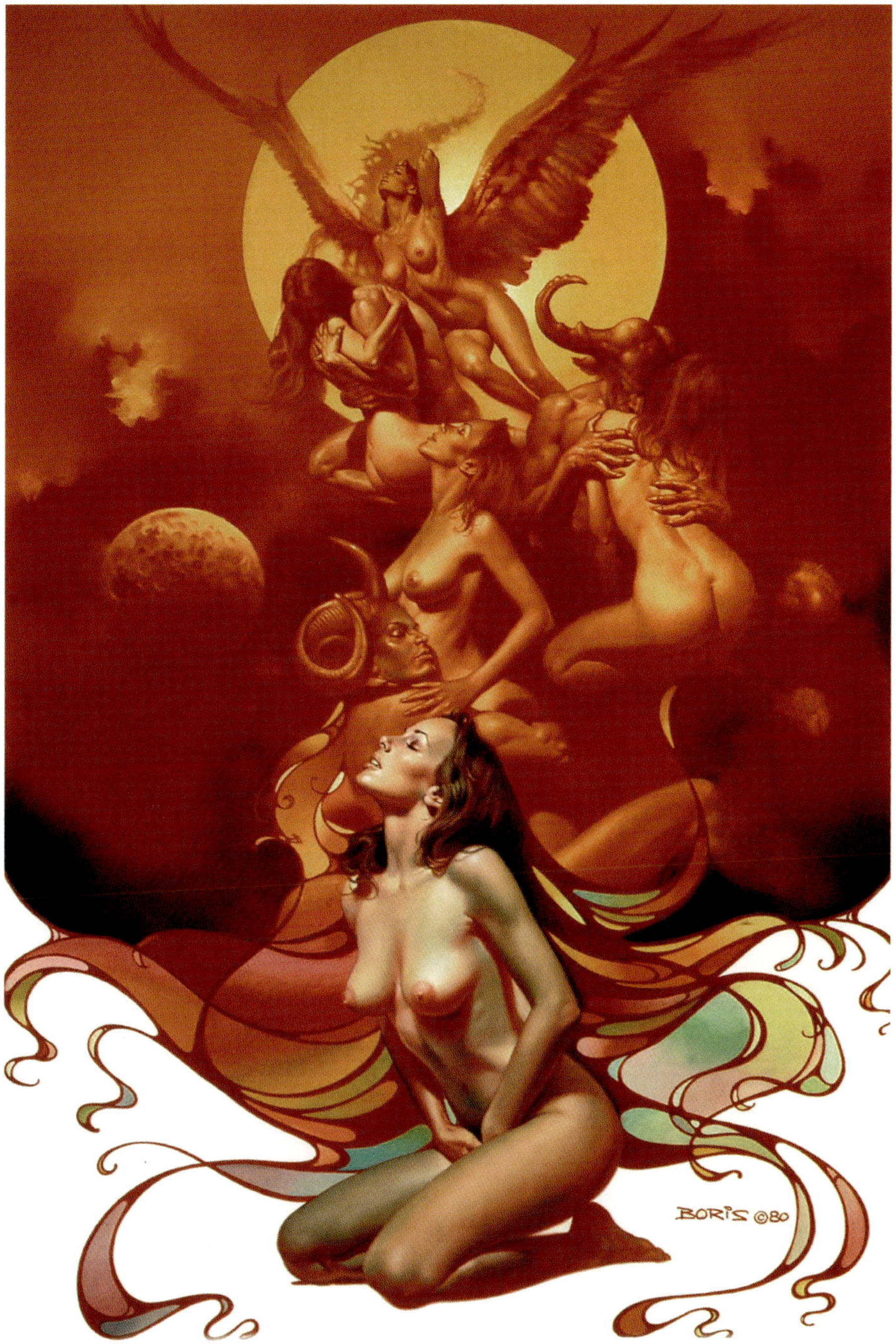

The Eye, Boris Vallejo, *1994, calendar*

Alone, Boris Vallejo, *1980,* Mirage *interior art*

"All of the paintings I did for *Mirage* were of an obviously sensual nature. The idea here, of course, is the woman's fantasy. The monochromatic red gives it a hot nature. The sun in the background makes it even hotter."

Breaking Through, Boris Vallejo, *1983, magazine cover*

"A cover for *Heavy Metal* magazine, one of the first times that I thought of using the image of a very powerful and aggressive woman. I was still under the influence of *Mirage*, hence the hair. It was a lot of fun working on that crushed starship door. I looked at a crumpled pie plate for reference. *Heavy Metal* is a wonderful avenue for illustrators and comic artists to showcase their work." says Boris. "They don't try to put limits on the artist." adds Julie.

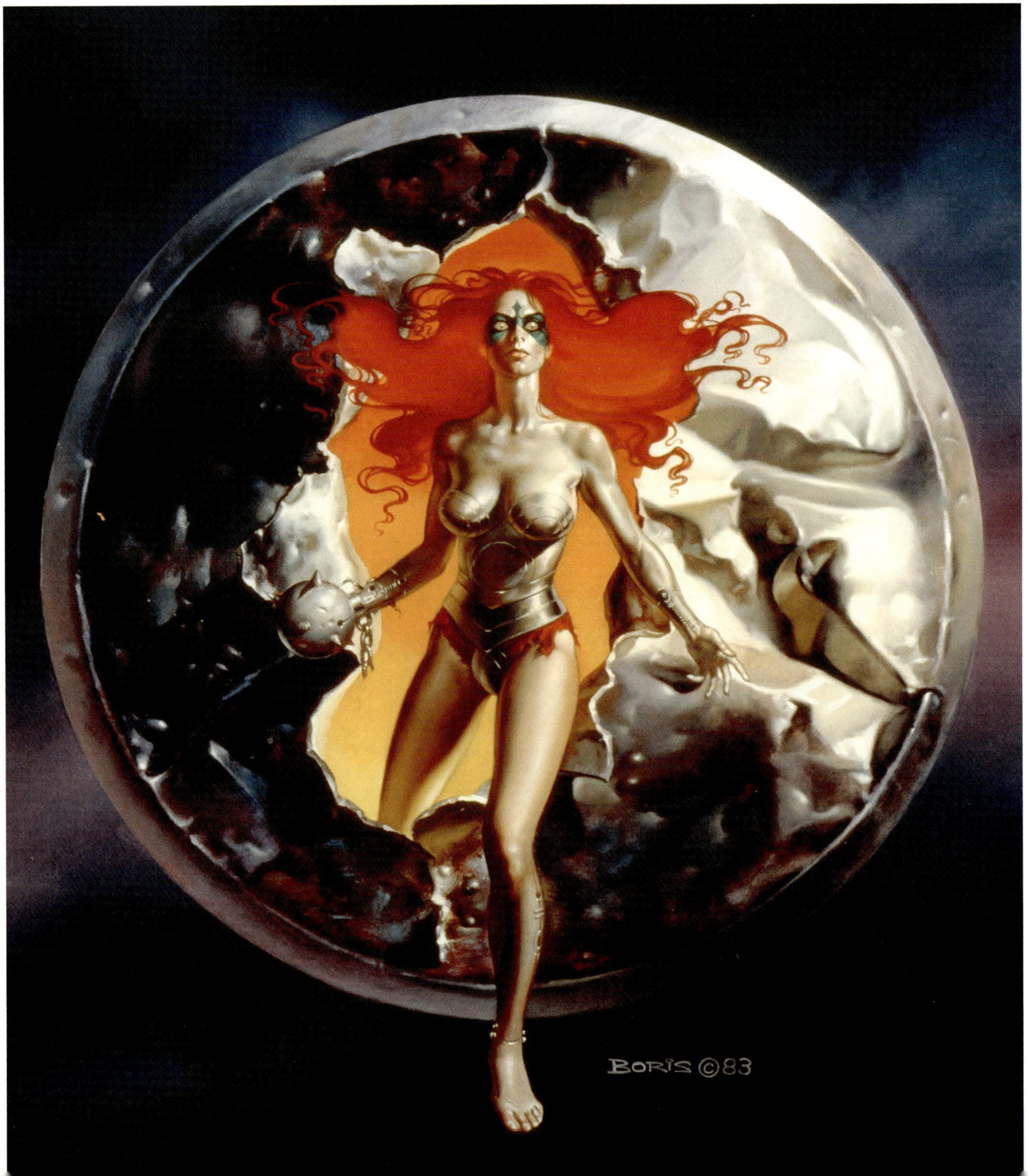

"I FEEL VERY CONNECTED TO THIS CHARACTER. SHE'S VERY NATURAL AND WILD, LIKE THE WOLF, AND I PUT A LOT OF MYSELF INTO HER.

JULIE

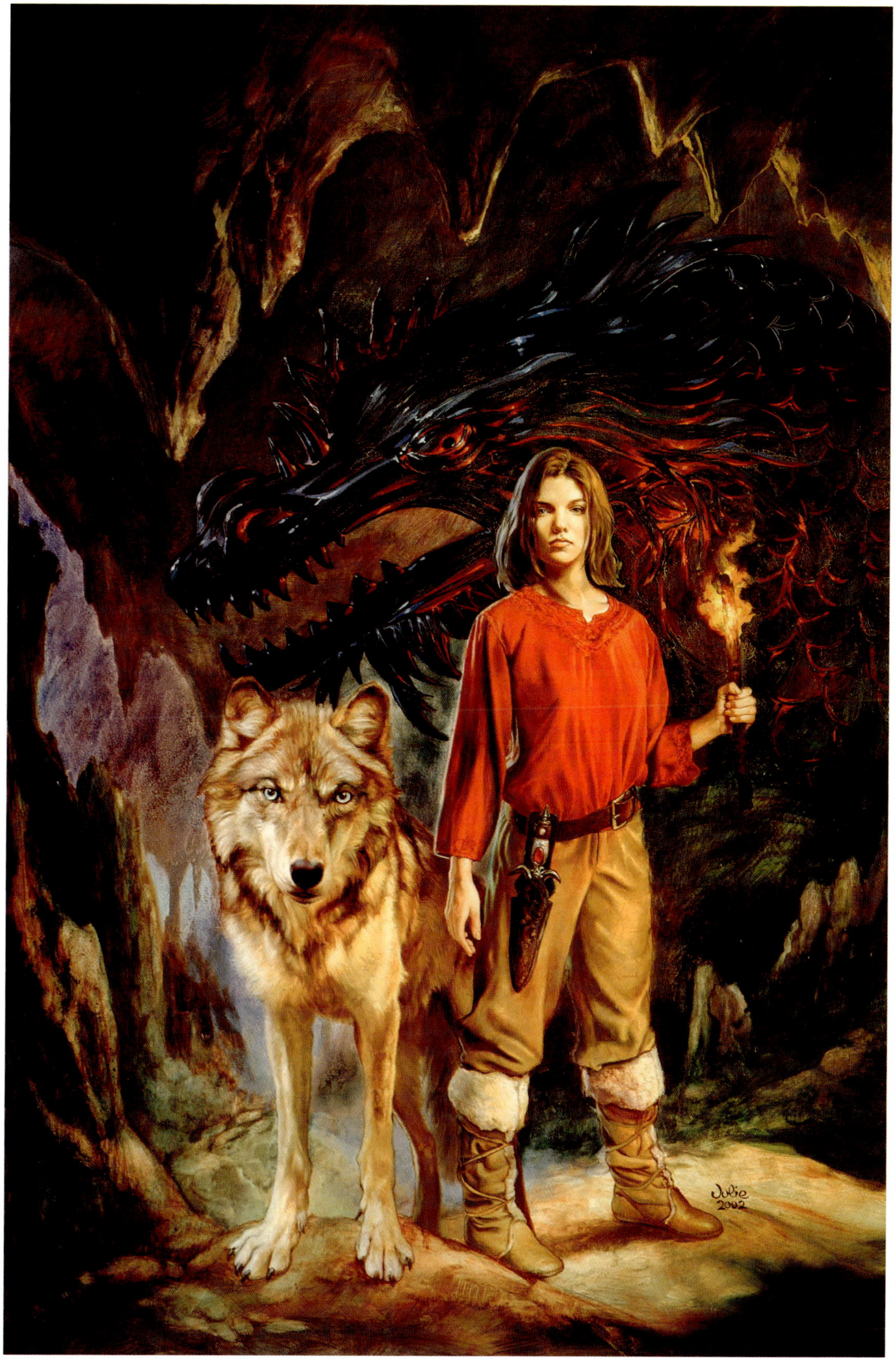

Obsidian Dragon,
Julie Bell, *2002, book cover*

We see here a dramatic divergence from Julie's typical heroic female. "I feel very connected to this character. She's very natural and wild, like the wolf, and I put a lot of myself into her. I even painted her in my own clothes." This painting was where Julie discovered her love for painting animals, wolves in particular.

The Locusts, Boris Vallejo, *1998, calendar* ▸▸

"Insects really intrigue me. I like the jewel-like quality of an insect's body and the colors in their wings. I used to be phobic of spiders, but not any more. One time, going to bed, I looked at the ceiling and saw hundreds of little spiders. I thought of them dropping on me in the night. The only thing I could do was go with my thumb and squish 'em. So that's what I did. I decided I had to get over my irrational fear."

"INSECTS REALLY INTRIGUE ME. I LIKE THE JEWEL-LIKE QUALITY OF AN INSECT'S BODY AND THE COLORS IN THEIR WINGS. I USED TO BE PHOBIC OF SPIDERS, BUT NOT ANYMORE."

BORIS

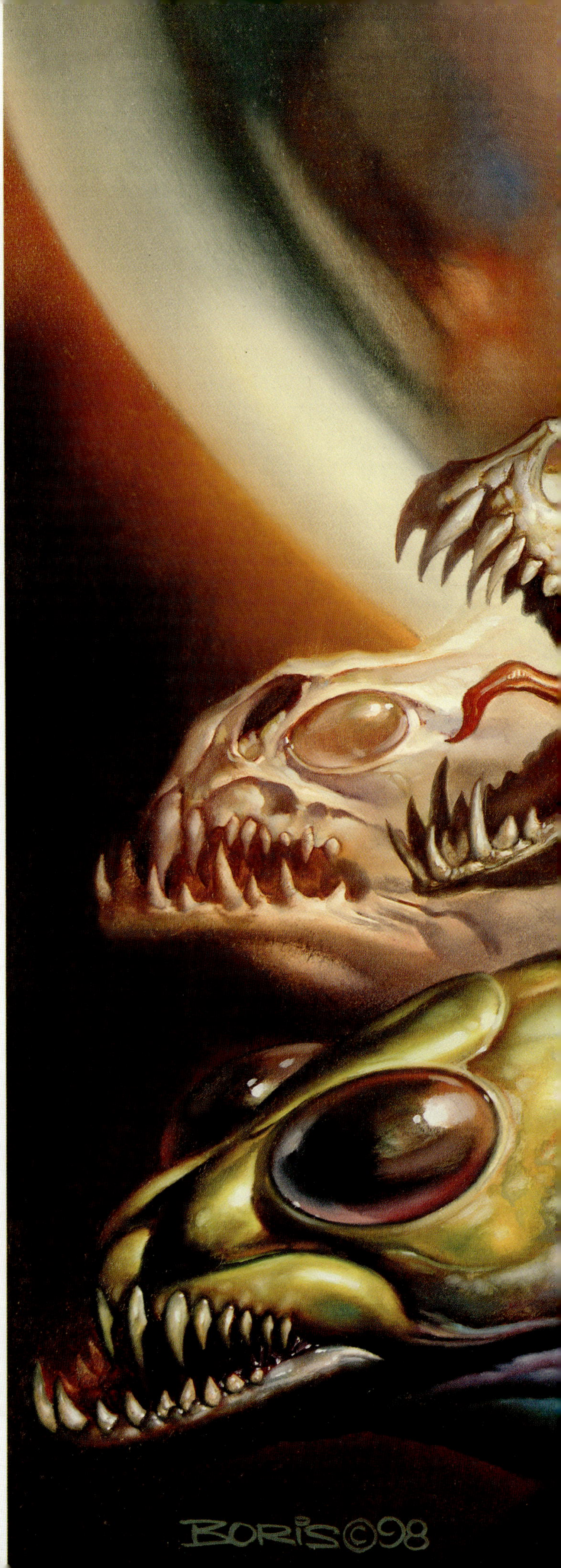

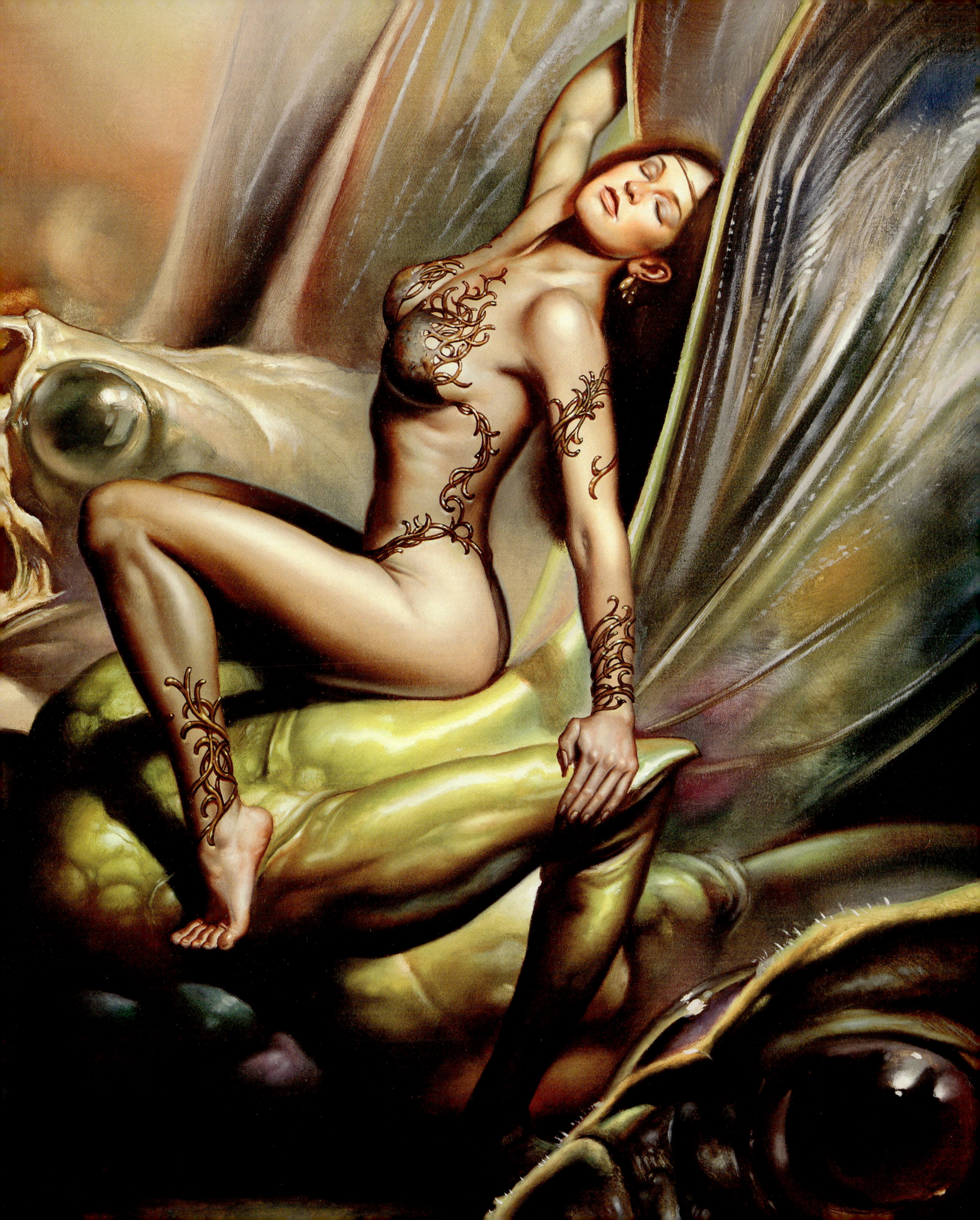

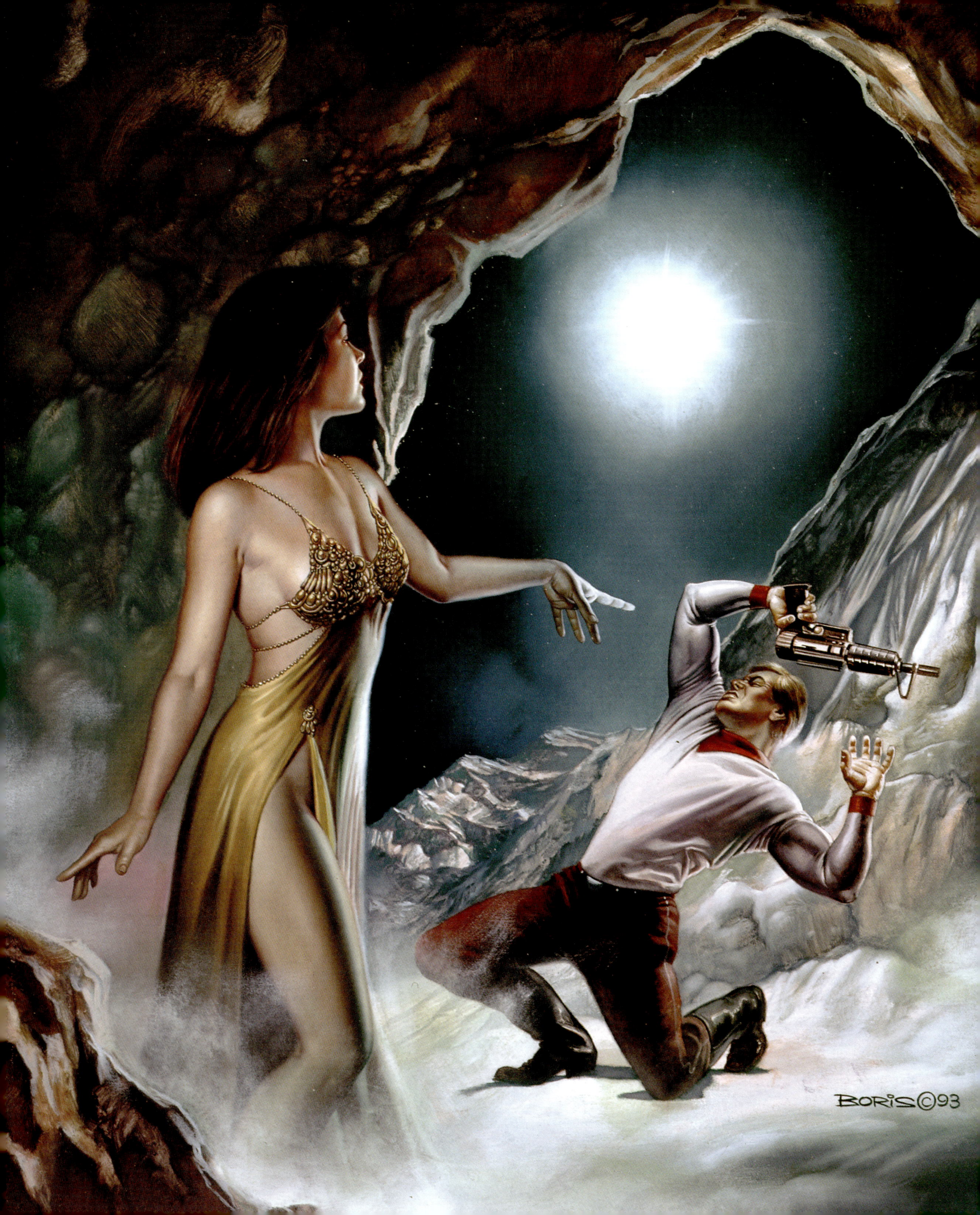
BORIS©93

Cave Fairy,
Boris Vallejo, *1993, book cover*

"It is great fun to paint book jackets. All the details are spelled out and you just have to figure out how to work the scene into a composition."

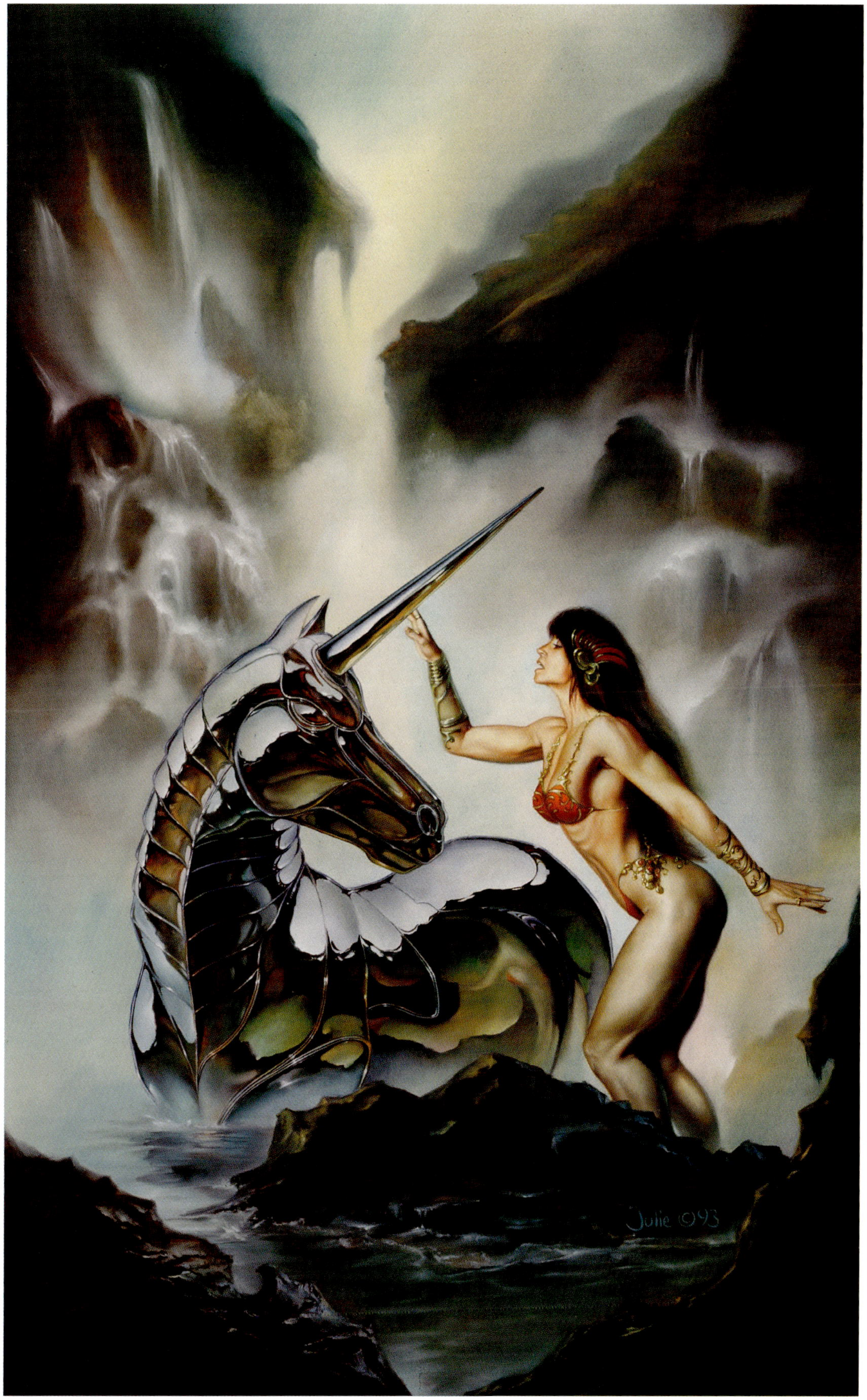

First Touch, Julie Bell,
1993, personal work

This piece was painted while Julie was preparing her first book. She was encouraged by the publisher to complete more metal paintings. "This painting is about how first experiences are unique, like a first kiss."

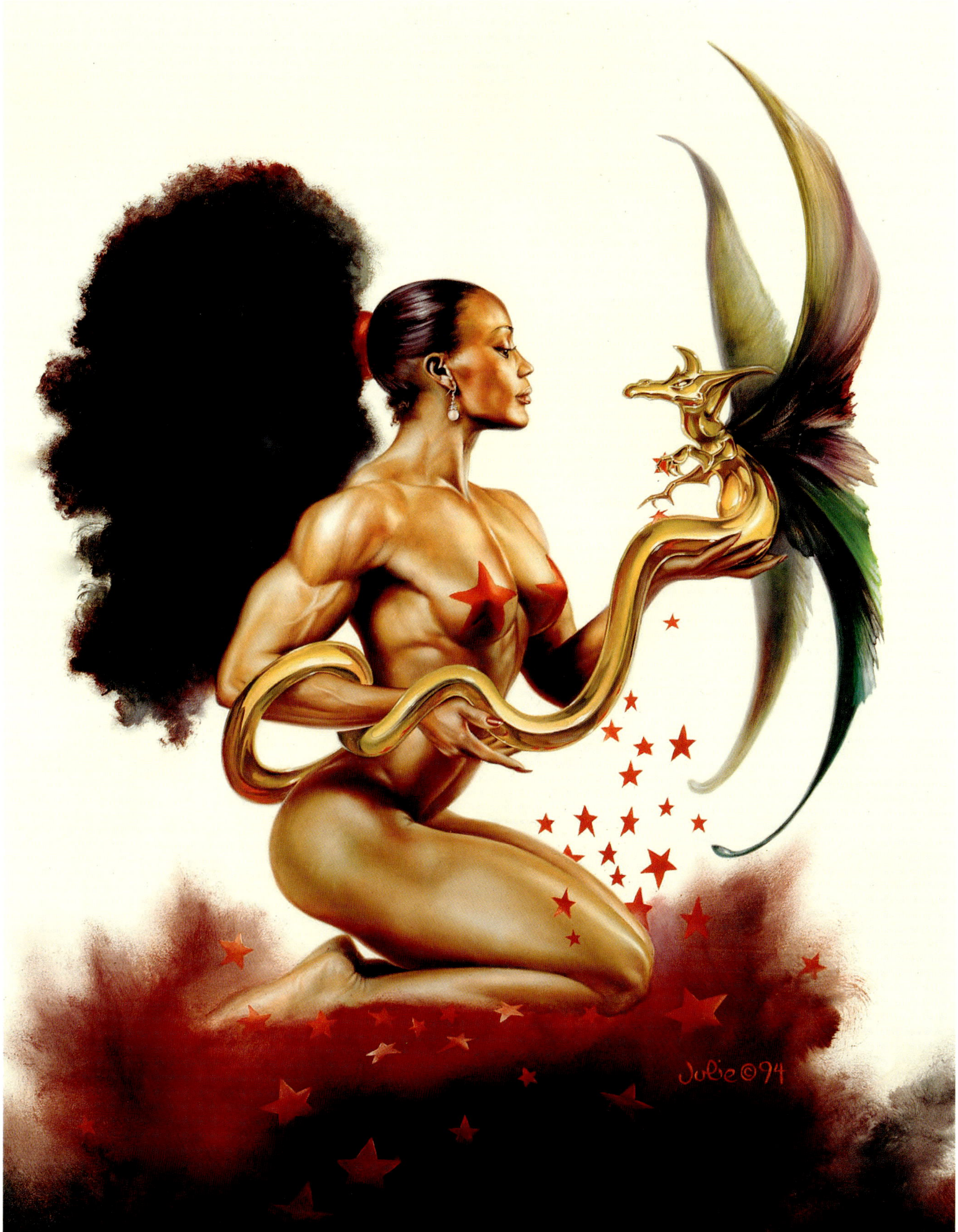
Julie©94

Star Giver,
Julie Bell, *1994, trading card*

An early example of a theme common to Julie's paintings: a strong woman with a small creature. Lenda Murray, eight-time Miss Olympia, was the model. "She's a very graceful woman," says Julie.

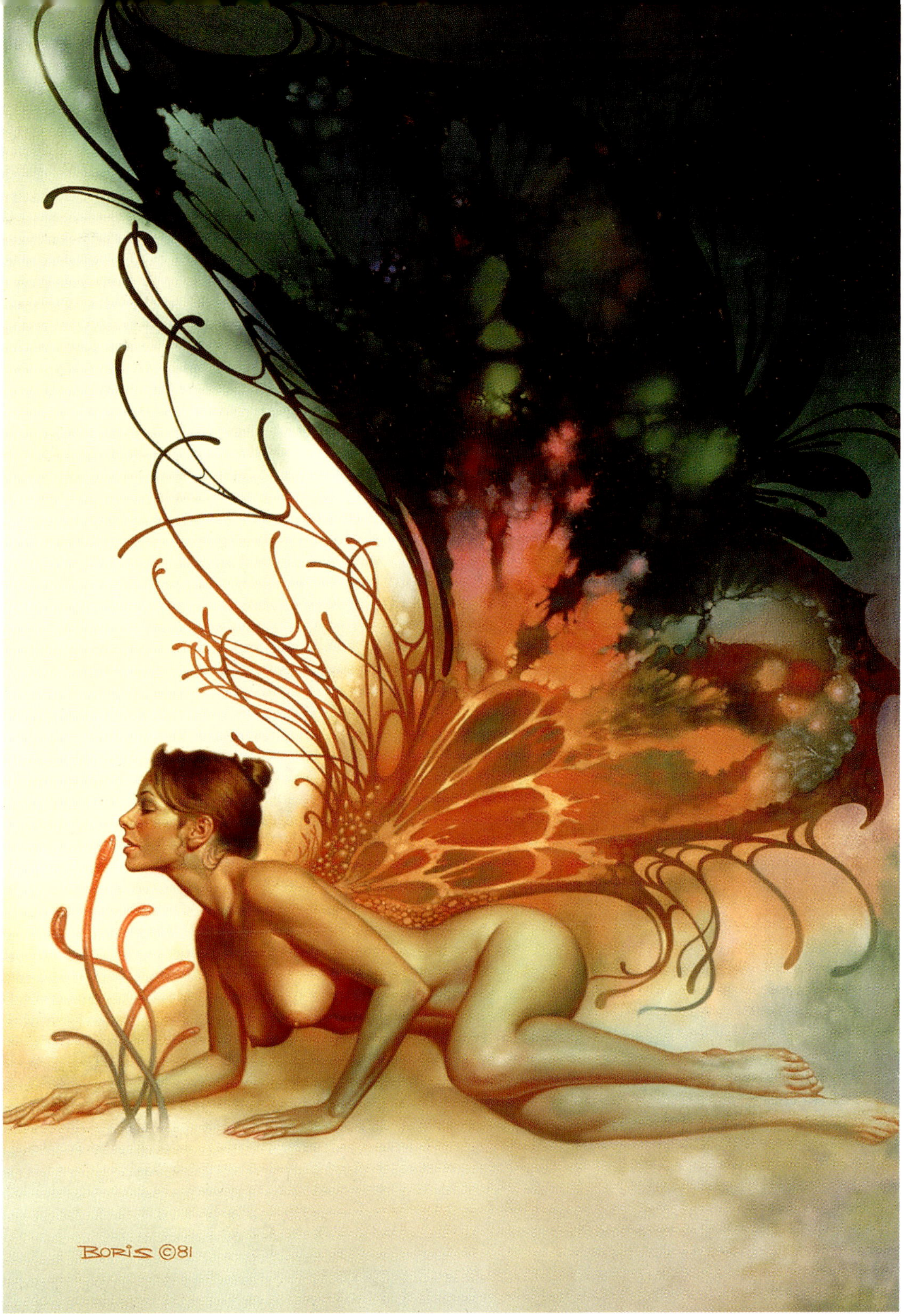

Spring Garden, Boris Vallejo, *1981,* Mirage *interior artwork*

Julie cites this piece as one of her favorites from the time before she ever met Boris, saying that she had always been attracted to its Art Nouveau style. According to Boris, this quality resulted from his desire to combine an abstract and graphic representation of the wings with the sensual realism of the woman.

"THIS WORK WAS SUPPOSED TO SHOW NEW YORK, SOMETHING LIKE 1,000 YEARS FROM NOW. I ASSUMED THAT, THOUGH THE BUILDINGS COULD BE ABANDONED AND COVERED IN MOSS, THE TWIN TOWERS WOULD STILL BE THERE."

BORIS

Debbie in New York,
Boris Vallejo, *1997, calendar*

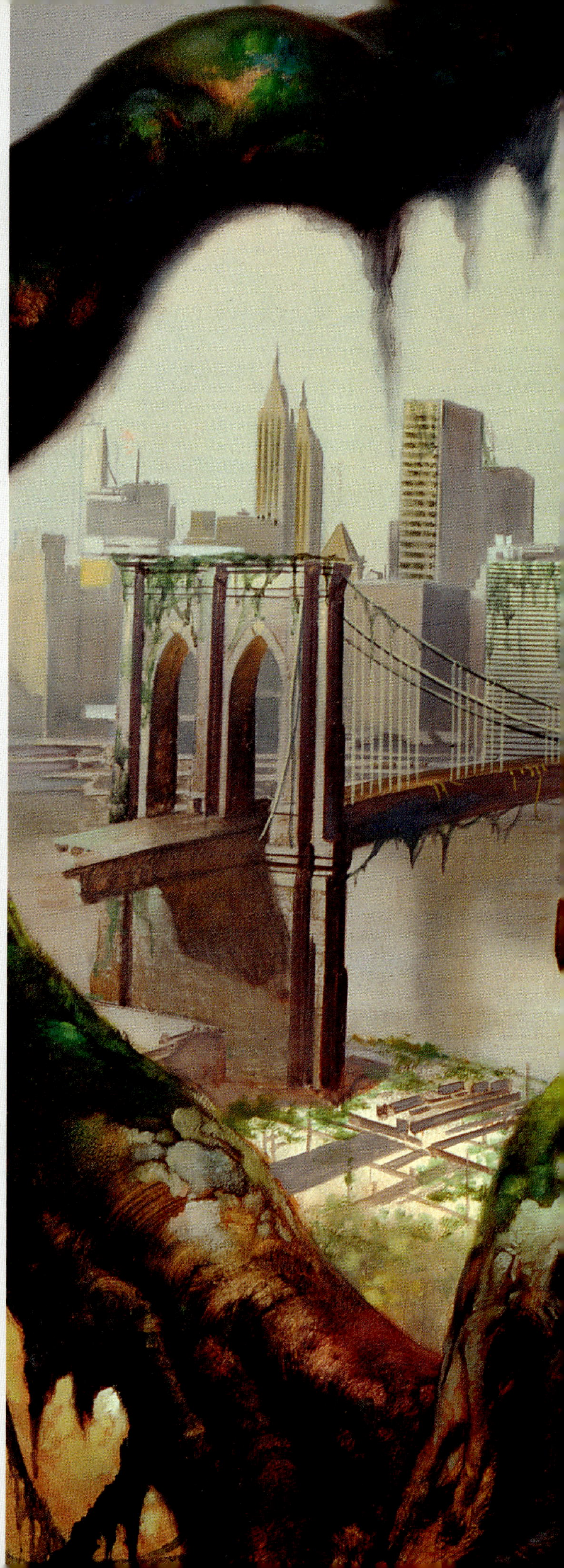

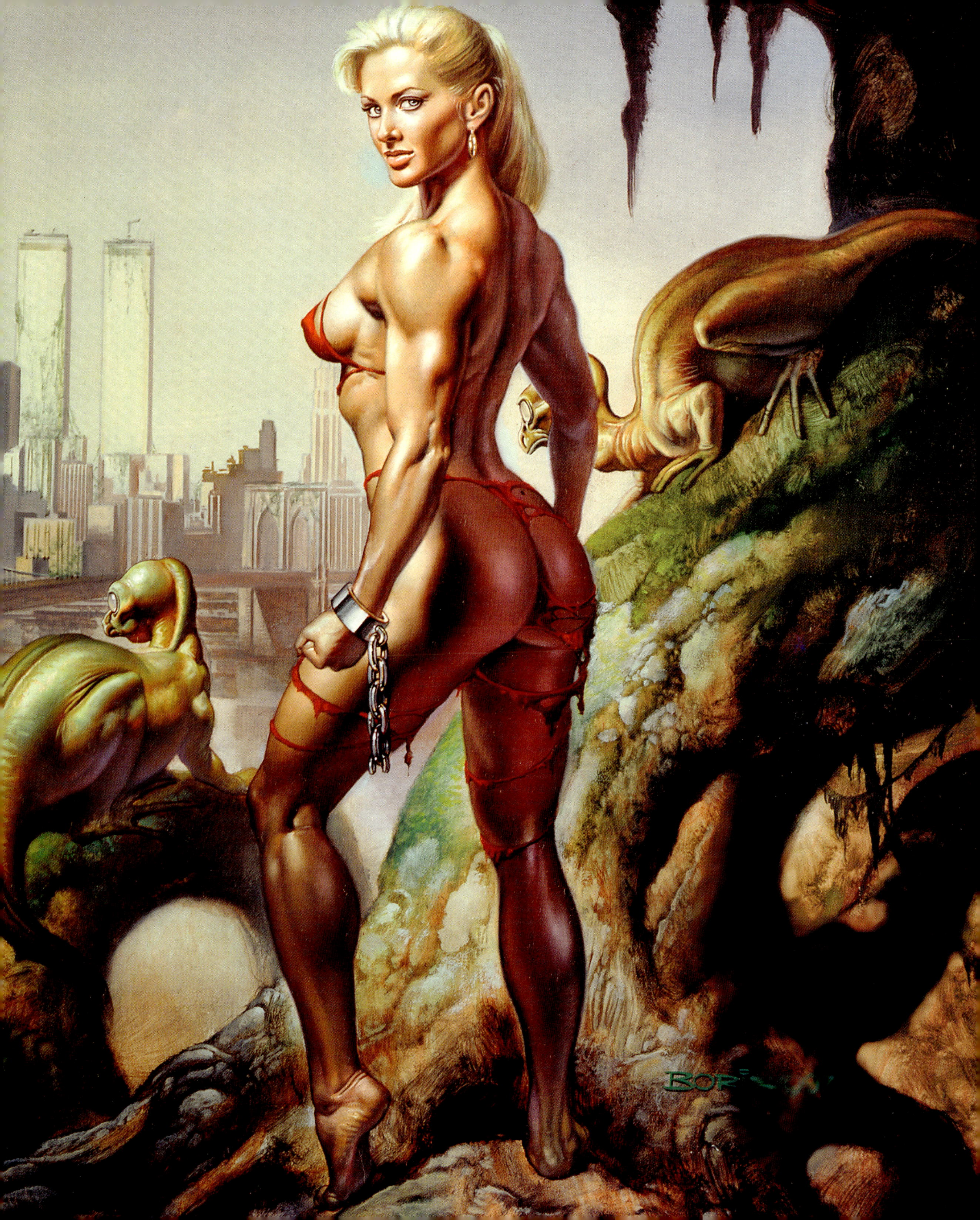

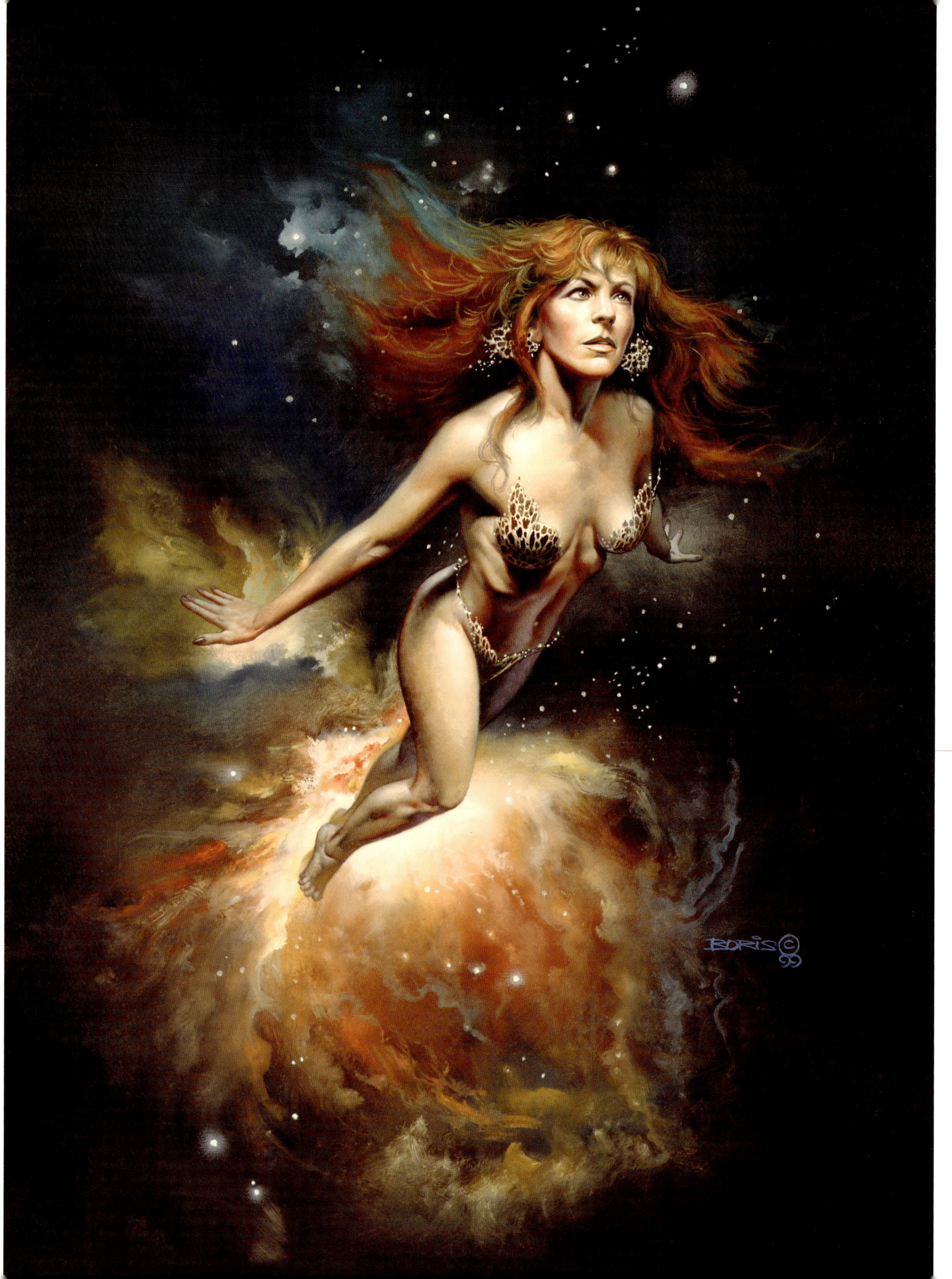
BORIS ©
99

Queen of the Galaxy,
Boris Vallejo, *1999, calendar*

"This is the nebula M-42 from Orion. It is my favorite celestial object. It was an unusual approach for me to paint this woman with such exaggerated foreshortening, but it just felt right."

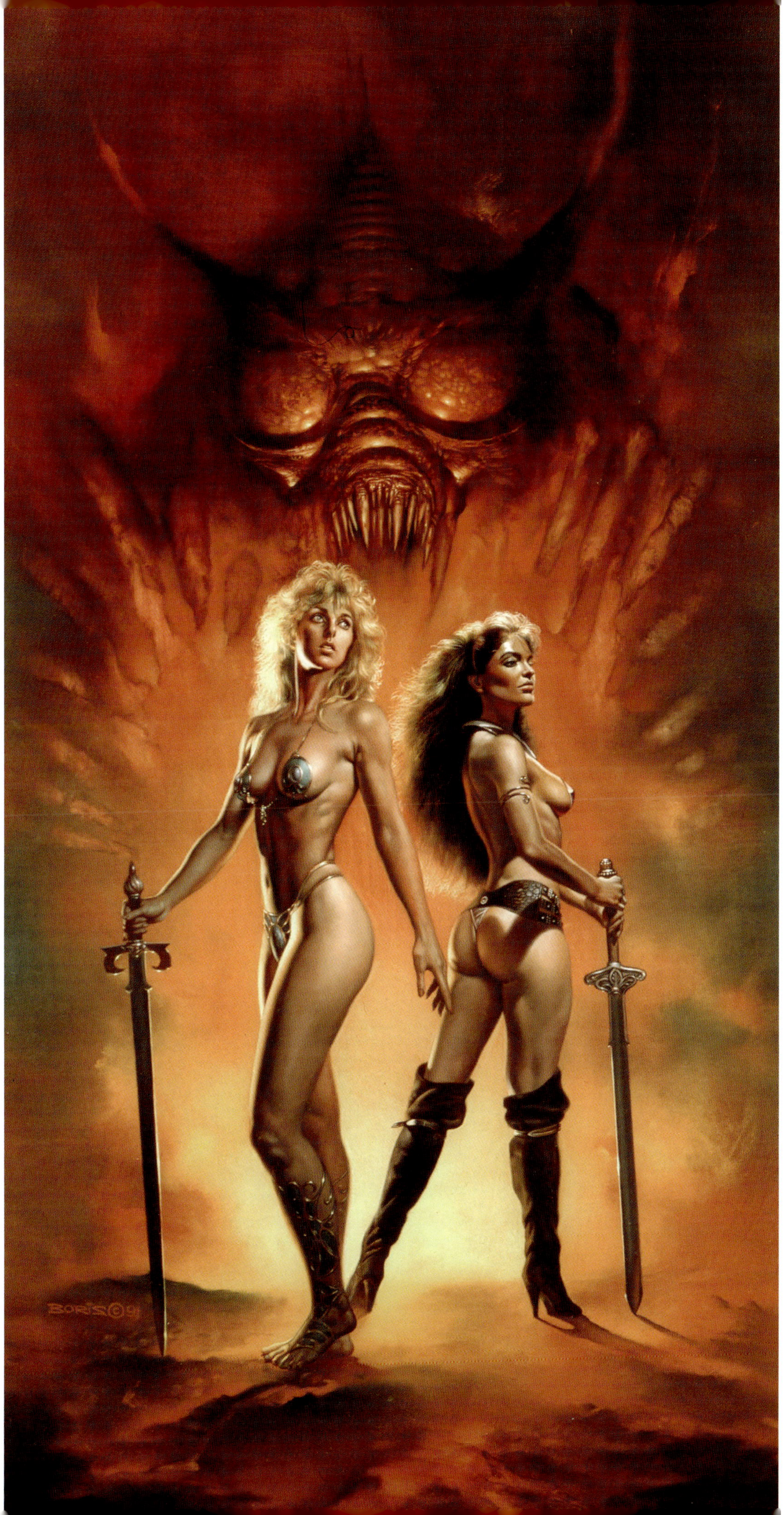

Cherufe, Boris Vallejo, *1991, calendar*

"Brinke Stevens [on the right] is a horror movie actress we've known for many years. I met her through a *Playboy* photographer named Ken Marcus whom she was dating. She speaks something like seven languages."

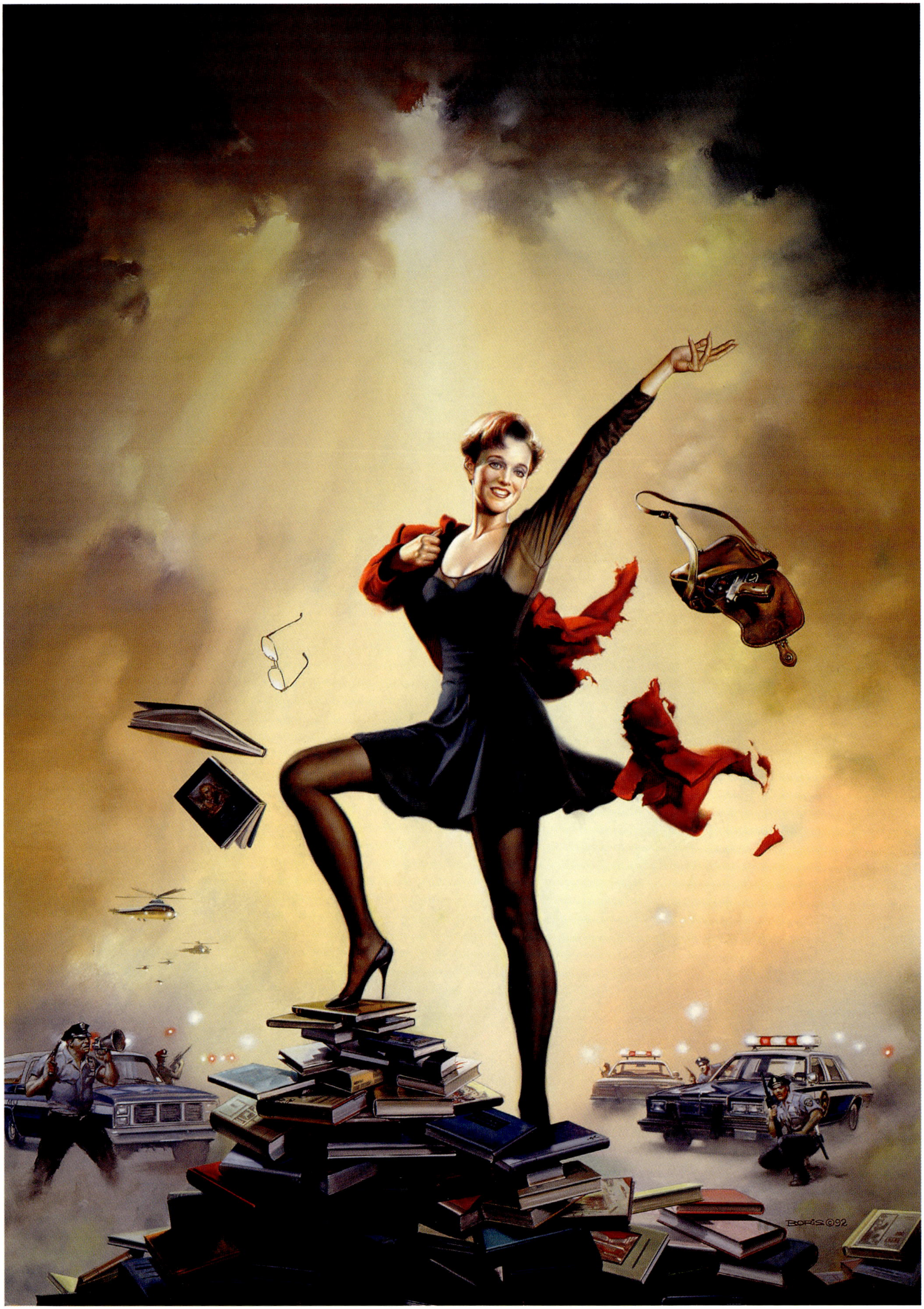
BORIS ©92

The Librarian,
Boris Vallejo, *1992, film poster*

"I was asked to do something like the poster I painted for *National Lampoon's Vacation*. What they really stressed was that I 'give her good legs'." Unfortunately, this painting was never used for the film.

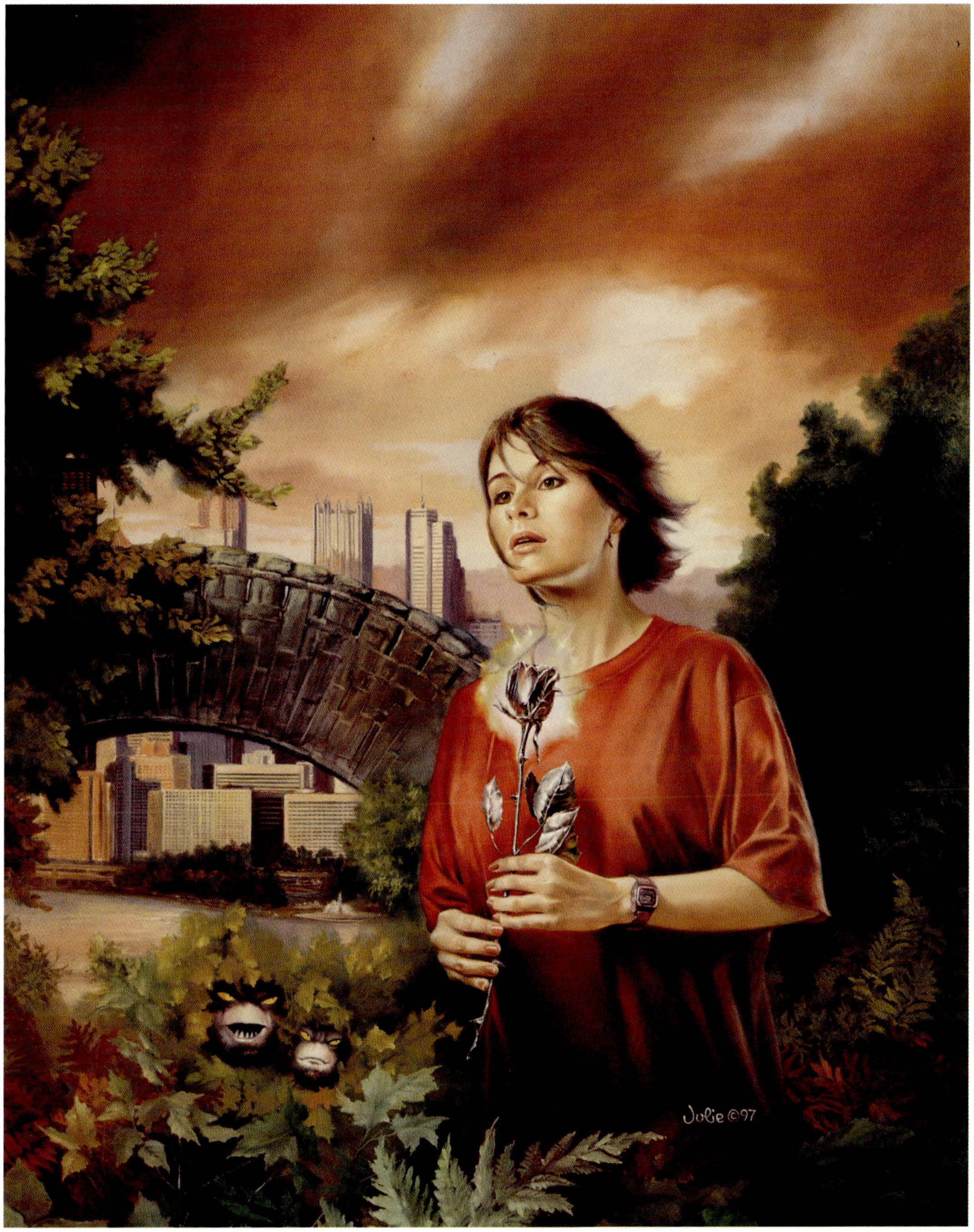

Shannon's Fantasy, Julie Bell, *1997, book cover*

At a time when her work-load consisted primarily of superhero paintings, Julie found it difficult to change gears for this quiet scene. "I kept myself focused by painting familiar things. I used my niece, Shannon, as the model for the girl and based the background on Schenley Park, in Pittsburgh, where I used to go for walks."

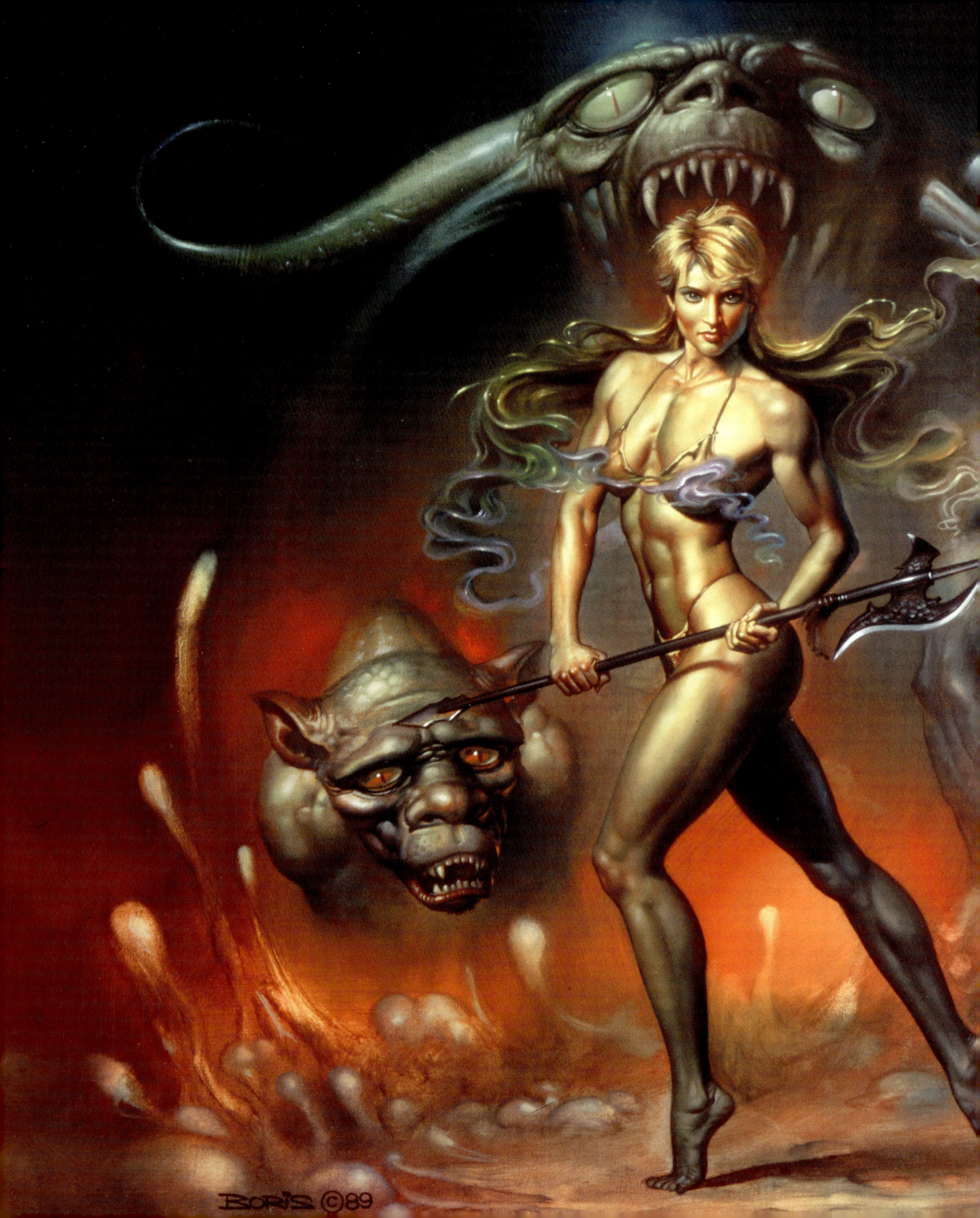
BORIS ©89

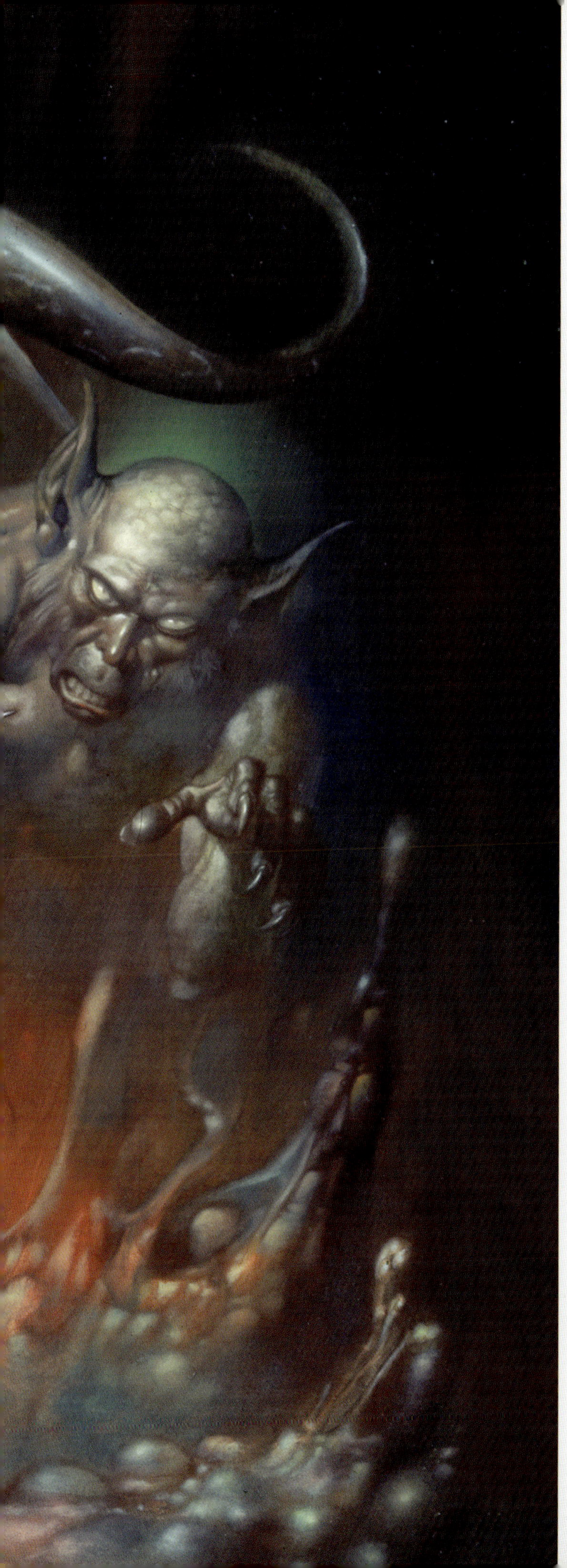

"IT WAS A TURNING POINT FOR ME. I SAW JULIE AS THE IDEAL OF FEMALE BEAUTY. SHE CHANGED MY WHOLE INTERPRETATION OF THE FEMALE, AND MADE IT THE EMPHASIS OF MY WORK EVER SINCE."

BORIS

Alpnu, Boris Vallejo, *1989, calendar*

Noteworthy not only as the first painting that Boris ever did of Julie, this painting also foreshadows the changes in his style over the years to come.

"IT'S A STILL LIFE, AND THERE IS THIS LITTLE ANGEL TRAPPED IN IT, FROZEN IN TIME." BORIS

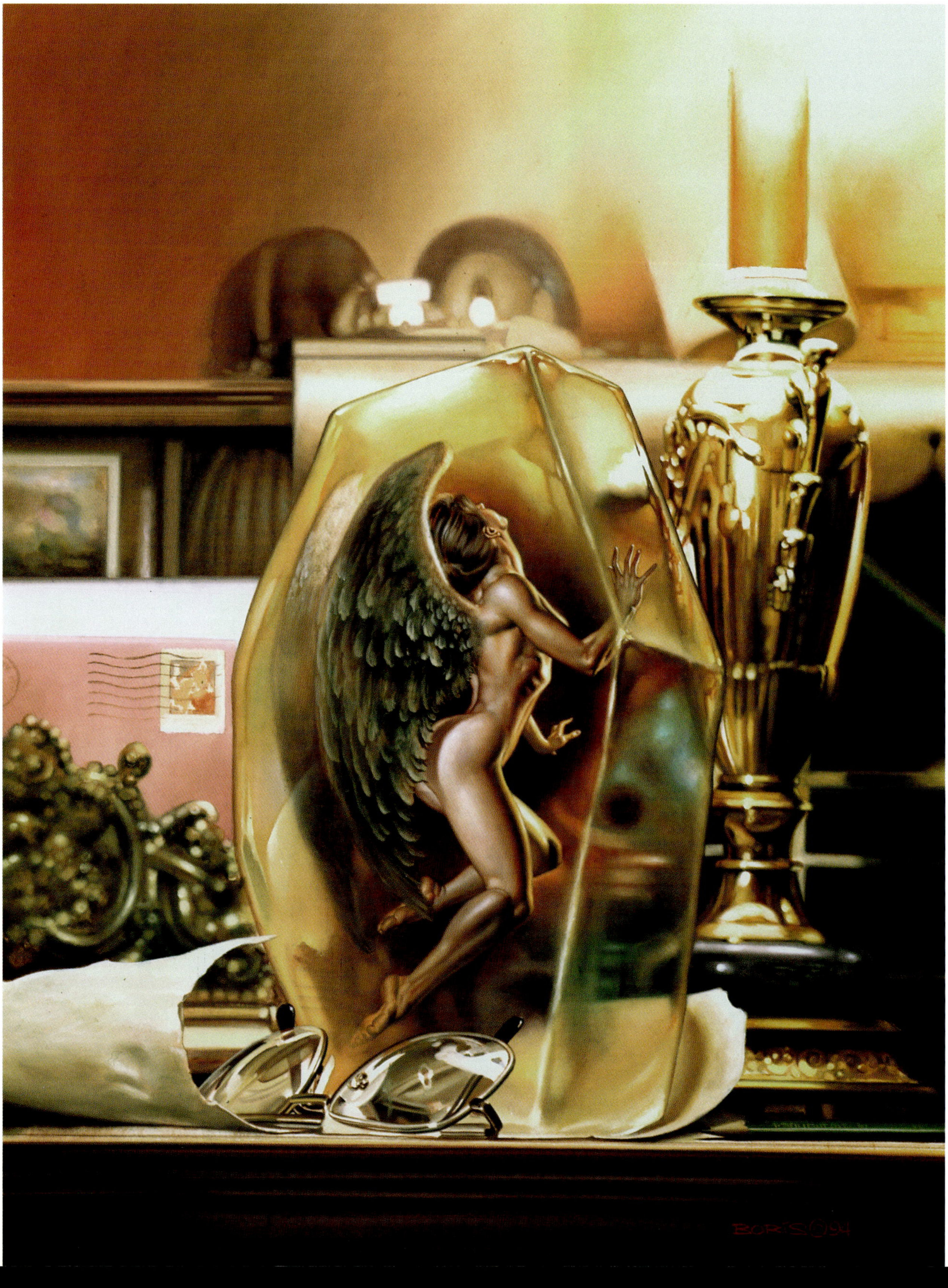

Amber,
Boris Vallejo, *1994, book cover*

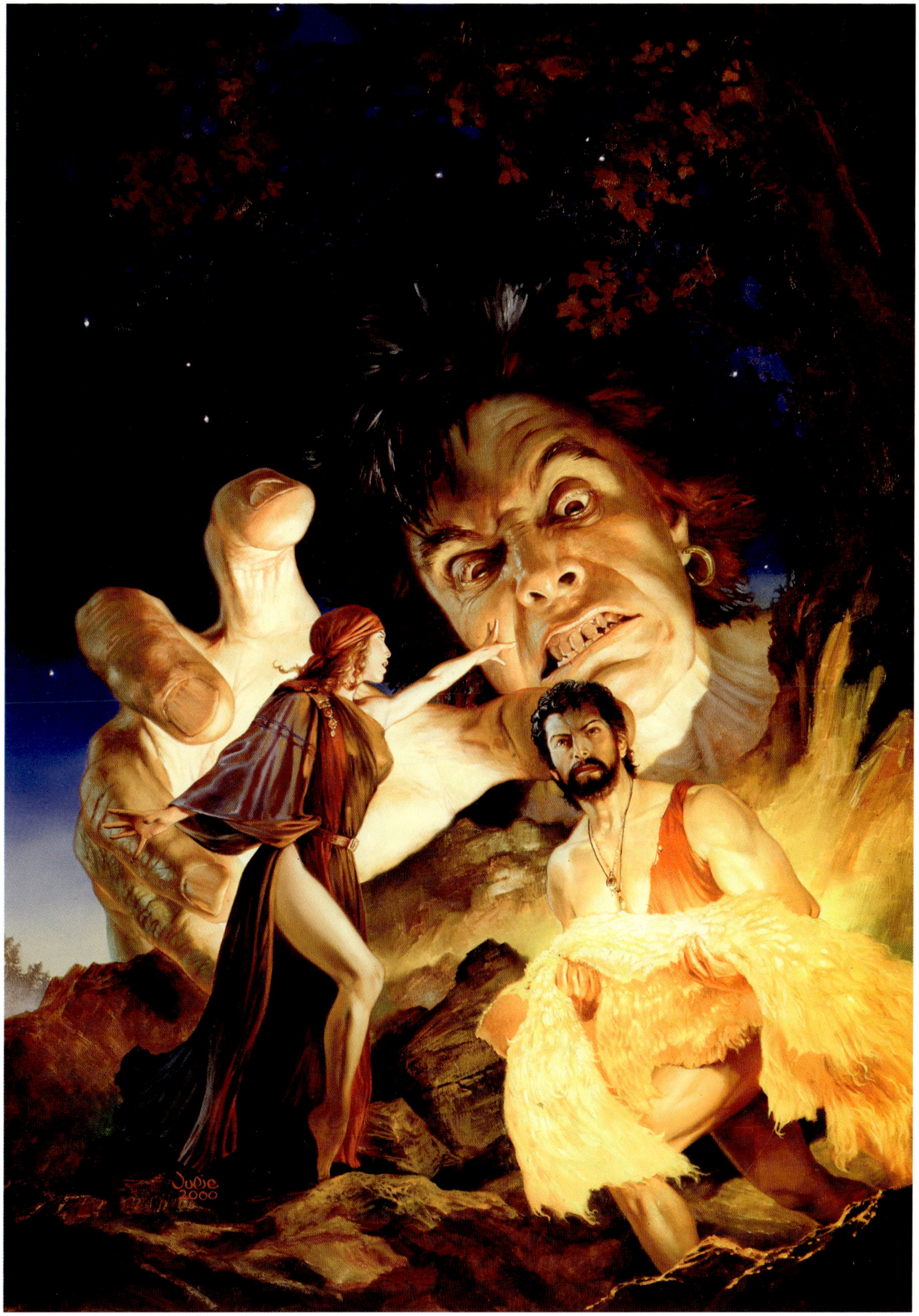

Jason and the Golden Fleece,
Julie Bell, *2000, book cover*

"Jason and the Argonauts was one of my favorite movies when I was a kid, so I was very excited about doing this painting. I also remember starting this just after seeing a Maxfield Parrish show, which really influenced me."

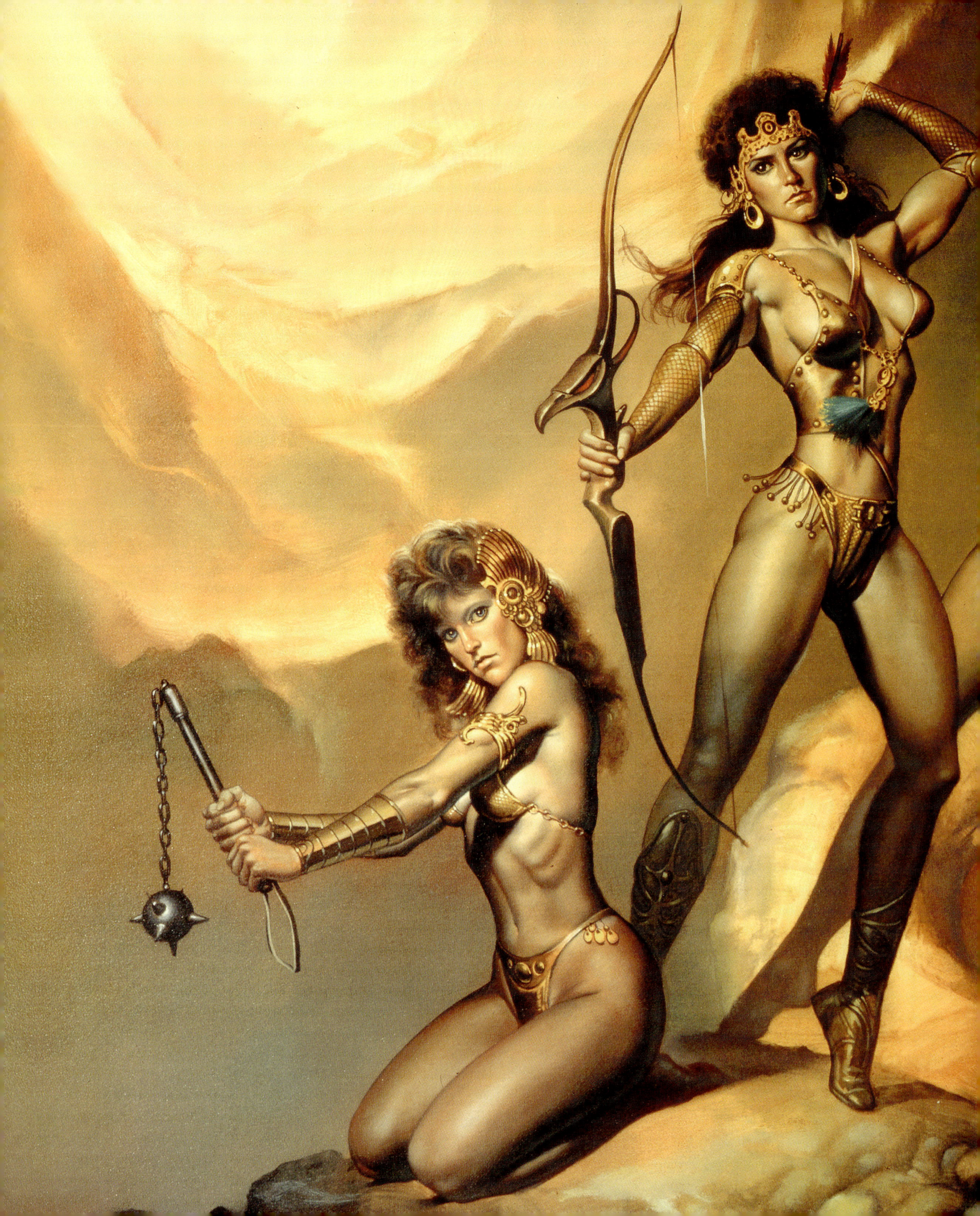

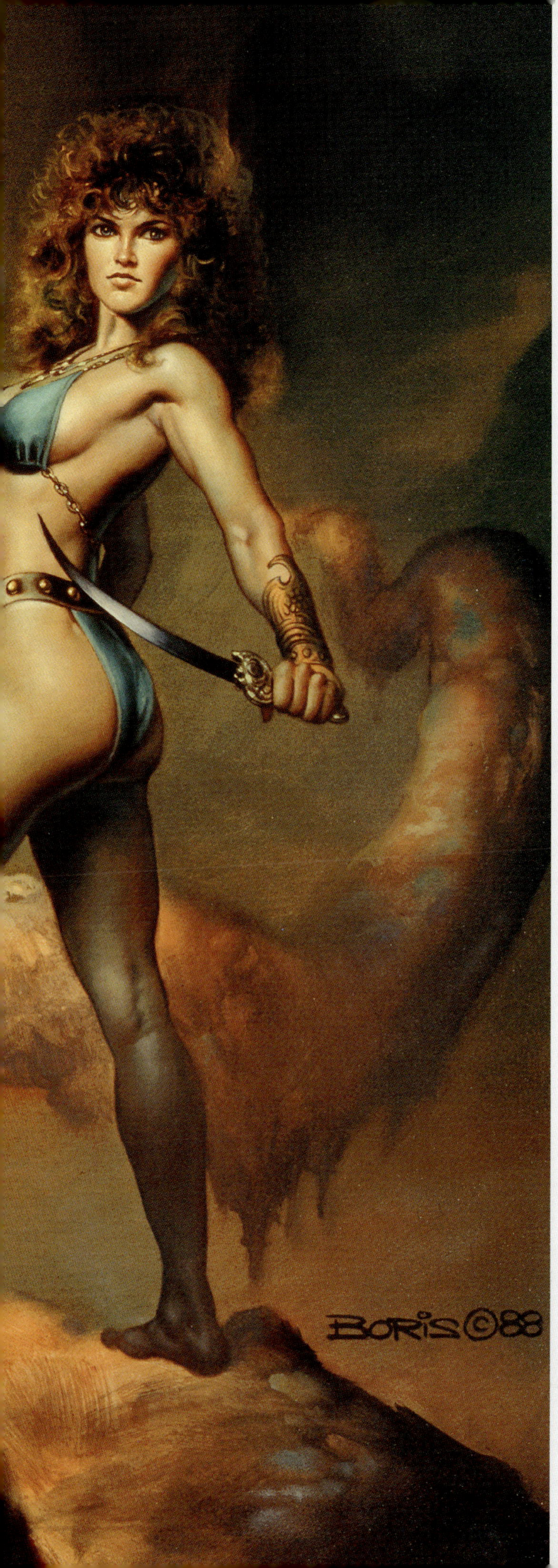

"ONE INTERESTING THING I FIND IN PAINTING AMAZON WOMEN: YOU CAN GO ON INFINITELY WITH DIFFERENT VARIATIONS ON THE THEME. THE CHALLENGE IS IN FINDING DIFFERENT WAYS TO DO IT. YOU WORK WITH DIFFERENT SETTINGS, DIFFERENT COLORS, DIFFERENT LIGHTING... "

BORIS

Team, Boris Vallejo, *1988, calendar*

"One interesting thing I find in painting Amazon women: You can go on infinitely with different variations on the theme. The challenge is in finding different ways to do it. You work with different settings, different colors, different lighting... You can get many things from the same model. Elvgren painted the same subject hundreds of times and all of his paintings were beautiful and different."

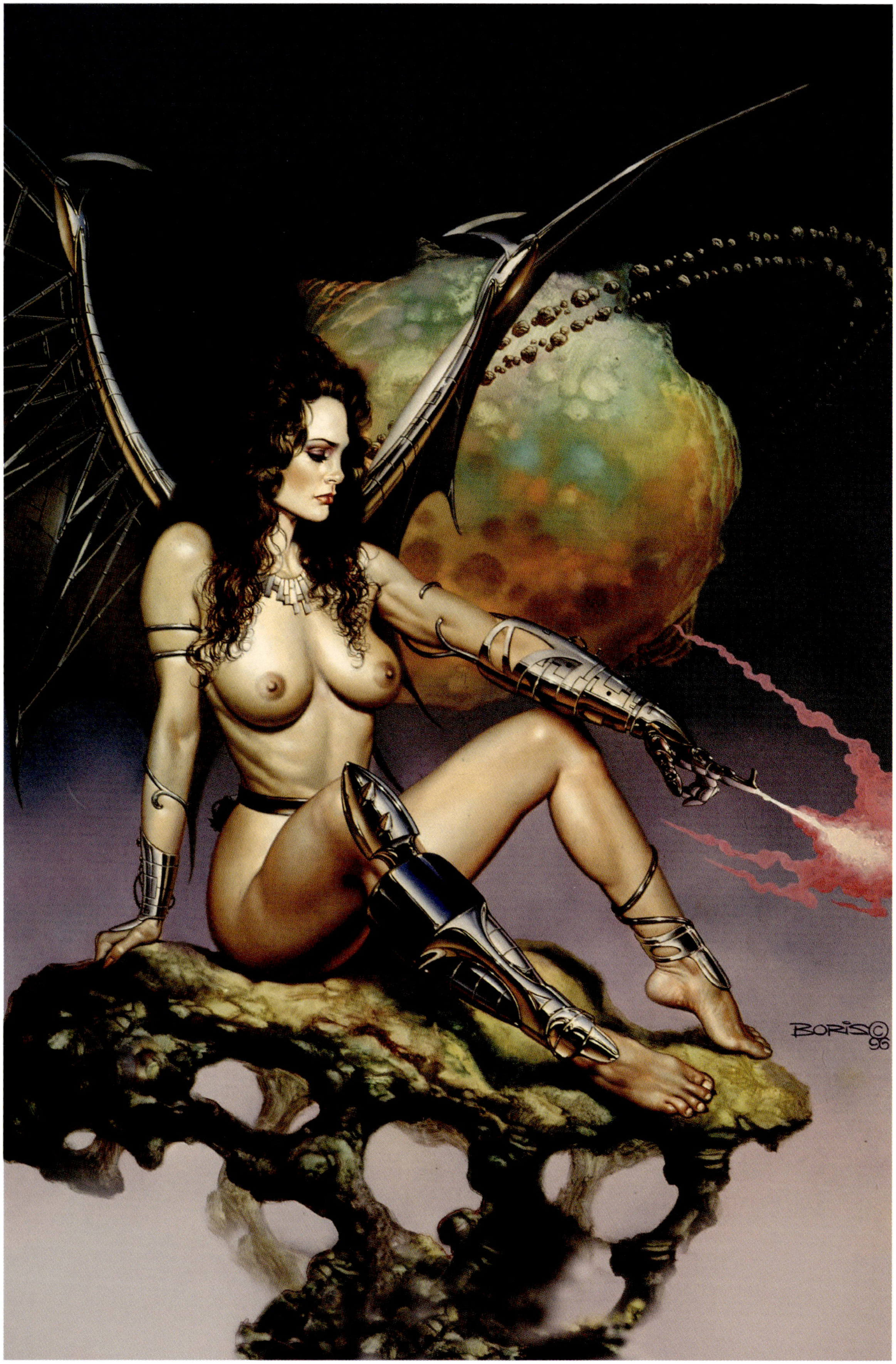

Julie Strain,
Boris Vallejo, *1996, calendar (Heavy Metal)*

"She really looks wicked. Julie Strain, who posed for this painting, seems to enjoy her wickedness quite a bit. That really appeals to me."

"IF I WERE TO DO A PAINTING FOR MYSELF... IT WOULD PROBABLY BE A VIGNETTE." BORIS

Corissa, Boris Vallejo, *1977, book cover*

"A very early book jacket. I had done a series of covers for Gor books. Due to the success of the Gor covers, the publisher had me do paintings for other books. I like this vignette approach. If I were to do a painting for myself, just for the heck of it, it would probably be a vignette."

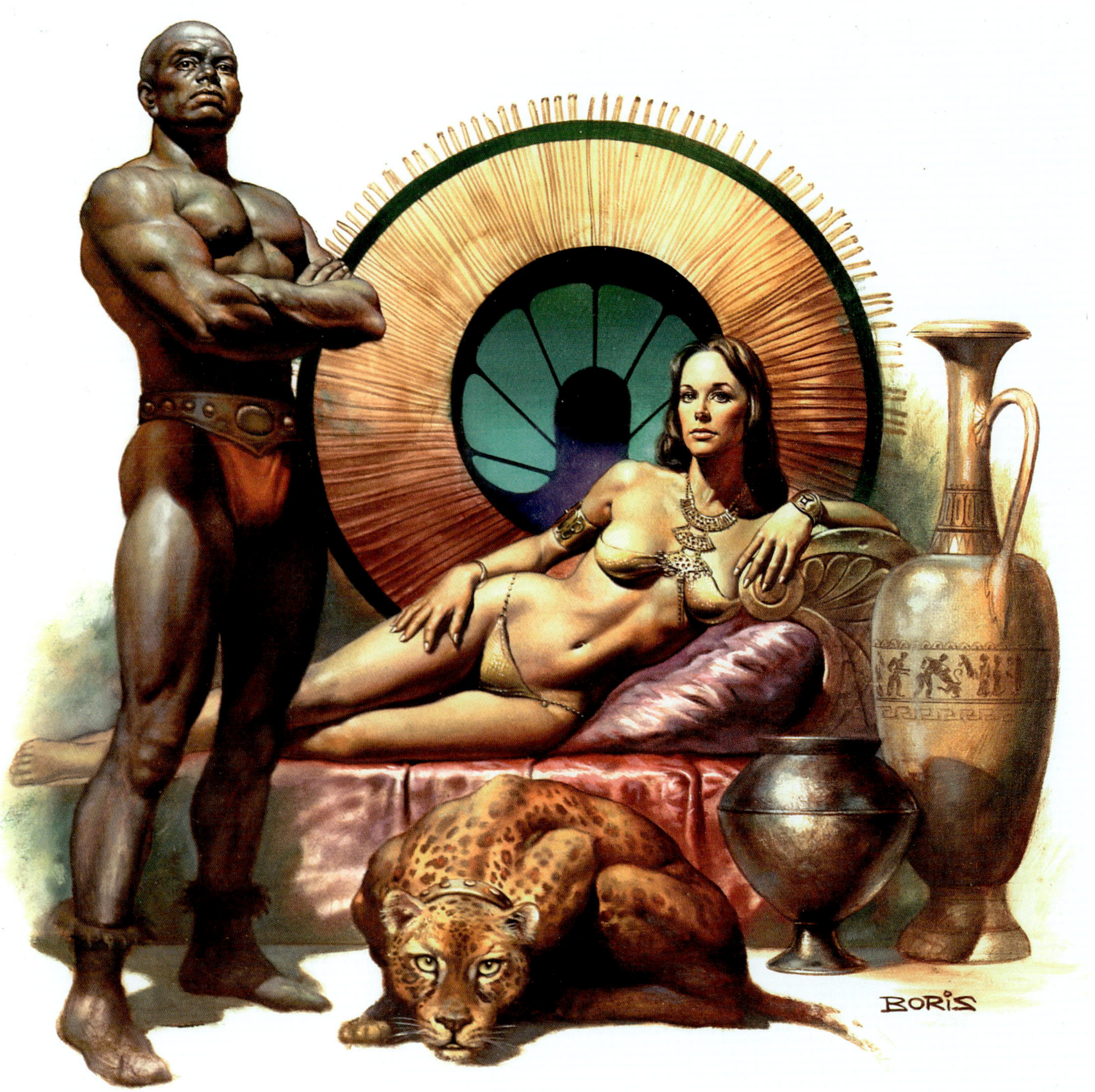

Dueling Bitches, Julie Bell, *1996, comic cover*

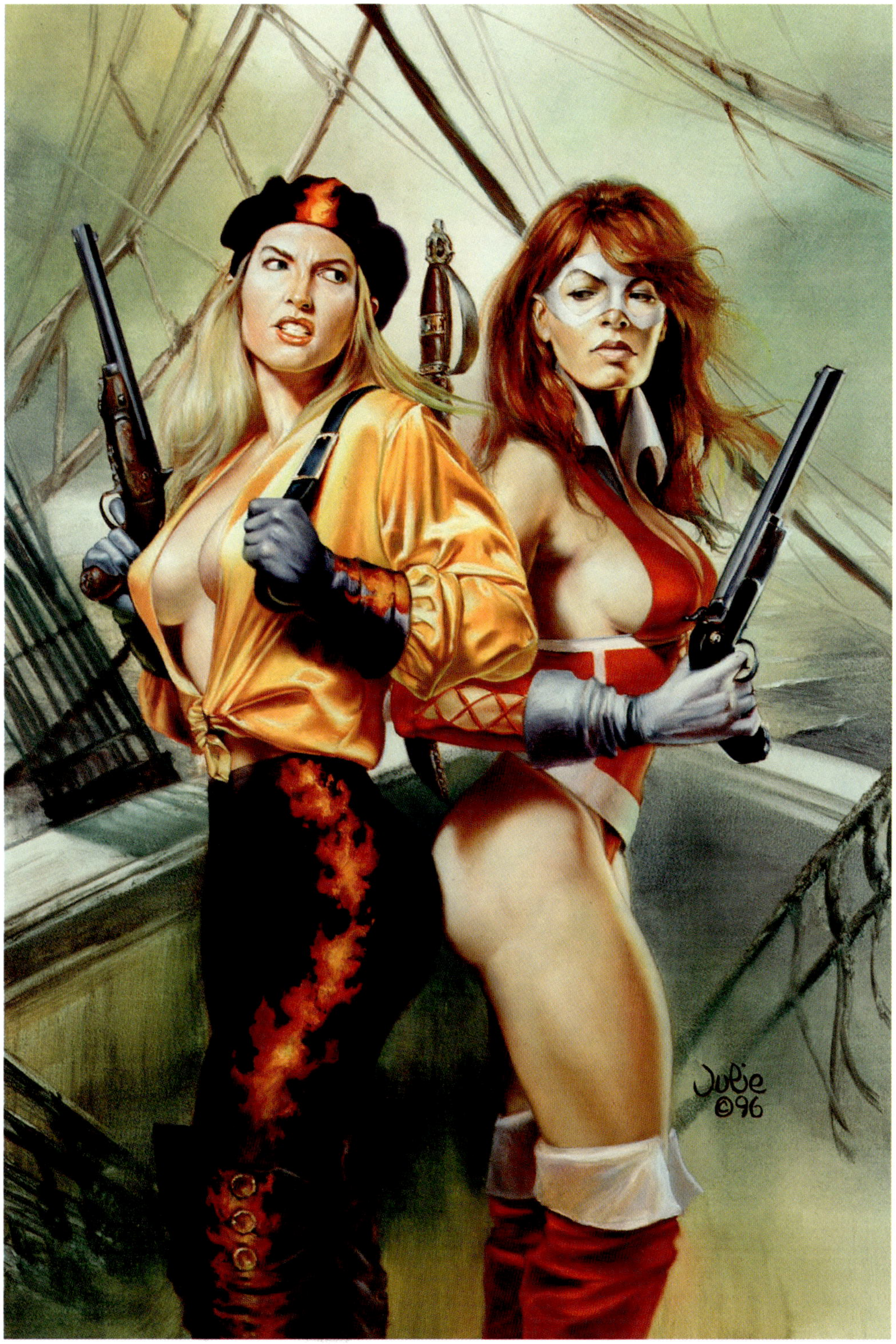

"PEOPLE LIKE TO SEE A GOOD CATFIGHT. IT'S UGLY TO SEE IN REAL LIFE, YET GLAMORIZED IN PAINTINGS AND MOVIES."

JULIE

Vampires, Boris Vallejo and Julie Bell, *2004, magazine cover*

This was one of the first paintings by Boris and Julie to be executed in separate pieces, which were later combined digitally. The man was painted by Boris while Julie worked on the woman.

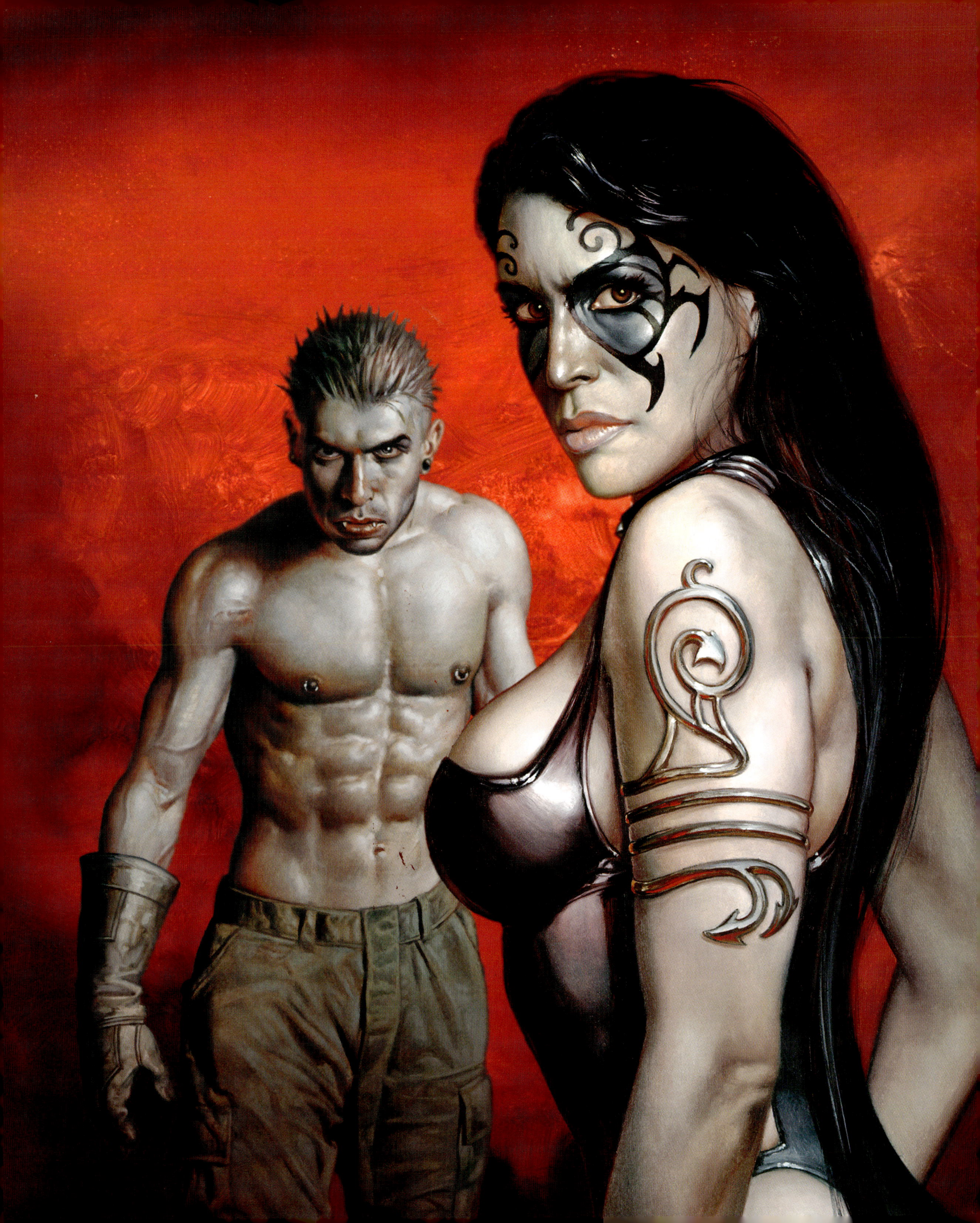

Andromeda, Boris Vallejo, *1988, calendar* ▸▸

When Boris paints mythological scenes, he often likes to expand on or alter the original story. "Since myths are not true, I have flexibility to interpret them as I please. In this piece, for example, there is no Perseus coming to Andromeda's rescue. I didn't want her to appear helpless and she is certainly not afraid."

"SINCE MYTHS ARE NOT TRUE, I HAVE FLEXIBILITY TO INTERPRET THEM AS I PLEASE."

BORIS

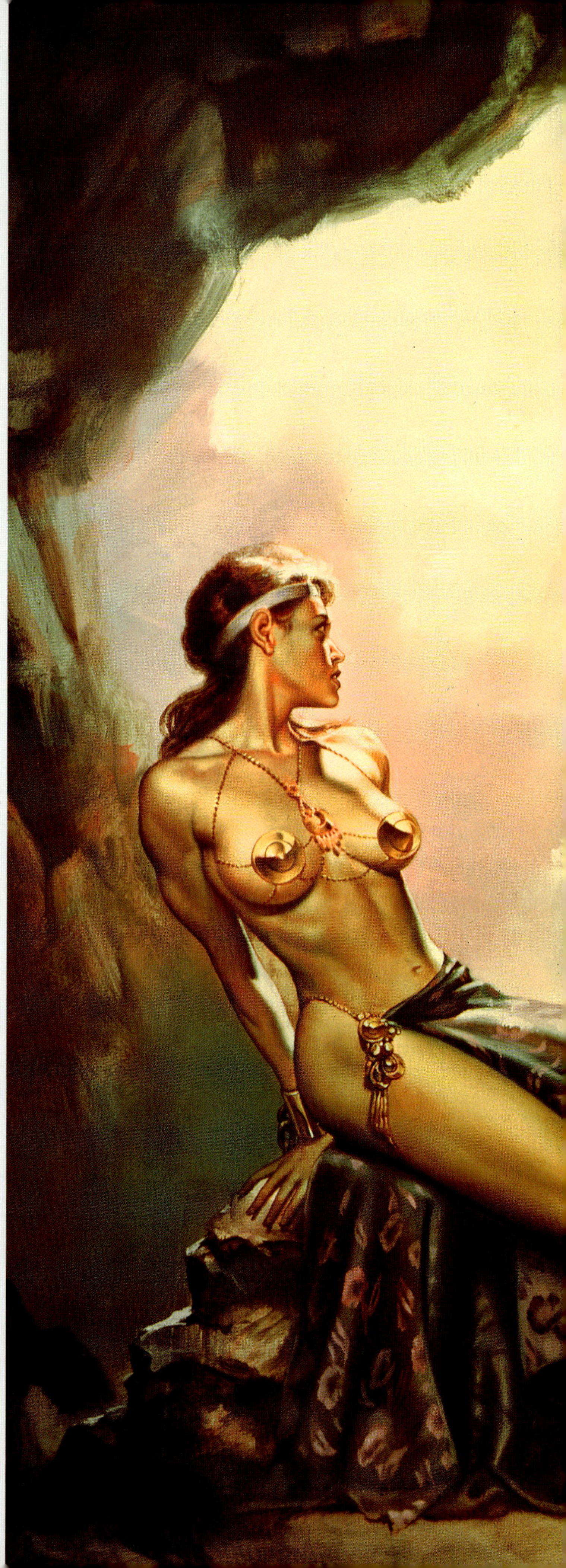

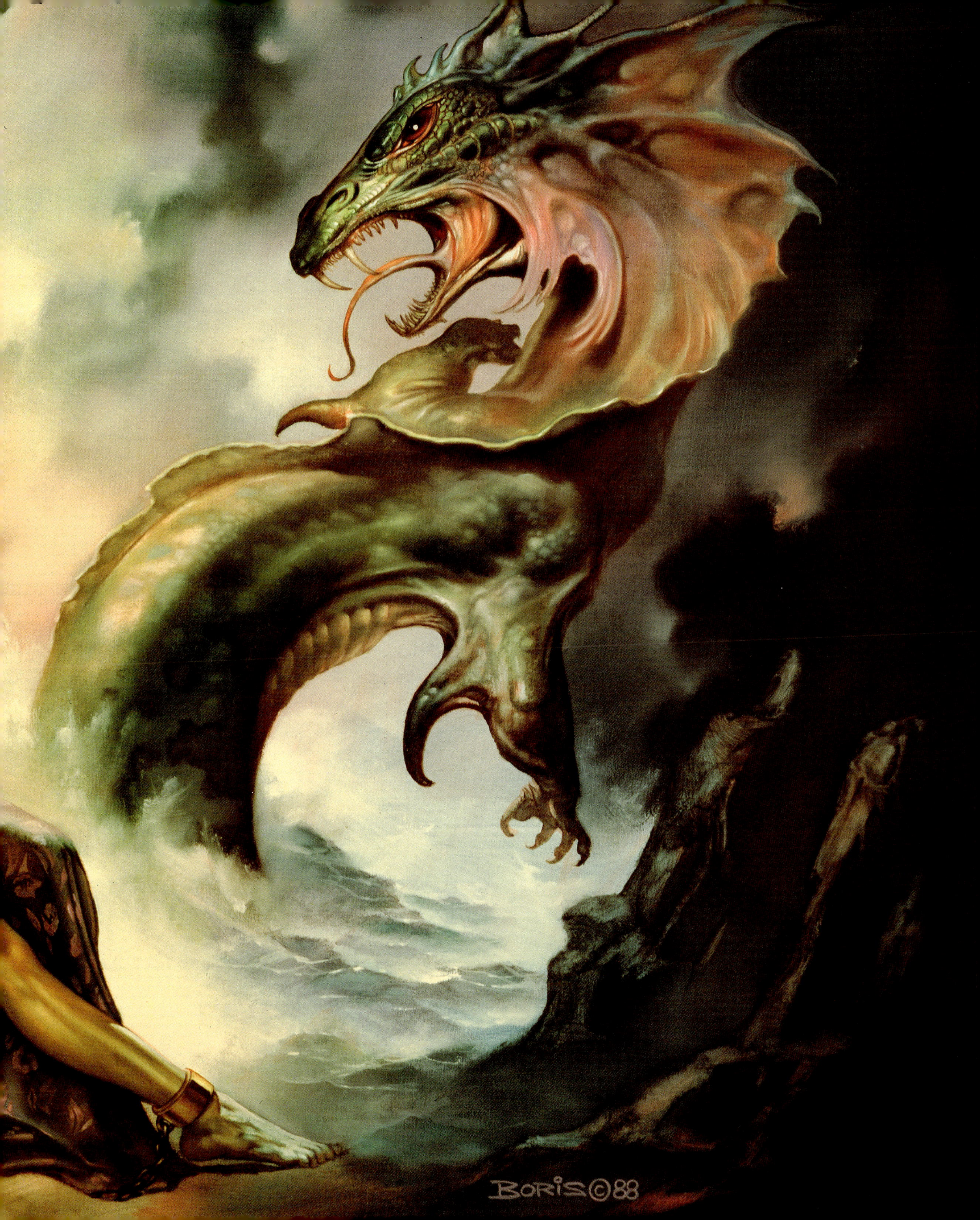
BORIS©88

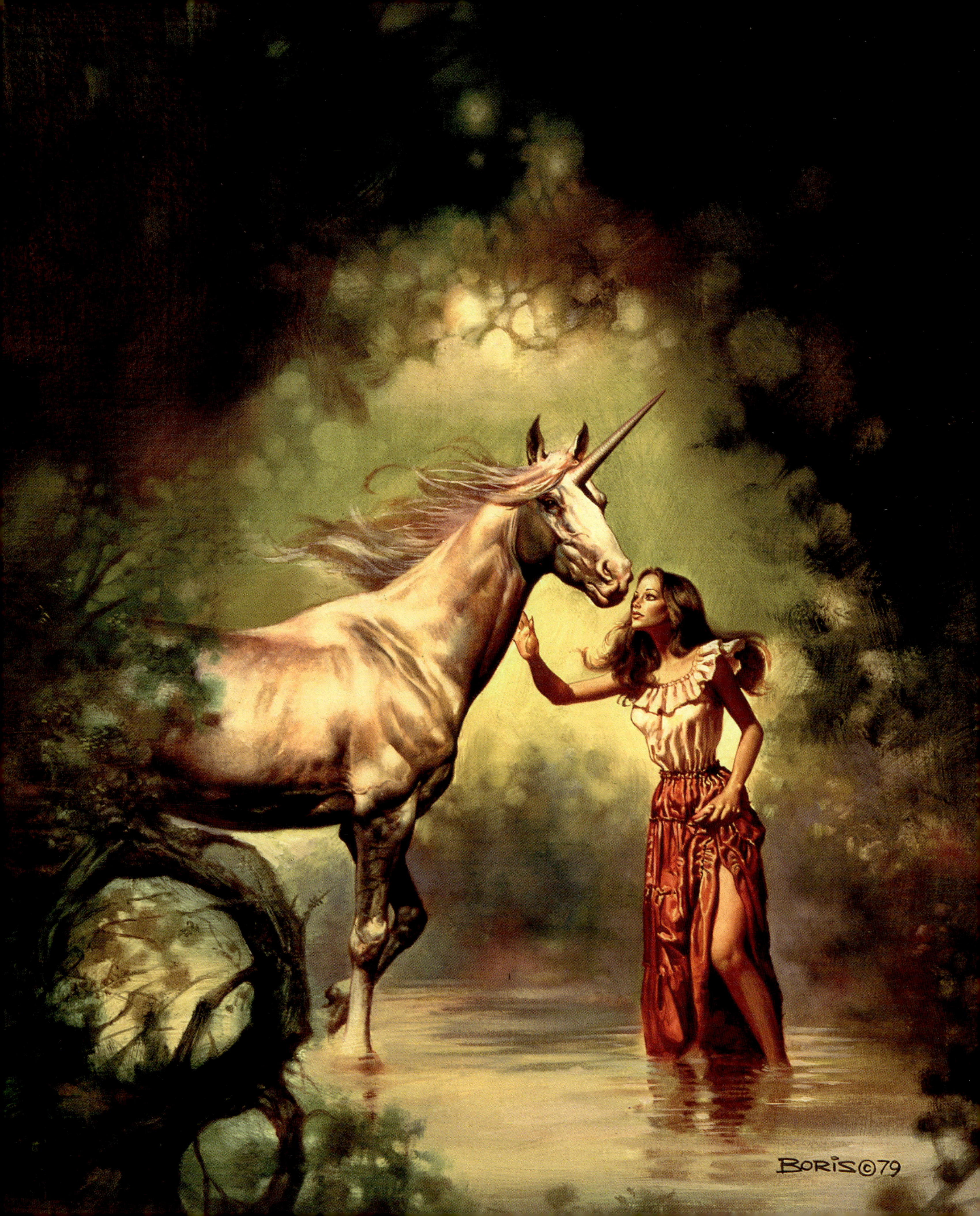
BORIS©79

New Beginnings, Julie Bell, ▸▸
2002, calendar

"I hadn't done anything with metal flesh in a few years and I wanted to come back to that with something different. This painting is reflective of who this model is. She became an Olympic cyclist. She is setting off on her life adventure."

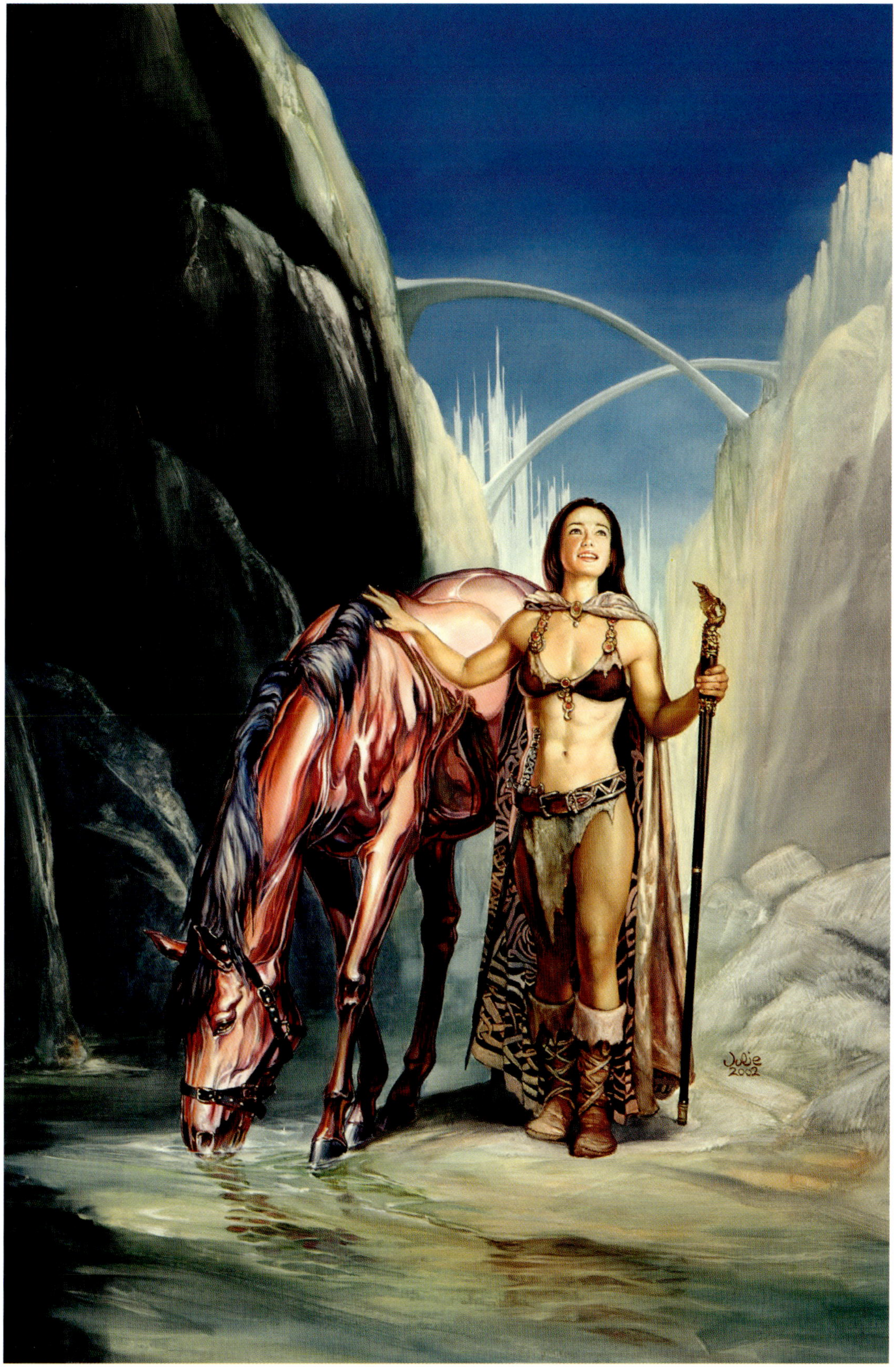

◂◂ **Unicorn and the Maiden,**
Boris Vallejo, *1979, book cover*

A rare occurrence in Boris' catalogue of paintings, we see here a fully clothed female. "Years ago I did a few romance pieces with period clothing. I'd much rather just paint the body." This piece would later provide an influence to Julie's painting, "First Touch".

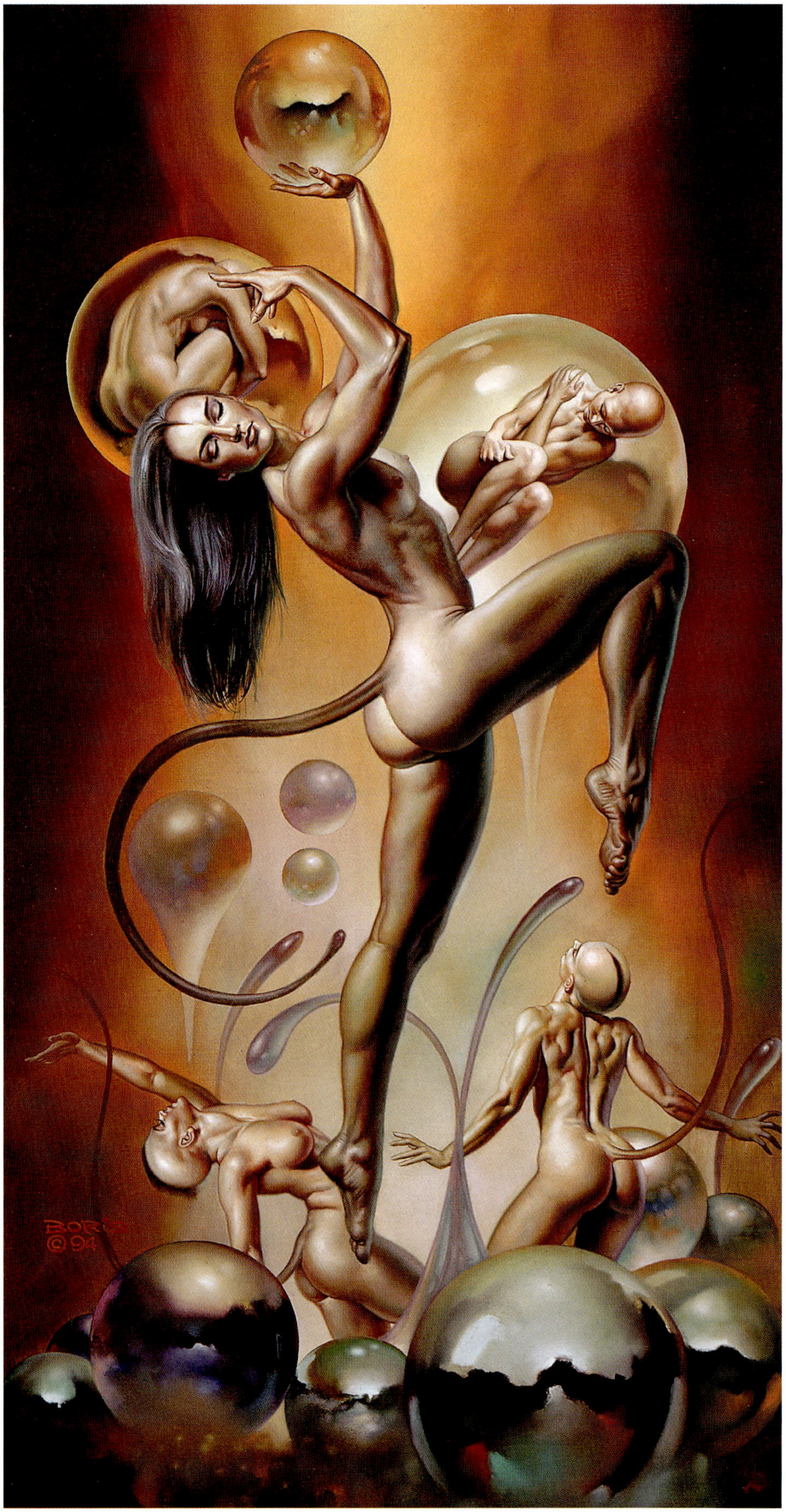

Clone Dance,
Boris Vallejo, *1994, calendar*

"WHEN I DID THIS PAINTING, THERE WAS TALK IN THE NEWS ABOUT CLONING. I THINK IT WILL HAPPEN ONE DAY. I DON'T OBJECT TO IT MORALLY, BUT I EXPECT THERE WILL BE PROBLEMS."

BORIS

Mermaid Love, Boris Vallejo & Julie Bell, *2004, advertisement*

Painted for a British deodorant ad, and once again a digital combination of several layers, Boris says, "It's tricky to keep the sense of depth between figure and background in mind when they're painted separately."

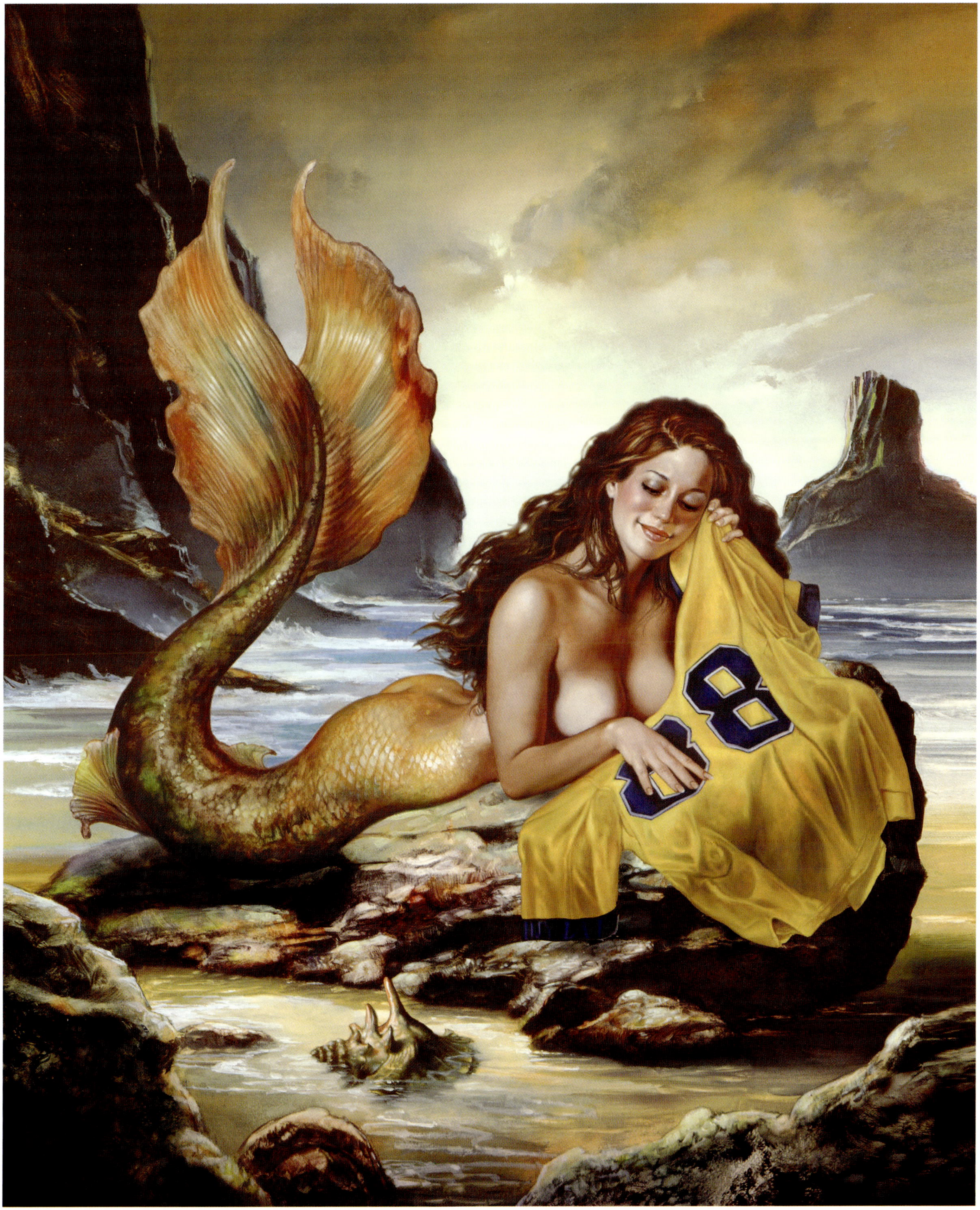

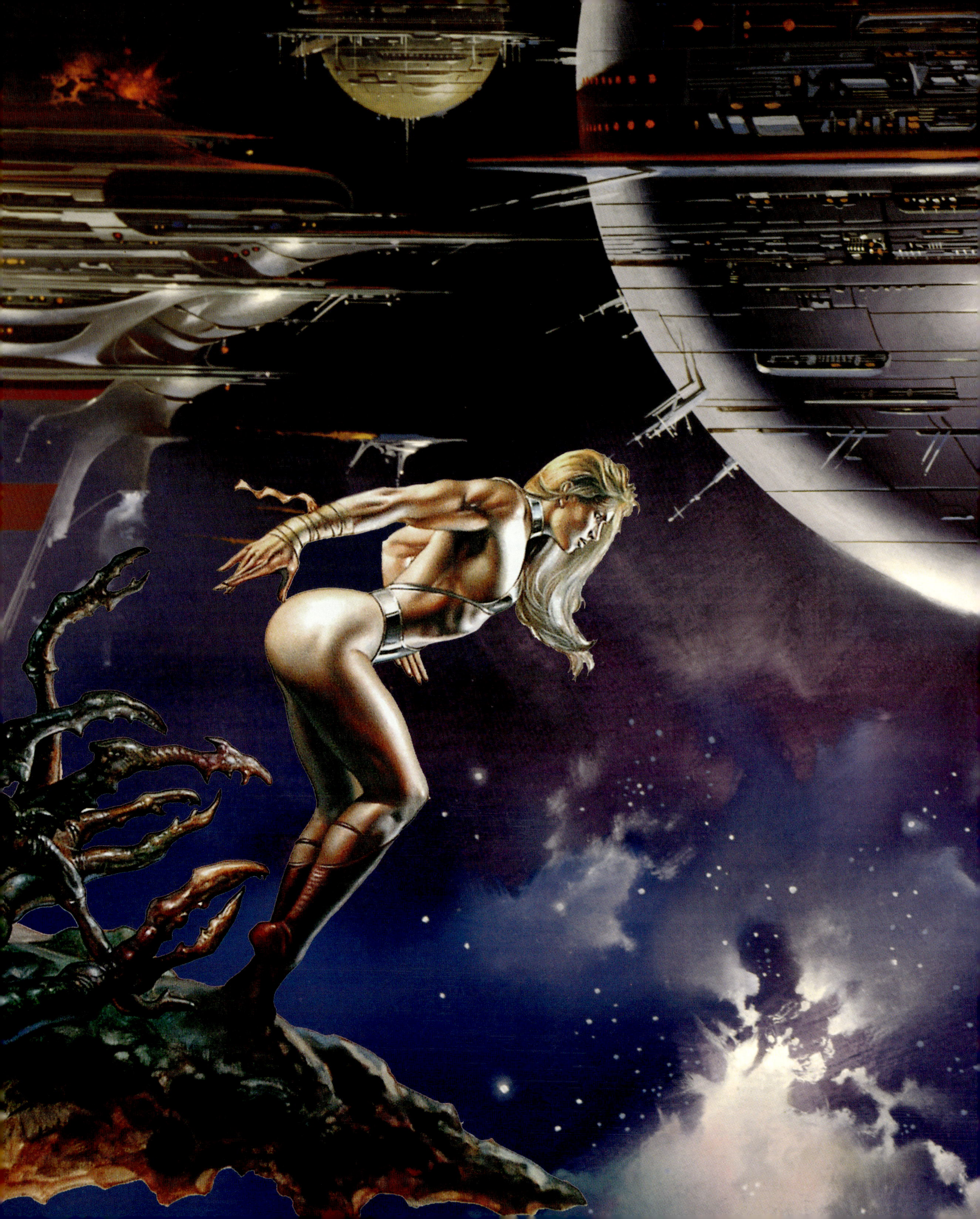

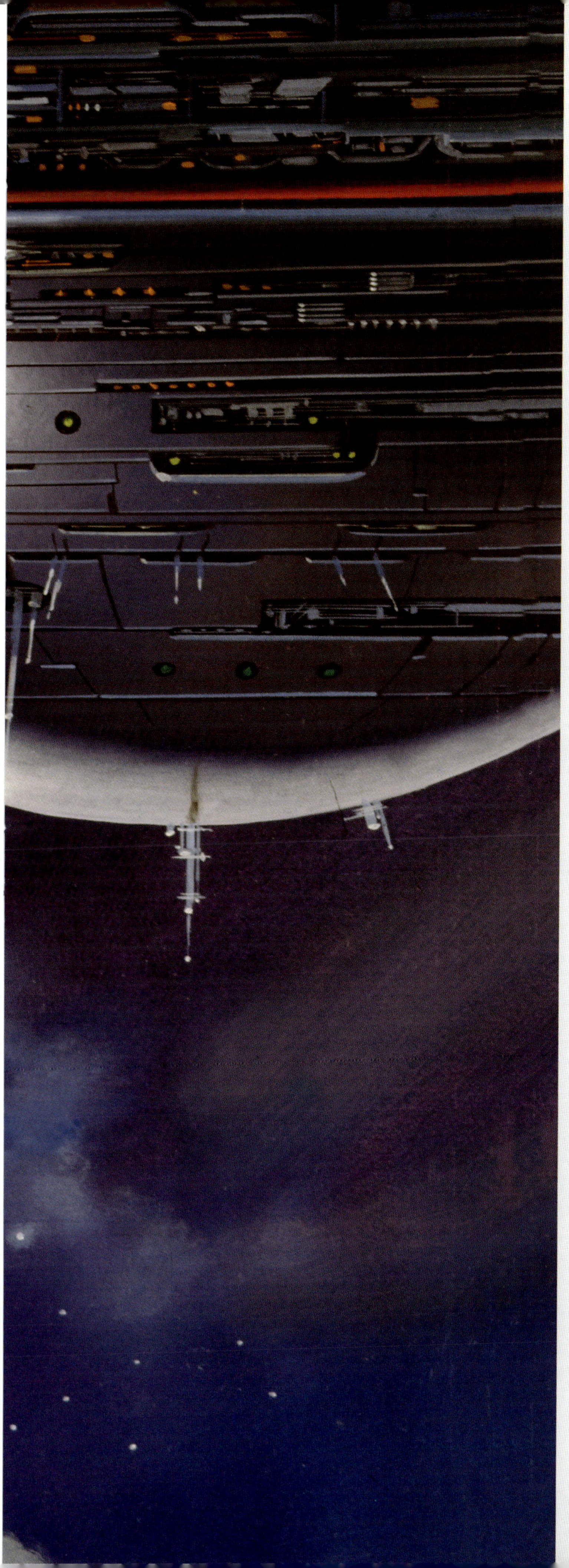

"IT'S ANOTHER DIGITAL COMPOSITE. YOU TURNED IT UPSIDE-DOWN!"

JULIE

The Void, Boris Vallejo, *1996*

"I think the computer is a tool like anything else, like airbrush. I used an airbrush a long time ago, in two or three paintings. I'm not against using any kind of digital help sparingly, though I wouldn't go totally digital. I like using real pencils and paints, and I like having an actual painting. One thing that bothers me when I finish a digital composition is that I don't end up with a physical painting."

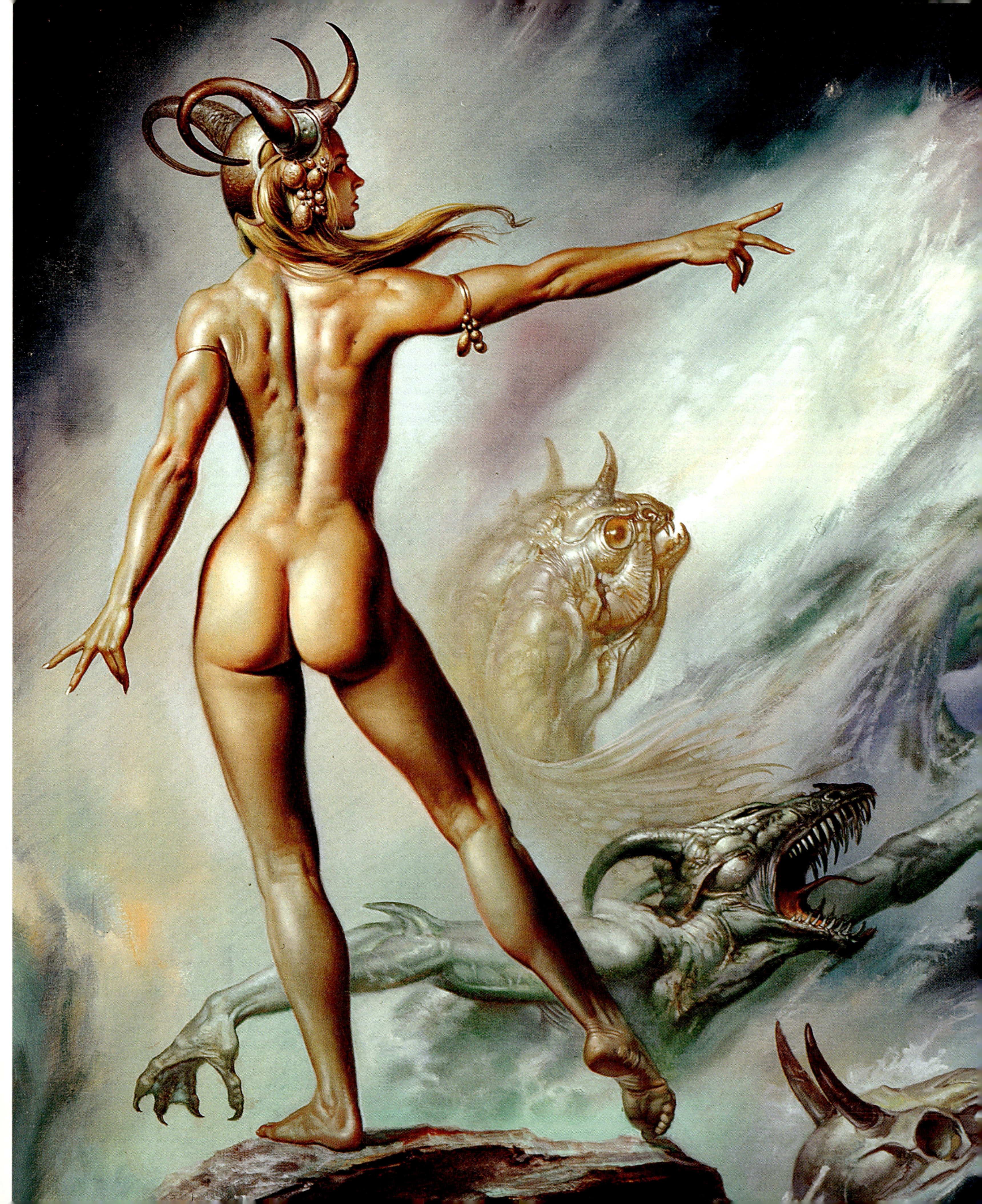

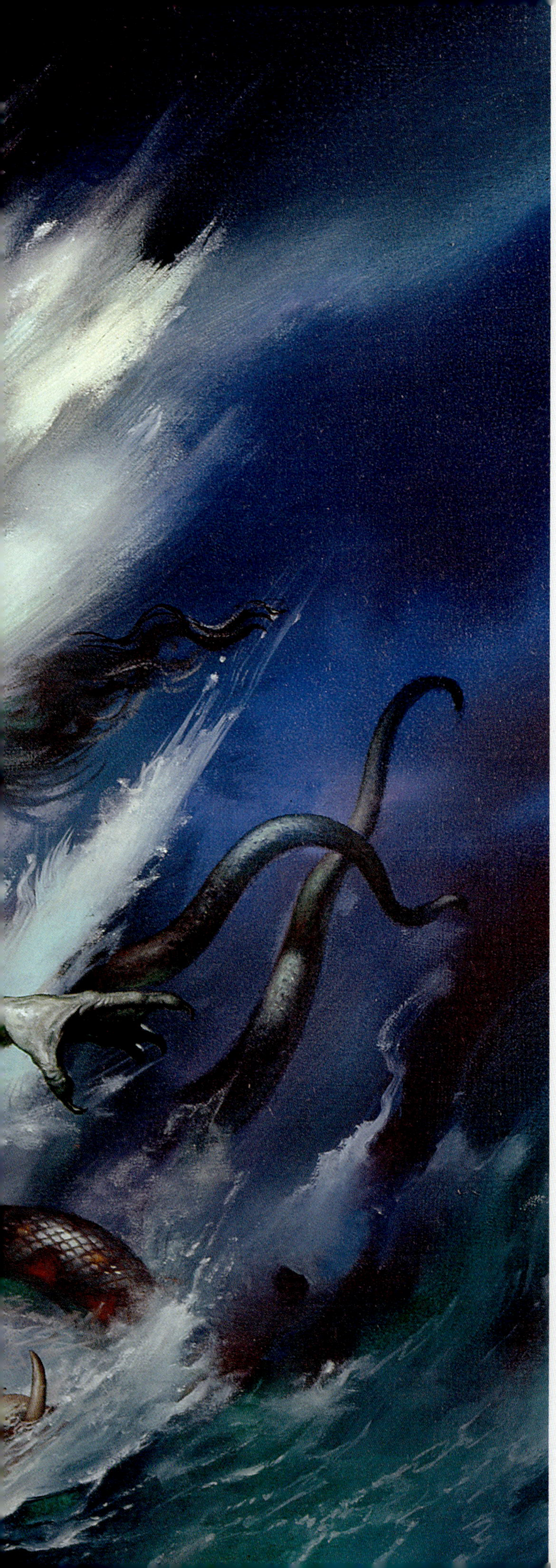

"I LOVE TO PAINT WATER. THE MOTION AND TEXTURE ARE VERY EXCITING TO REPRODUCE, ESPECIALLY WITH A VERY OMINOUS SEA LIKE THIS ONE."

BORIS

Sea Creatures, Boris Vallejo, *1993, calendar*

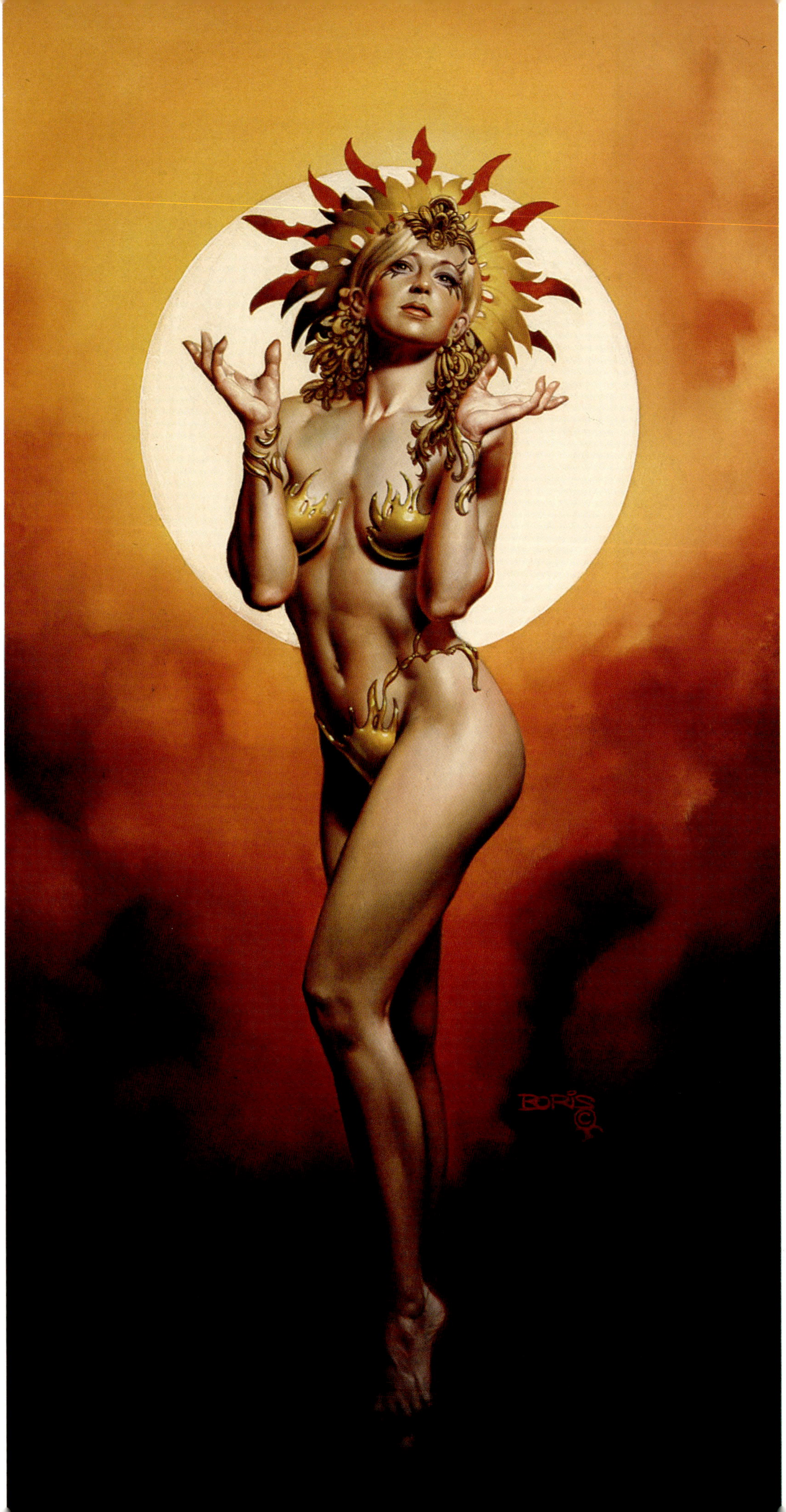

Sun Goddess,
Boris Vallejo, *1999,*
Franklin Mint pocket knife design

Boris admits that this headdress may have been inspired by the Incan imagery of his native Peru.

Warrior of Aries,
Julie Bell, *1994, trading card*

With such a high level of detail in the costume and figure, Julie decided to reduce her background to a simple field of colour. "That costume manages to hold your eye to the point that you don't really need more."

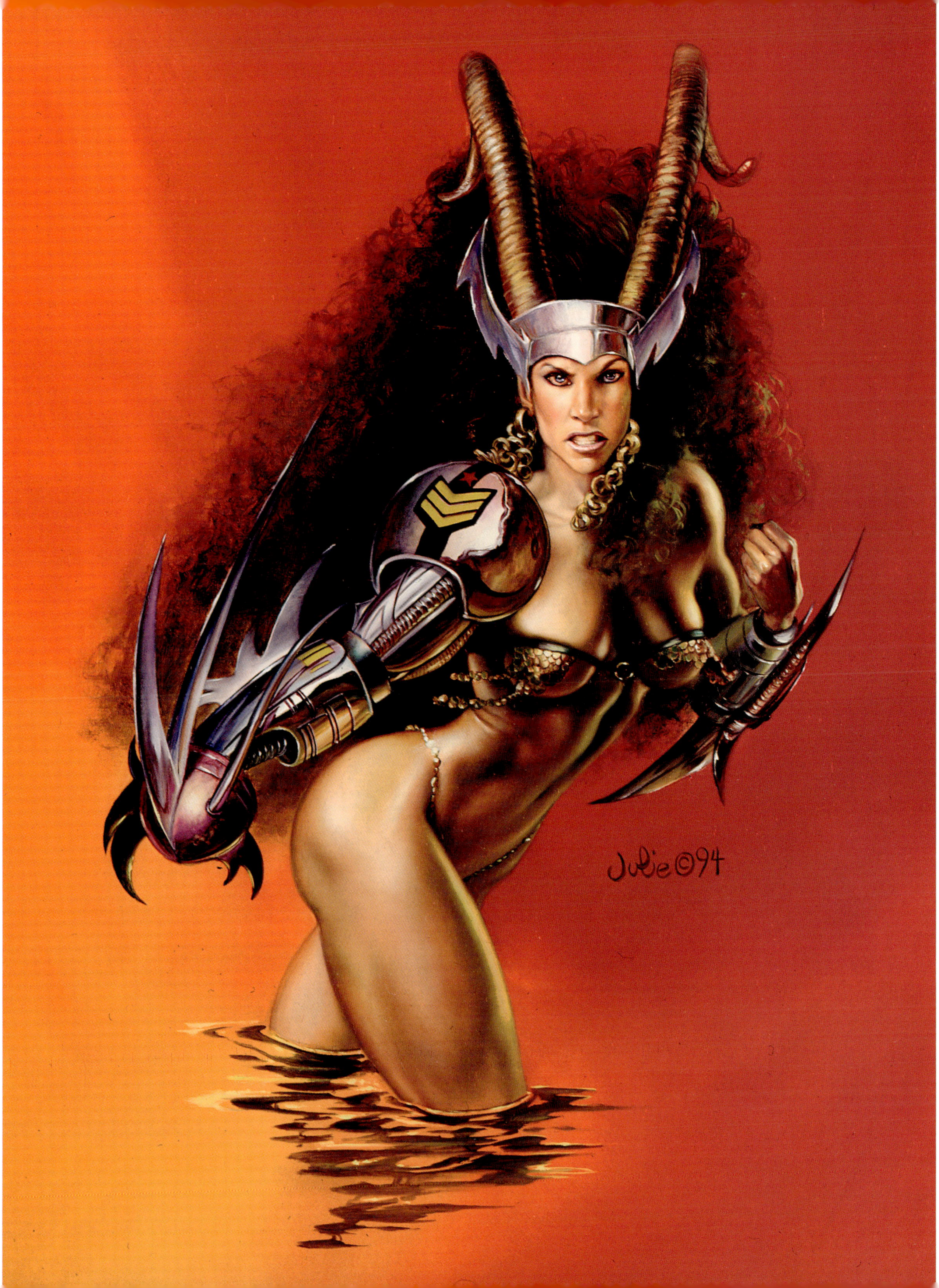
Julie ©94

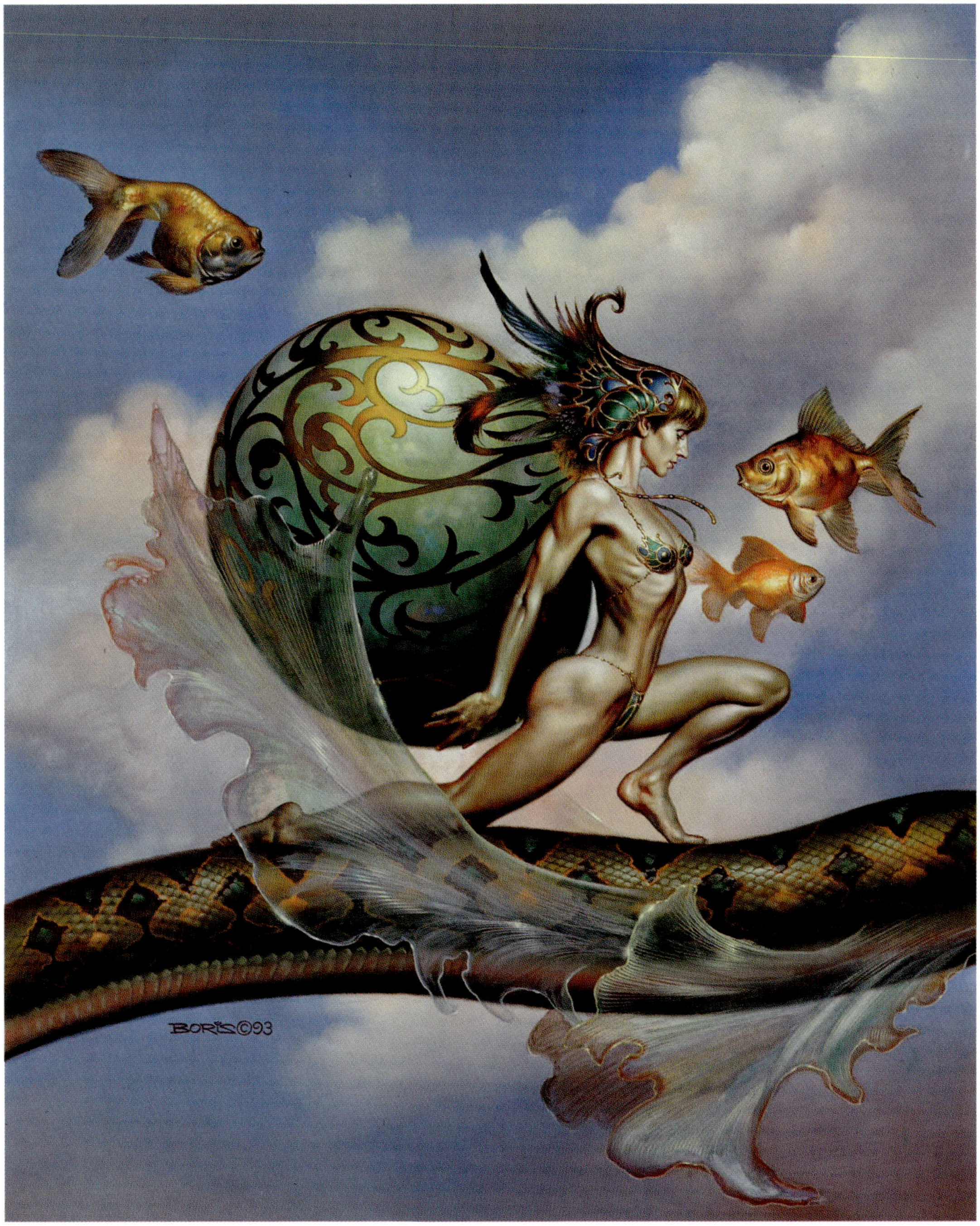

Egg of Life, Boris Vallejo, *1993, calendar*

"I get ideas for surreal paintings sometimes before I go to sleep, or even when I'm riding in a car late at night. I see odd things, like giant grasshoppers jumping down the roads."

Barbarian Queen, Boris Vallejo, *1986, film poster*

"This is another one of the Roger Corman movies. The two posters have basically the same elements: barbarian girls showing lots of skin and looking very pretty. It is certainly directed at a male audience. The idea is that you would see yourself getting into a fight with these girls. Is that something to look forward to, or something to be scared of?"

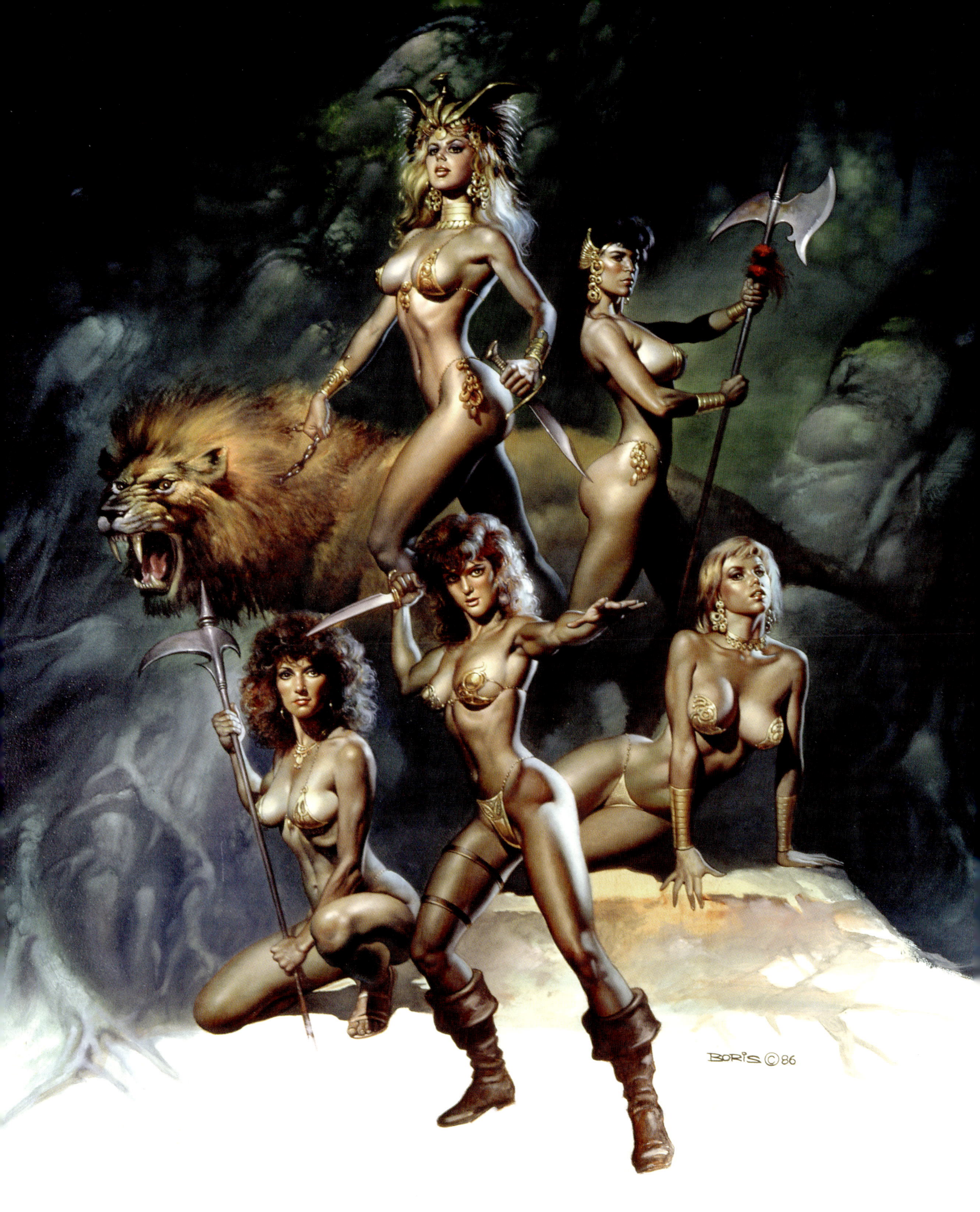
BORIS ©86

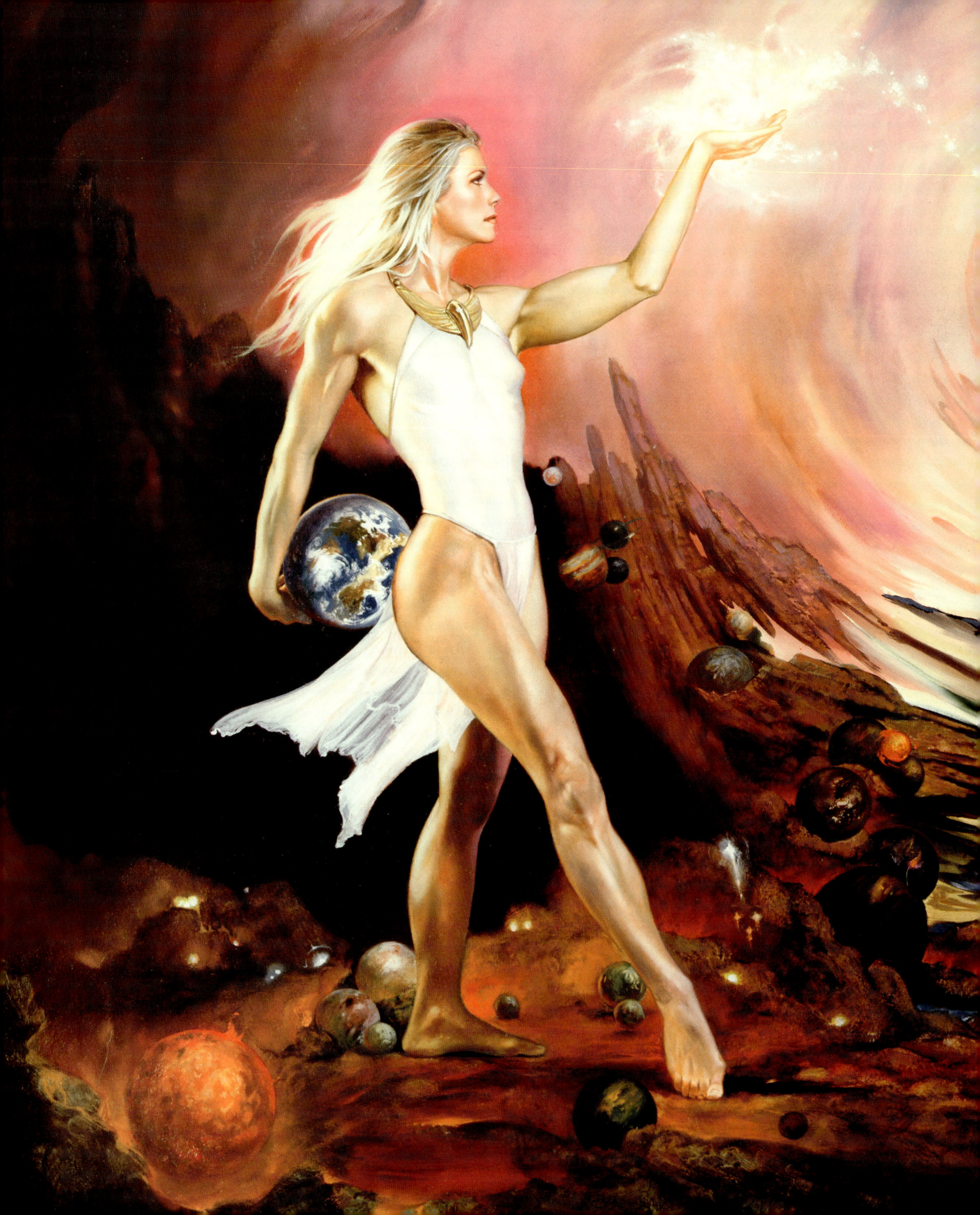

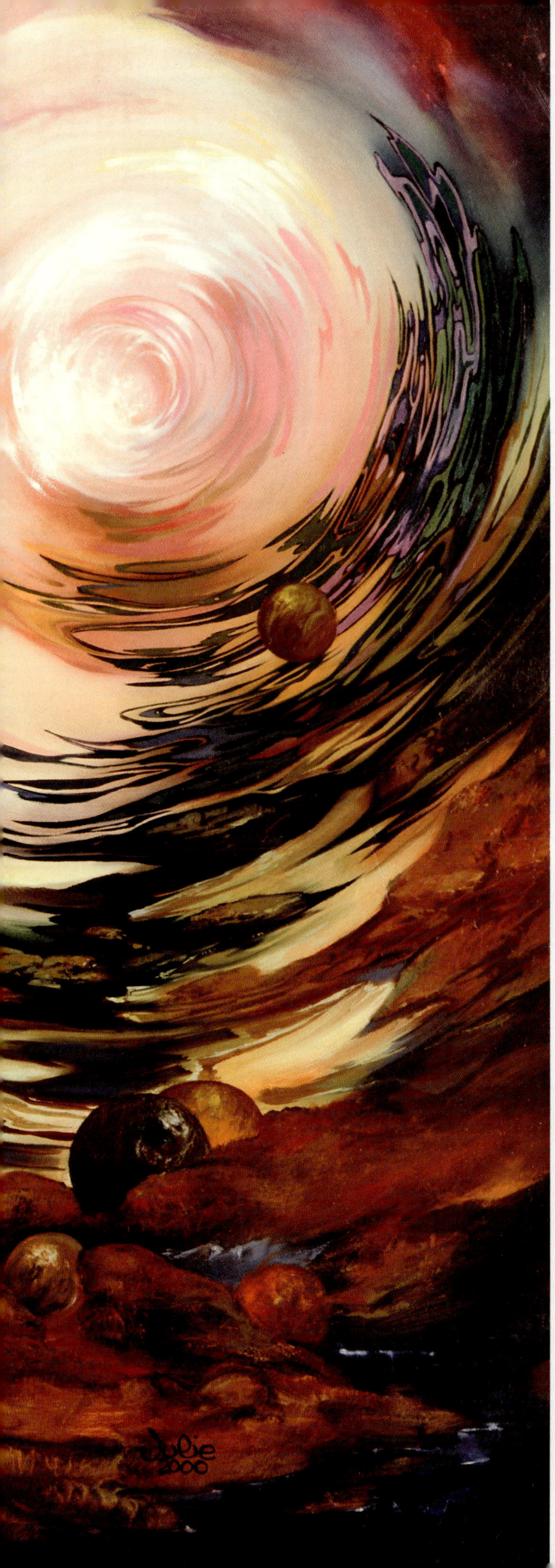

"THIS IS REALLY AN ALLUSION TO MY FEELINGS ON HAVING CHILDREN. IF EACH OF US IS OUR OWN UNIVERSE, THEN HAVING A CHILD IS LIKE SETTING A WHOLE NEW UNIVERSE INTO MOTION."

JULIE

Galaxy Weavers, Julie Bell, *2000, calendar*

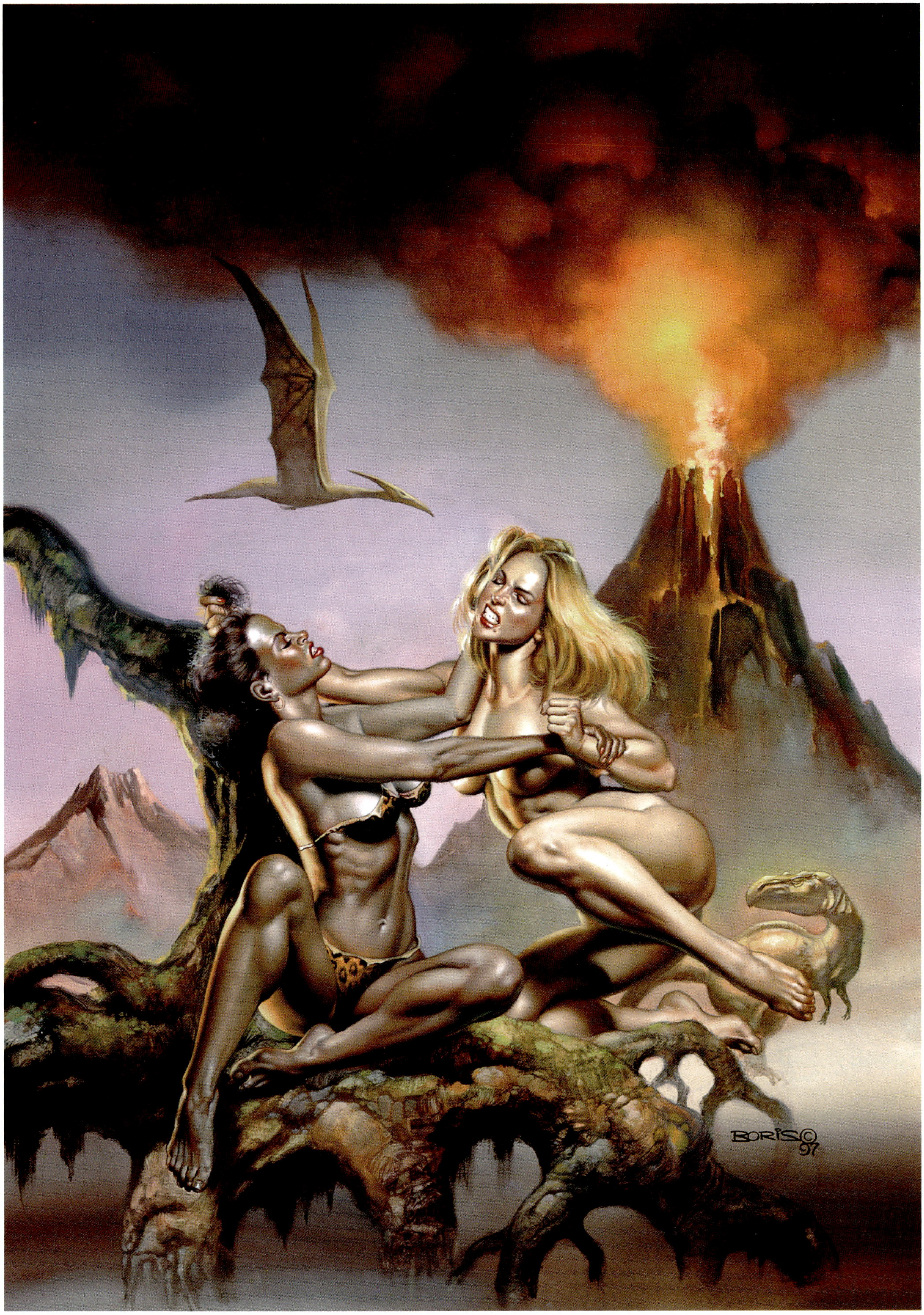
BORIS©
97

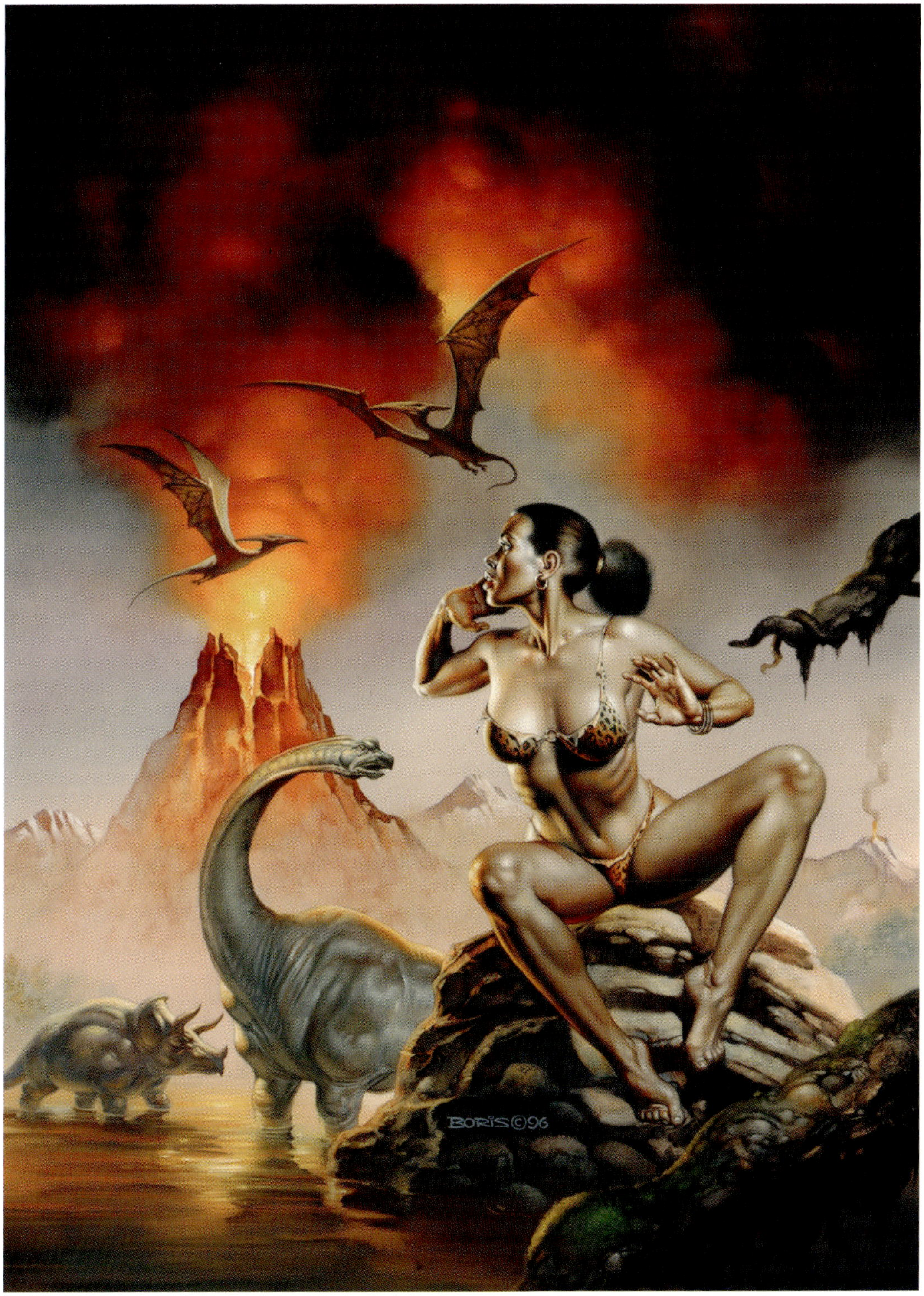

Primitive World I & II, Boris Vallejo, *1996, Penthouse Comix cover*

"It would bother me to have to paint something historically accurate, rather than fantasy... They probably aren't fighting about anything in particular, it's just the competitive nature of women." – Boris
"One time, somebody wanted me to participate in a professional wrestling match with another woman. I wouldn't do it. They wanted me to lose too. It was all choreographed, it was just too stupid." – Julie
"You didn't do it 'cause you didn't want to lose!" – Boris

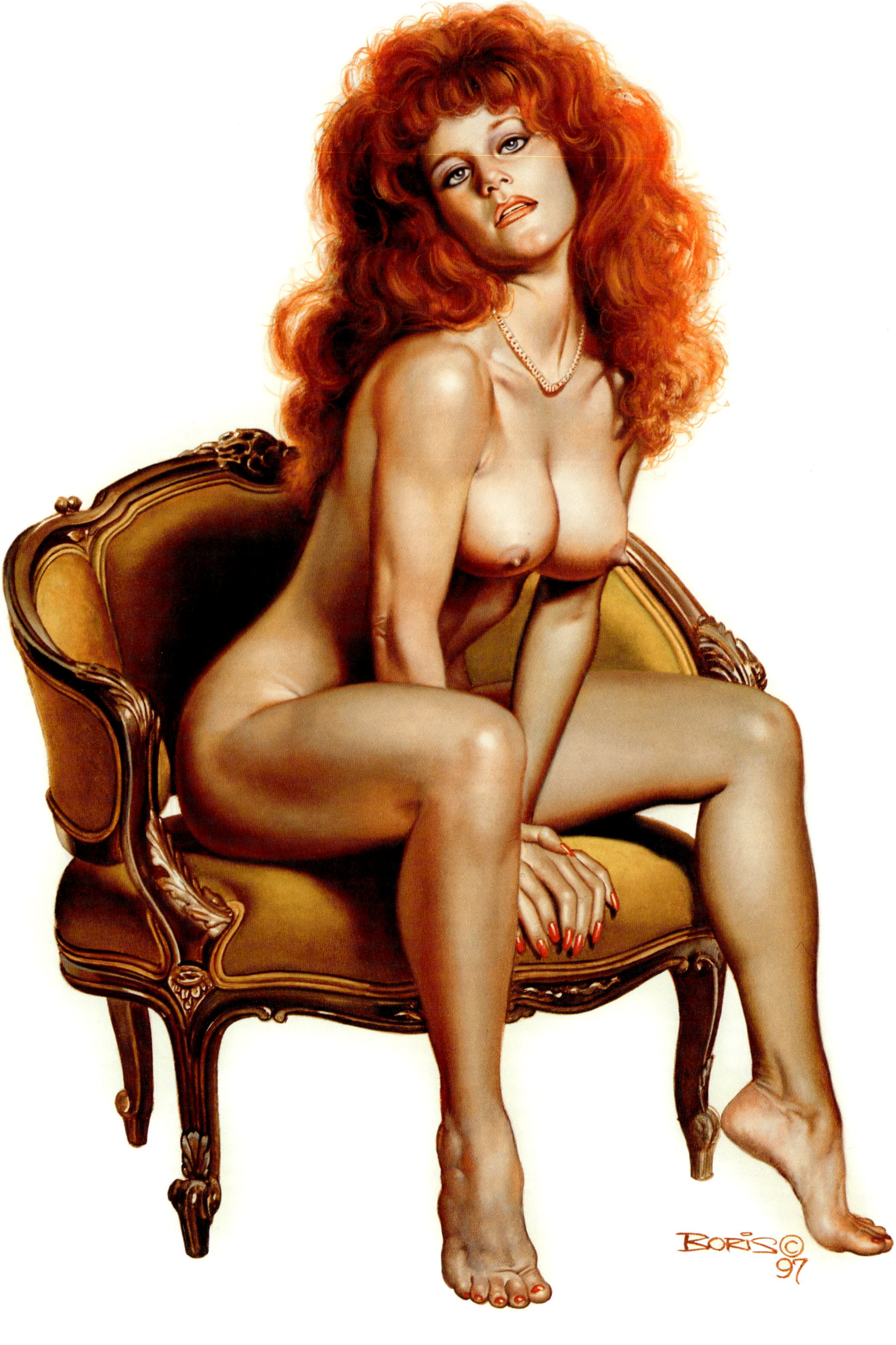
BORIS©
97

Flaming Hair, Boris Vallejo, *1997, Penthouse Comix pin-up*

"I had fun concentrating on the figure without having to worry about a background. The pin-up artists of the 50's influenced me a bit here."

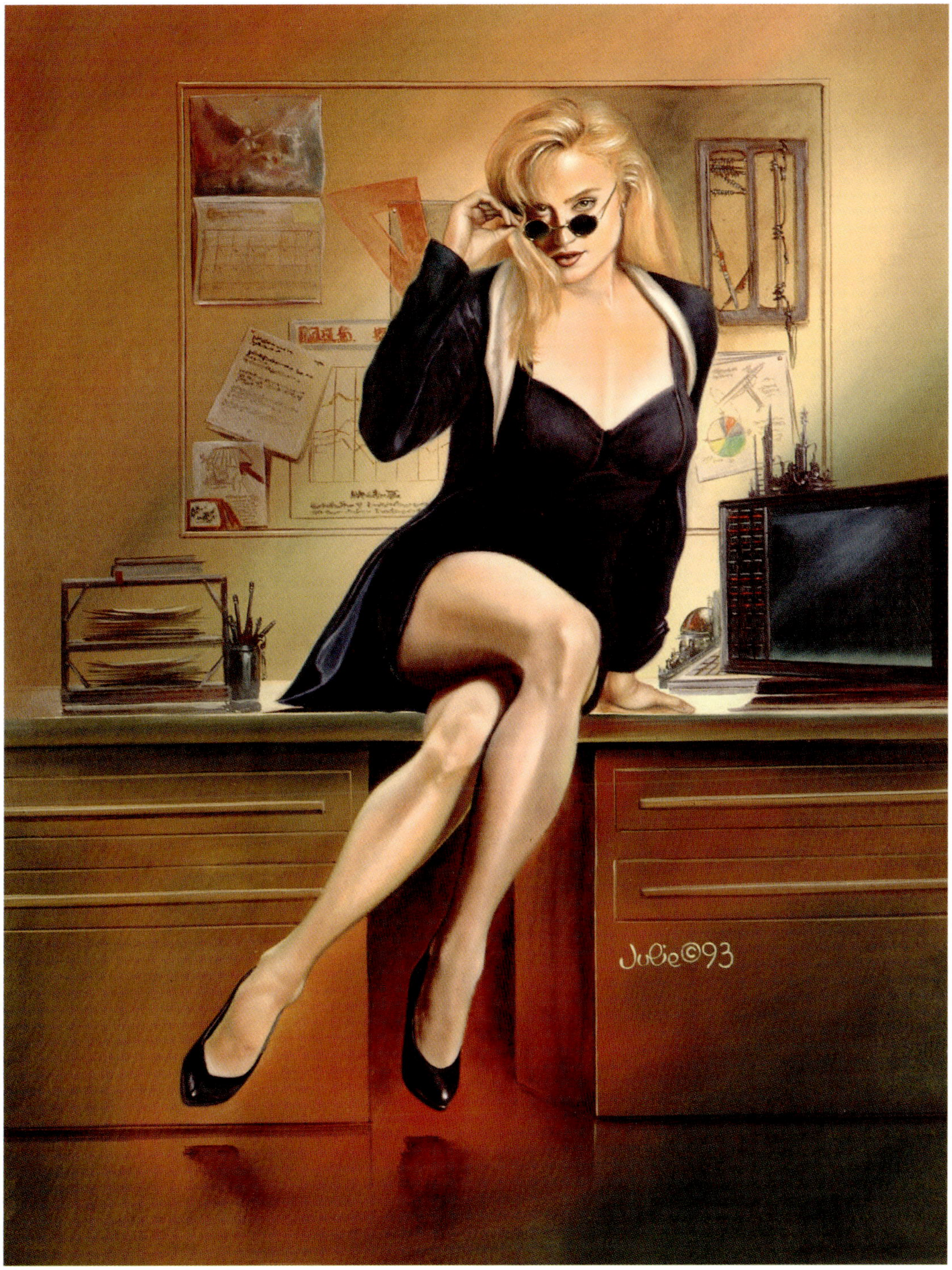

The Secretary, Julie Bell, *1993, trading card*

The workspace in this painting was based on the office of Julie's father, an architect in Texas. Boris' calendar can be seen hanging on the bulletin board.

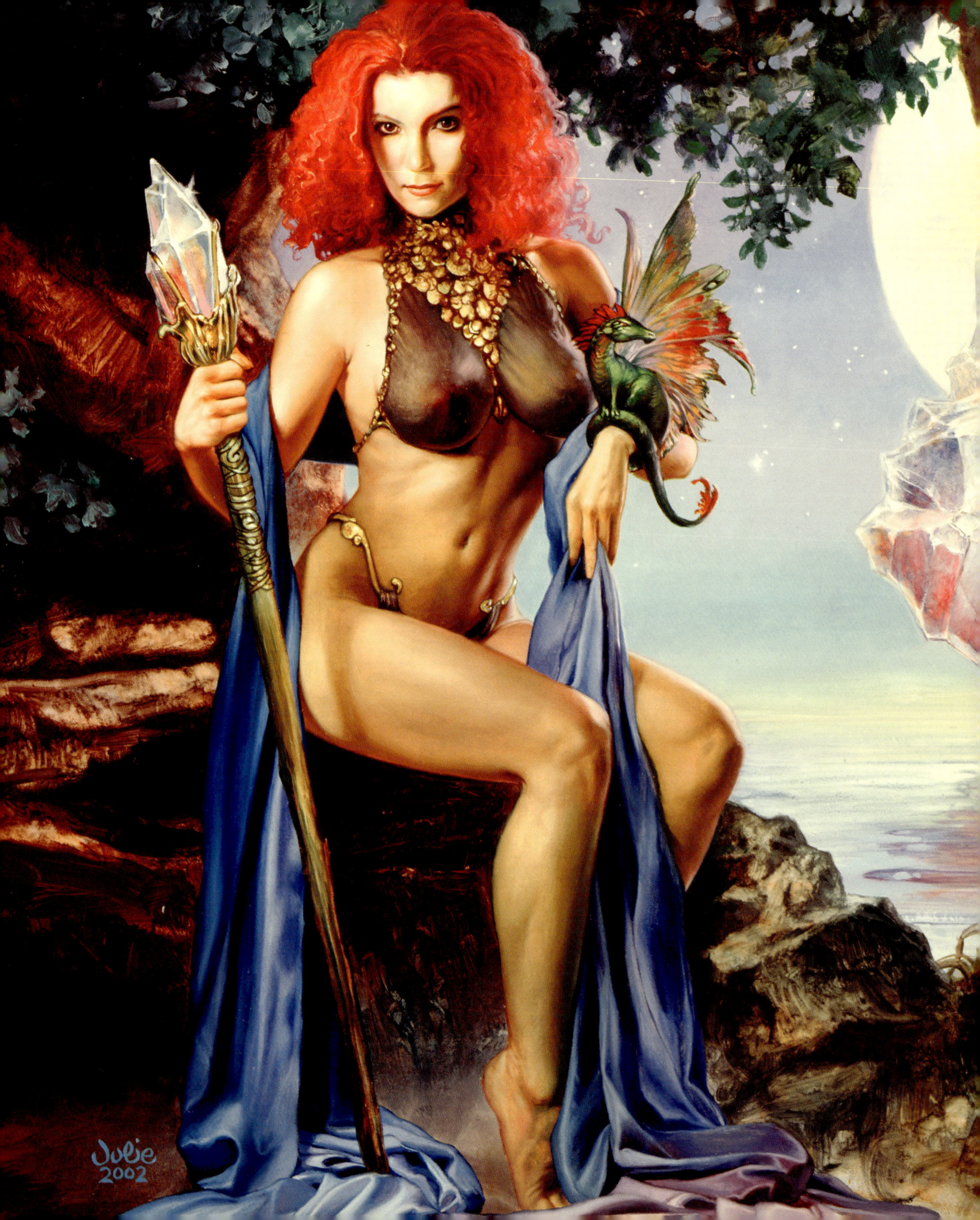
Julie
2002

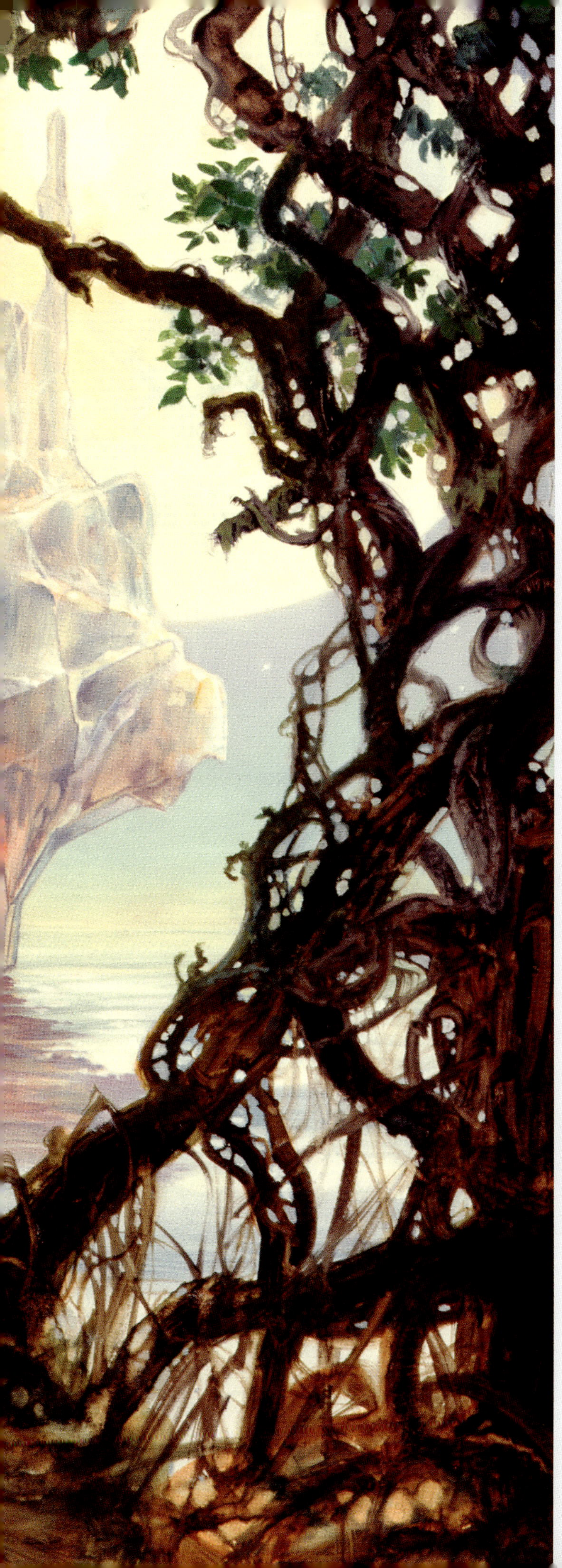

"WHEN I DO A CREATURE, IT'S FIERCE. WHEN JULIE DOES A CREATURE, IT NEEDS PROTECTION."

BORIS

The Storyteller, Julie Bell, *2002, calendar*

"The first time I met Julie, I instantly recognized that she is 100% Mommy. She really adores her kids. You can see it in her paintings. When I do a creature, it's fierce. When Julie does a creature, it needs protection." – Boris

Serpent Song, Boris Vallejo, *1994, calendar*

"That's a far cry from some girl just being pretty, there!" – Julie

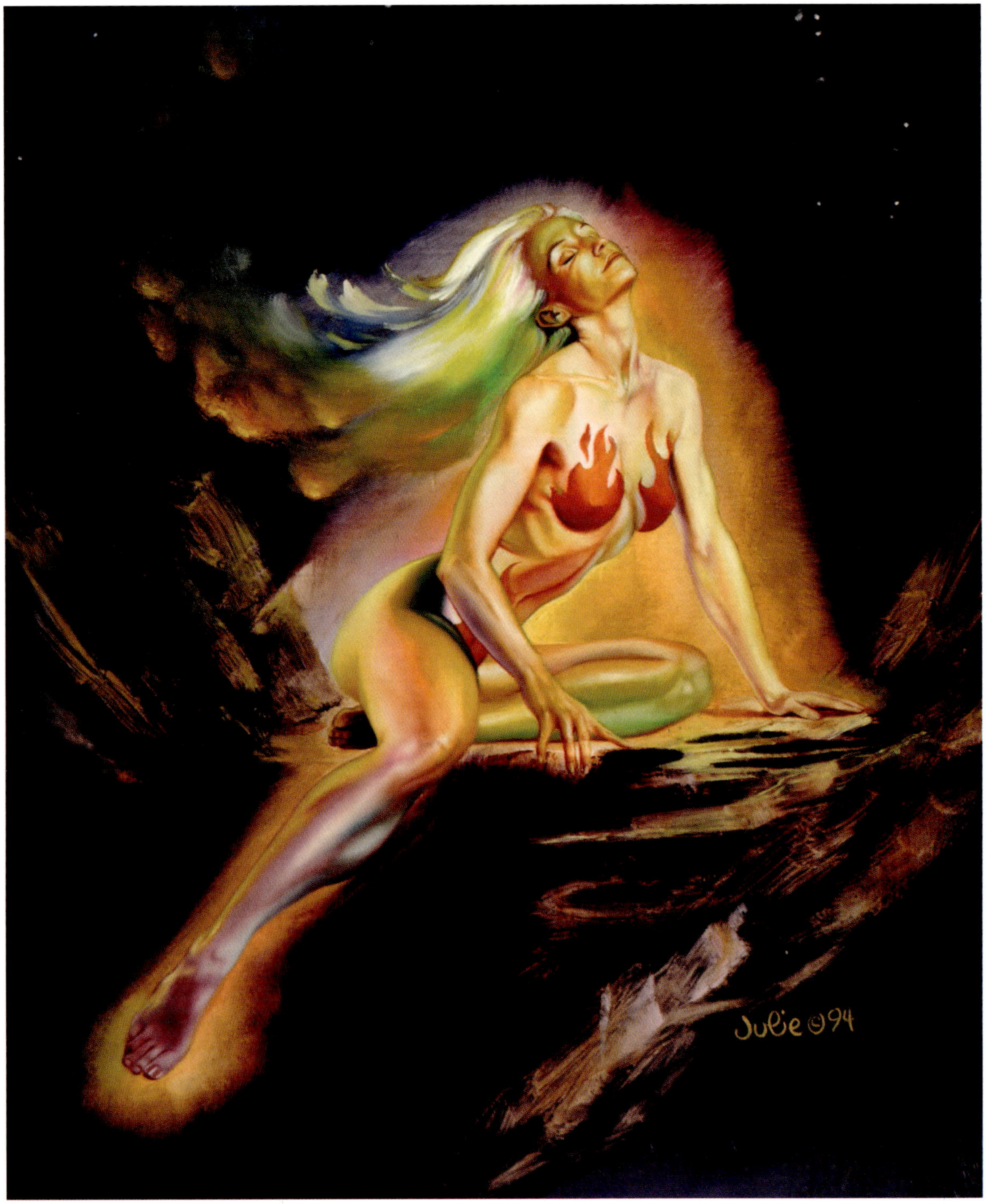

Ember, Julie Bell, *1994, trading card*

"I LIKE USING PERSONIFICATION IN MY WORK, HAVING A PERSON REPRESENT A CONCEPT OR IDEA." JULIE

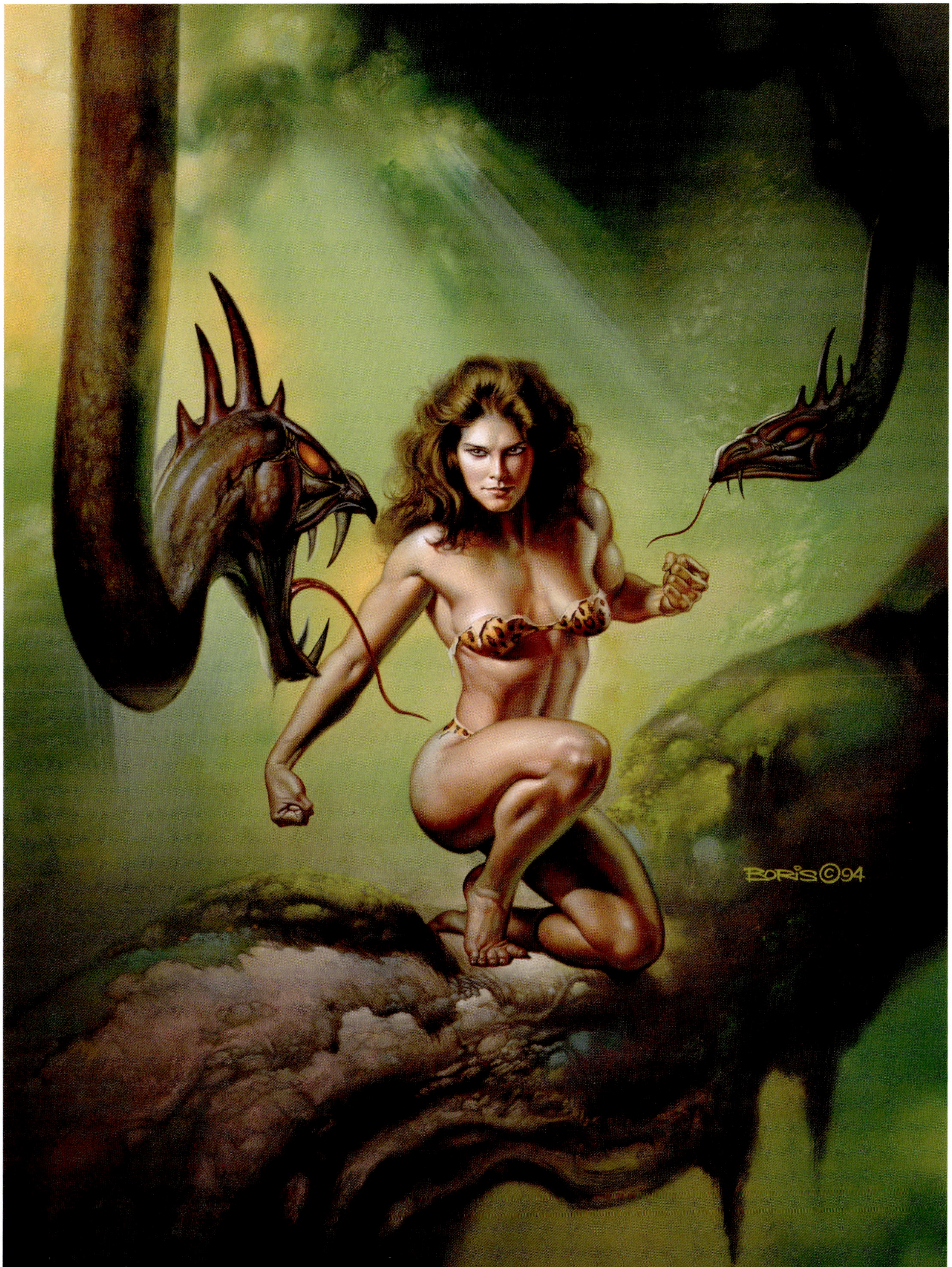
BORIS ©94

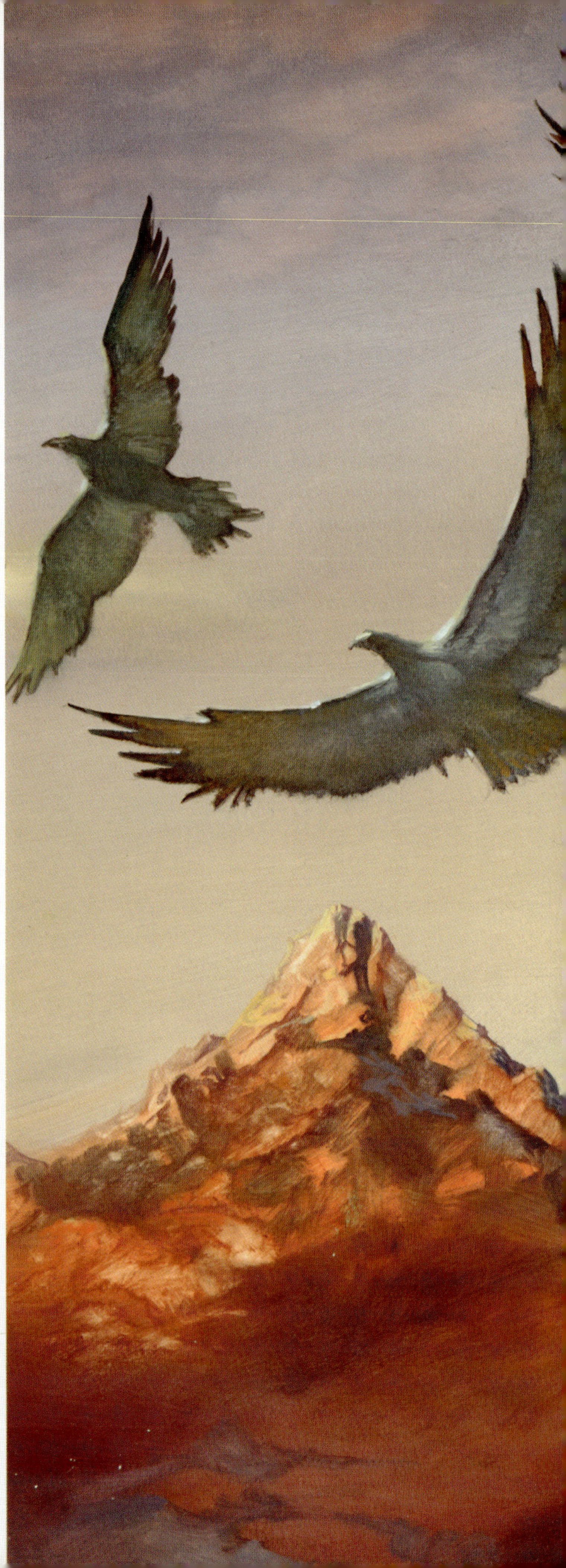

Bird Woman, Boris Vallejo, ▸▸
2002, Franklin Mint concept piece

Originally painted to be printed on a tankard, this piece ultimately found its way into Boris and Julie's calendar when that project fell through. This painting was originally a panoramic composition, but in the end it was cut down to fit its new purpose.

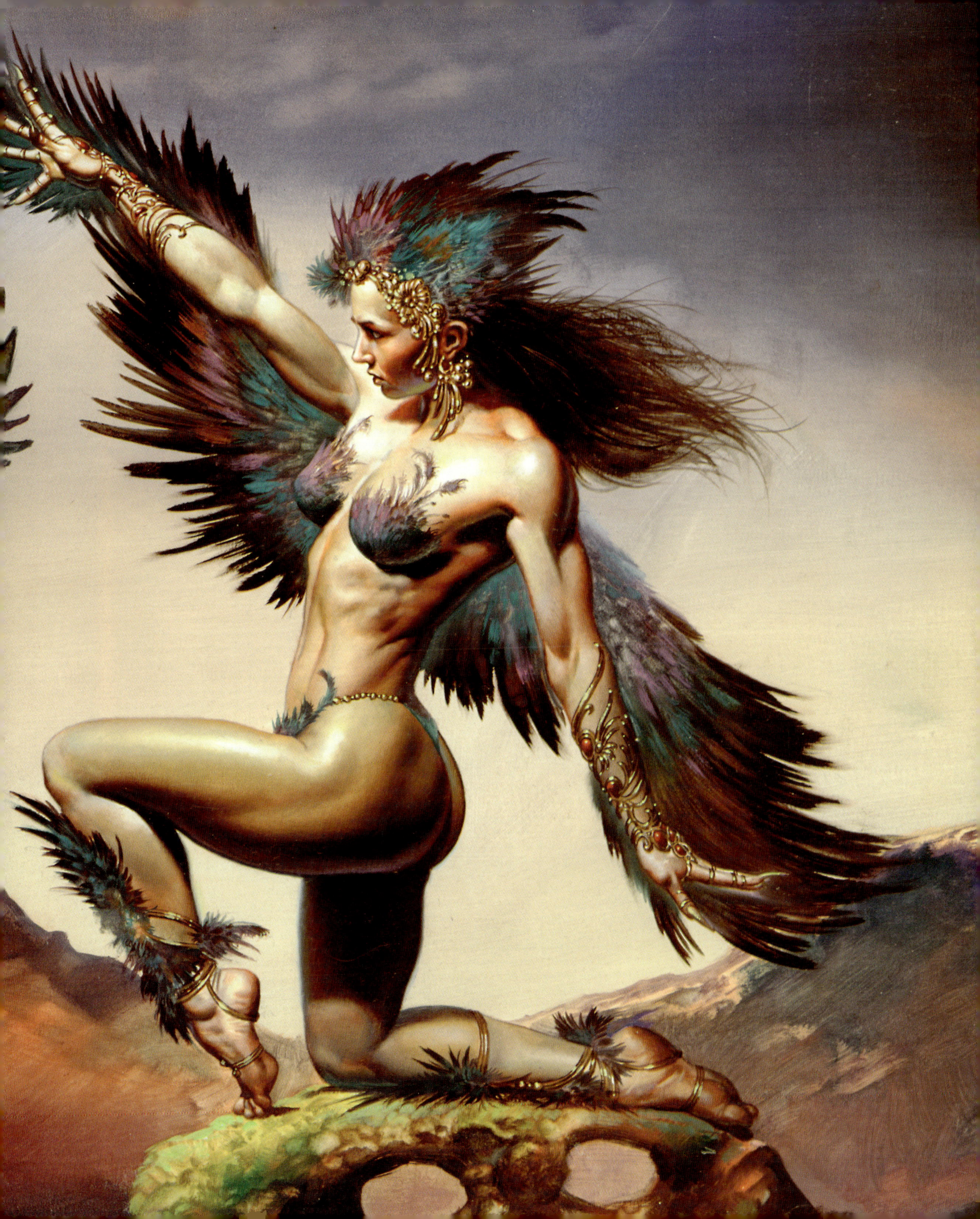

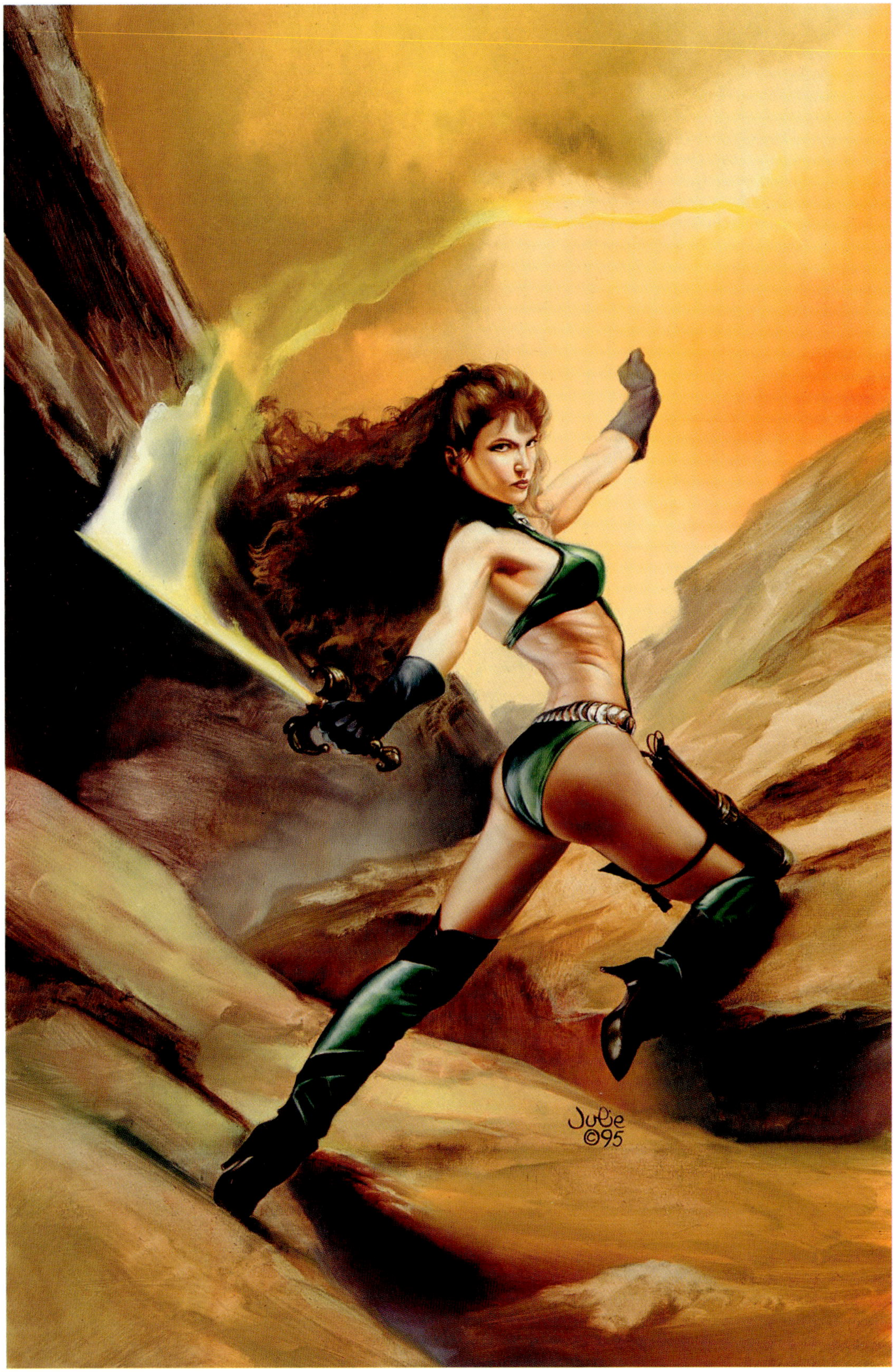

Brinke, Julie Bell,
1995, comic cover

As this was done for the cover of her own comic book (*Brinke of Destruction*), Brinke Stevens provided her own props and hand-made costume.

Mistress of the Cats,
Boris Vallejo, *1987, calendar*

A piece that has not been very widely reprinted, Boris questions why it was not more popular. "I really enjoy this one. I suppose it's an example of how the artist tends to like something for reasons other people may not see."

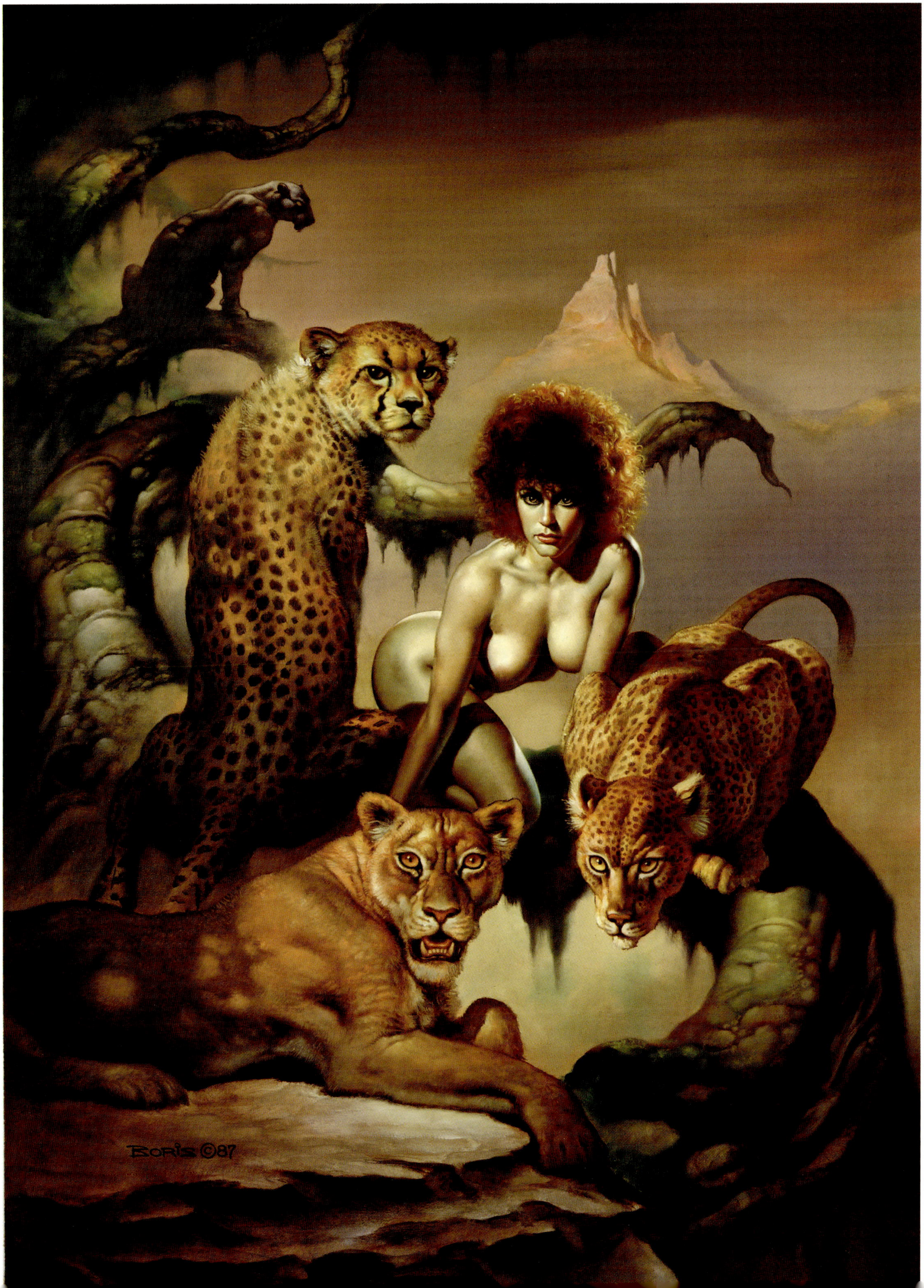
BORIS ©87

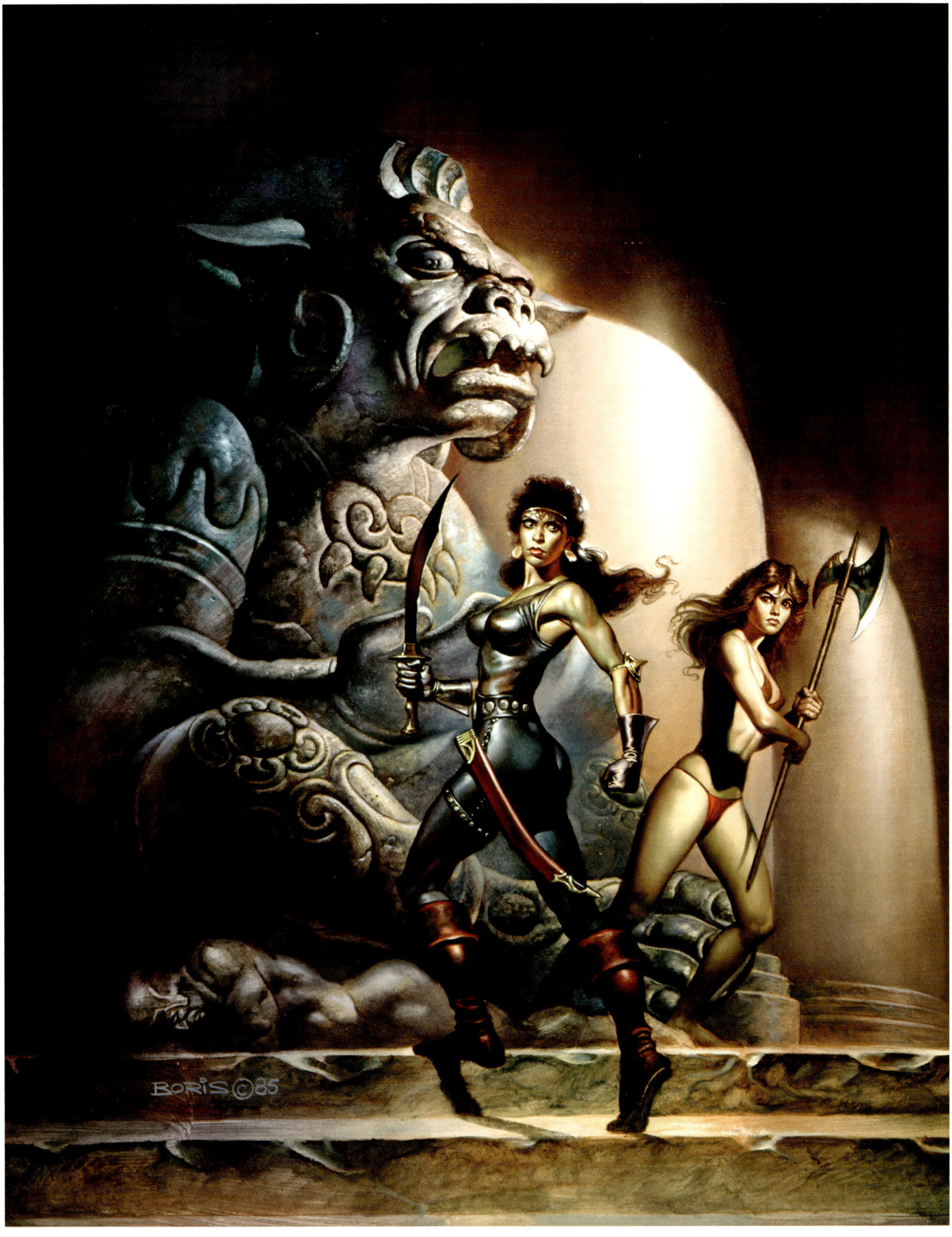
BORIS ©85

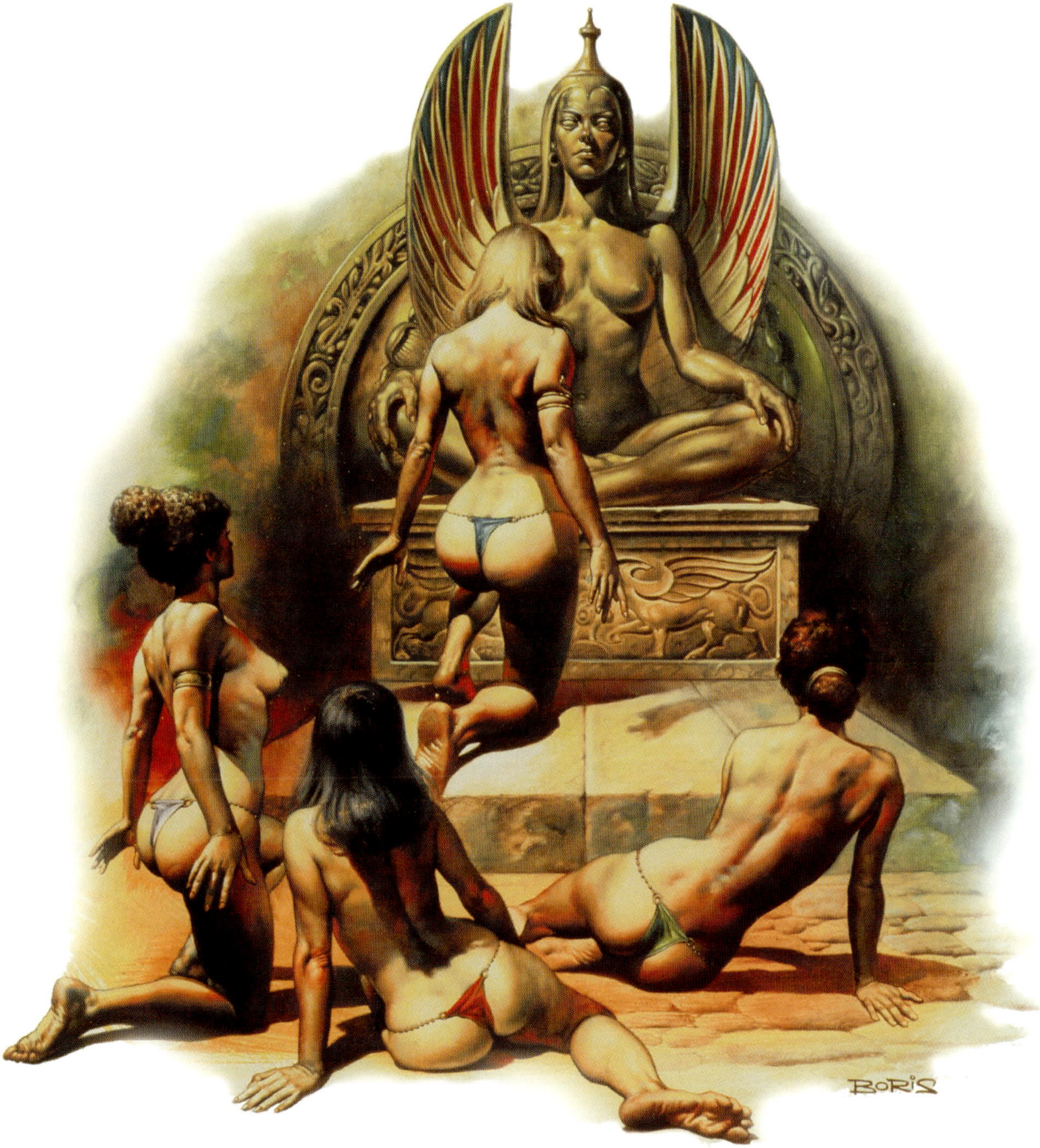

◂◂ **Bloodsong,** Boris Vallejo, *1985, book cover*

"Oh, the female warrior again..." Boris laughs when asked about this painting. "And the thing is, I could go on doing female warriors for the rest of my life!" Boris also recalls the invention of the stone idol, "I love painting the different textures. It was fun to design him."

Vestal Virgins, Boris Vallejo, *book cover* ▴

When presented with the opportunity, Boris is always ready and willing to paint more and more sexy women. "It is clear looking at this piece which anatomical feature I enjoy painting most," says Boris, "the butt."

By the Sword, Julie Bell, *2001, calendar* ▸▸

When this painting appeared in the calendar, the woman had to be clothed, so two separate versions exist.

"SOMETIMES I PREFER THE NATURAL BEAUTY OF NUDITY. ANIMALS LOOK BEAUTIFUL AS THEY ARE. IT'S A SHAME PEOPLE HAVE TO BE COVERED."

JULIE

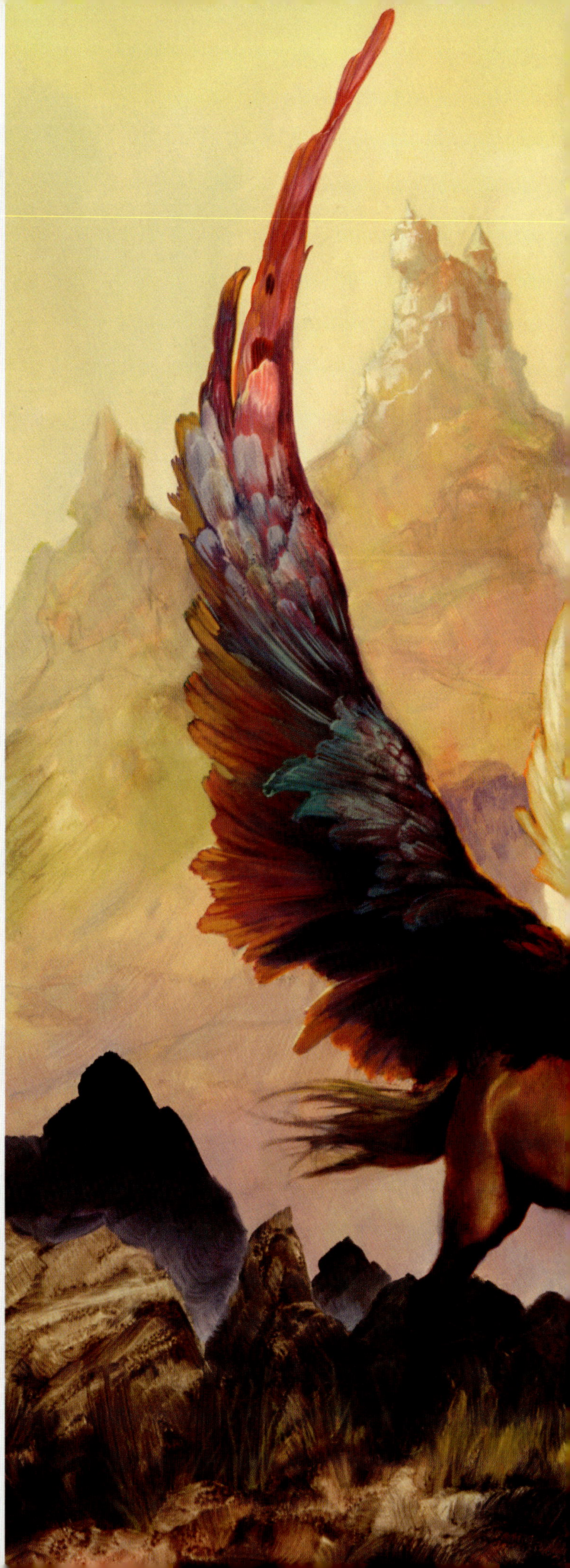

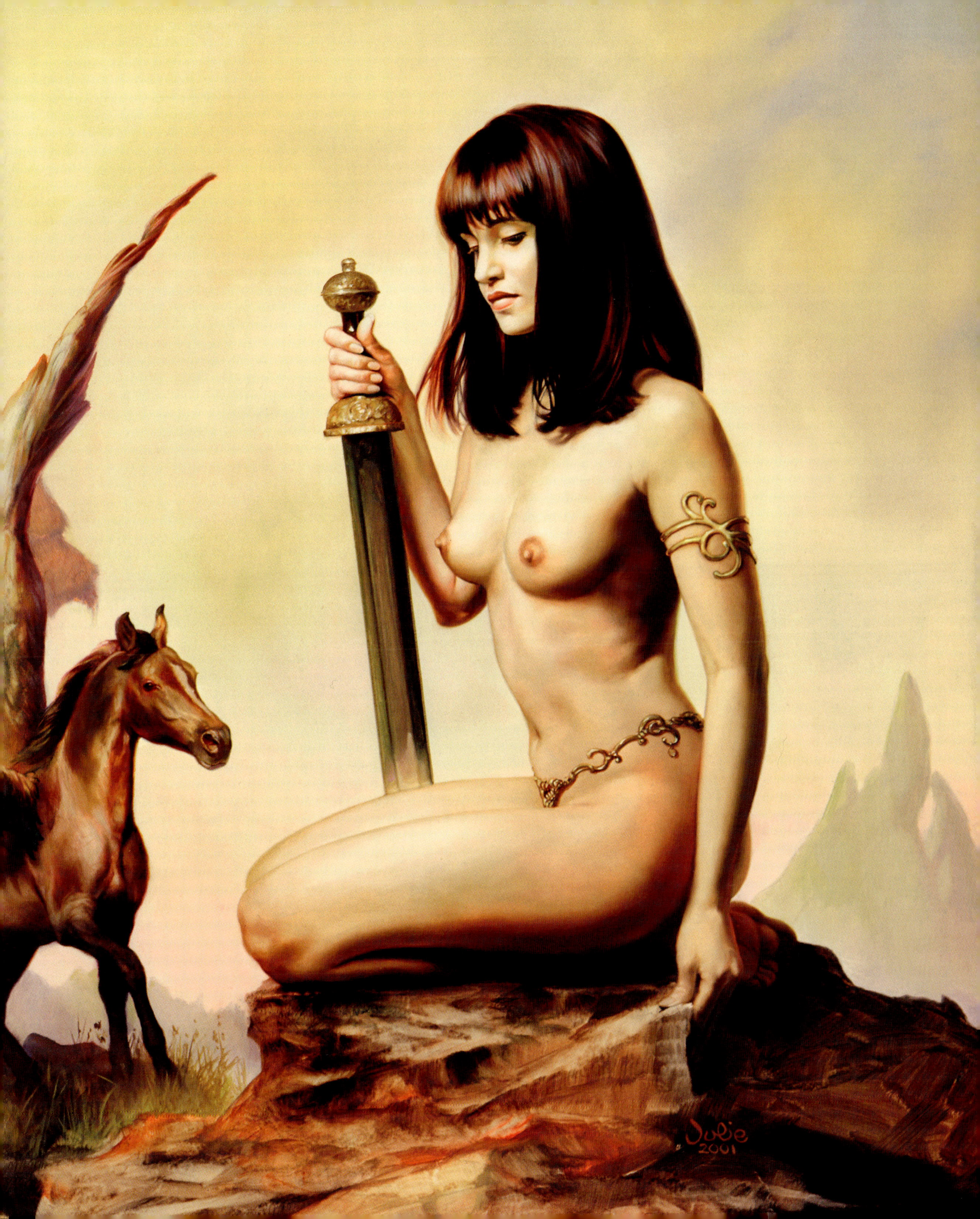
Julie
2001

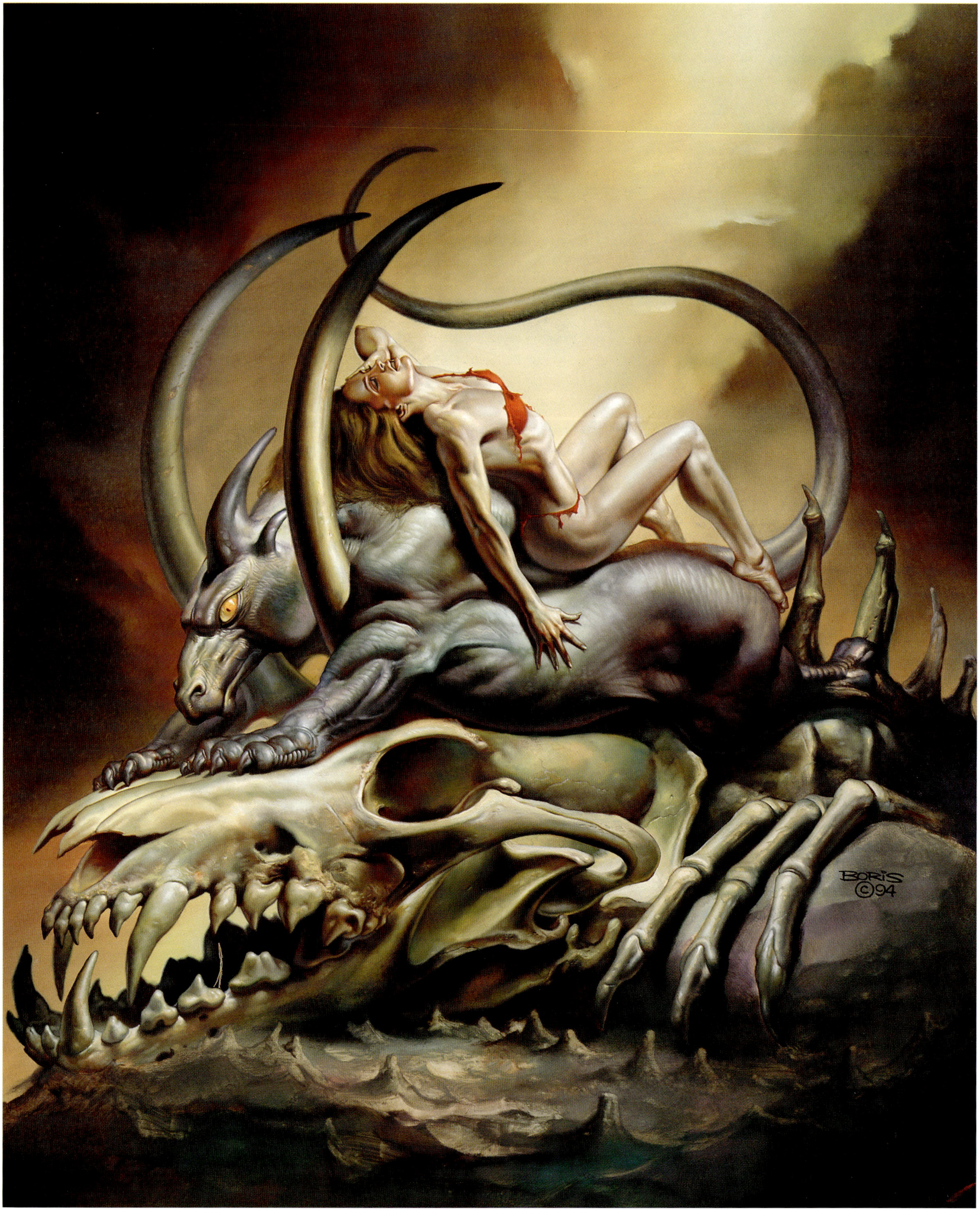
BORIS
©94

A Second of Forever,
Boris Vallejo, *1994, calendar*

Boris demonstrates here how he likes to build up an environment through a variety of bizarre textures and elements. "I like to be surprised at what comes out. I'll just start with the pose of the model and work from there."

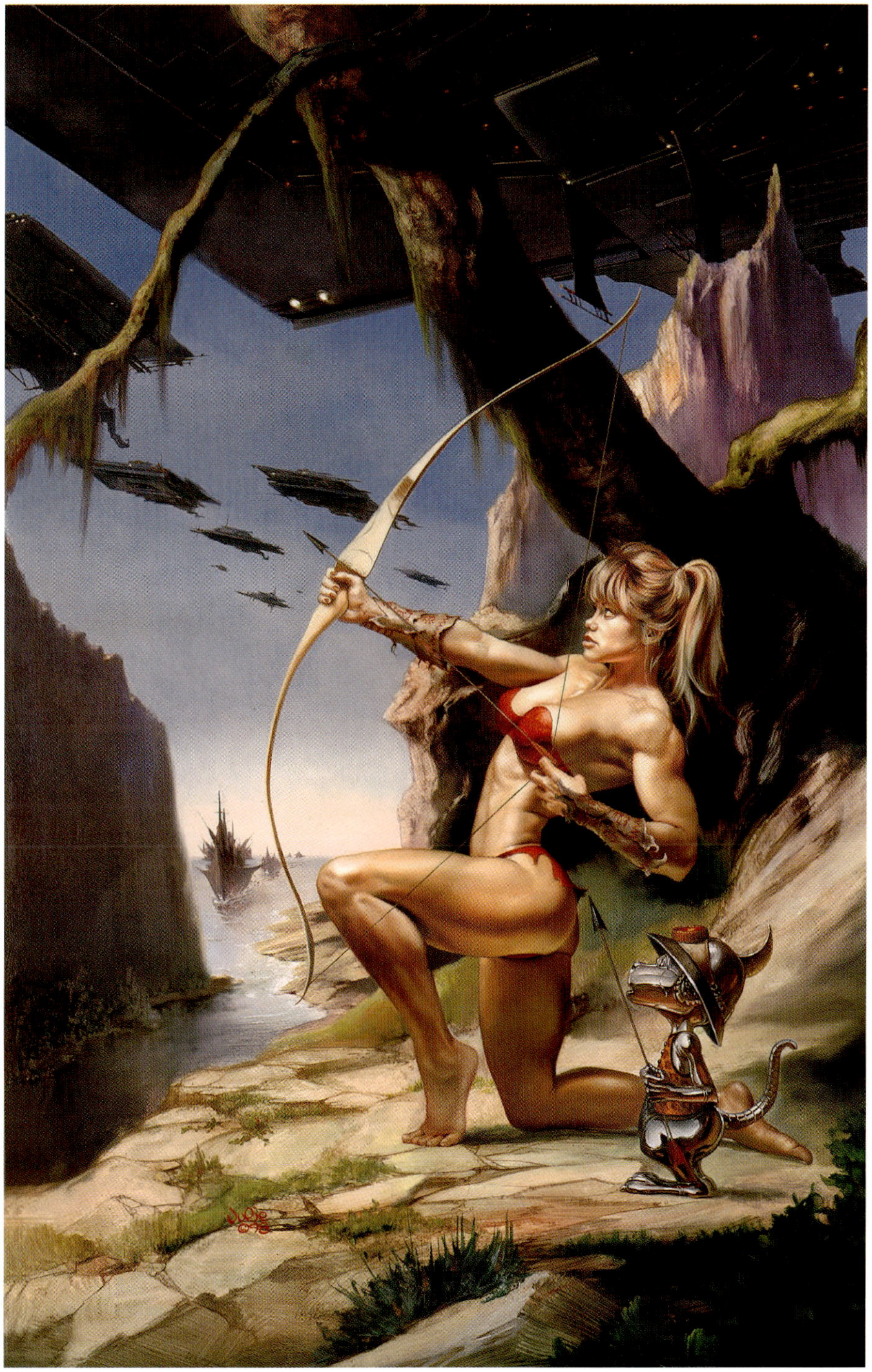

"I LIKE TO BE SURPRISED AT WHAT COMES OUT. I'LL JUST START WITH THE POSE OF THE MODEL AND WORK FROM THERE."

BORIS

Defenders of Paradise, Julie Bell, *1998, calendar*

In her paintings, Julie often enjoys injecting humour into what would otherwise be a tense situation. "It's so hilarious. They both look so serious with their primitive weapons against these high tech machines!" The small metal creature was inspired by Julie's pet rabbit.

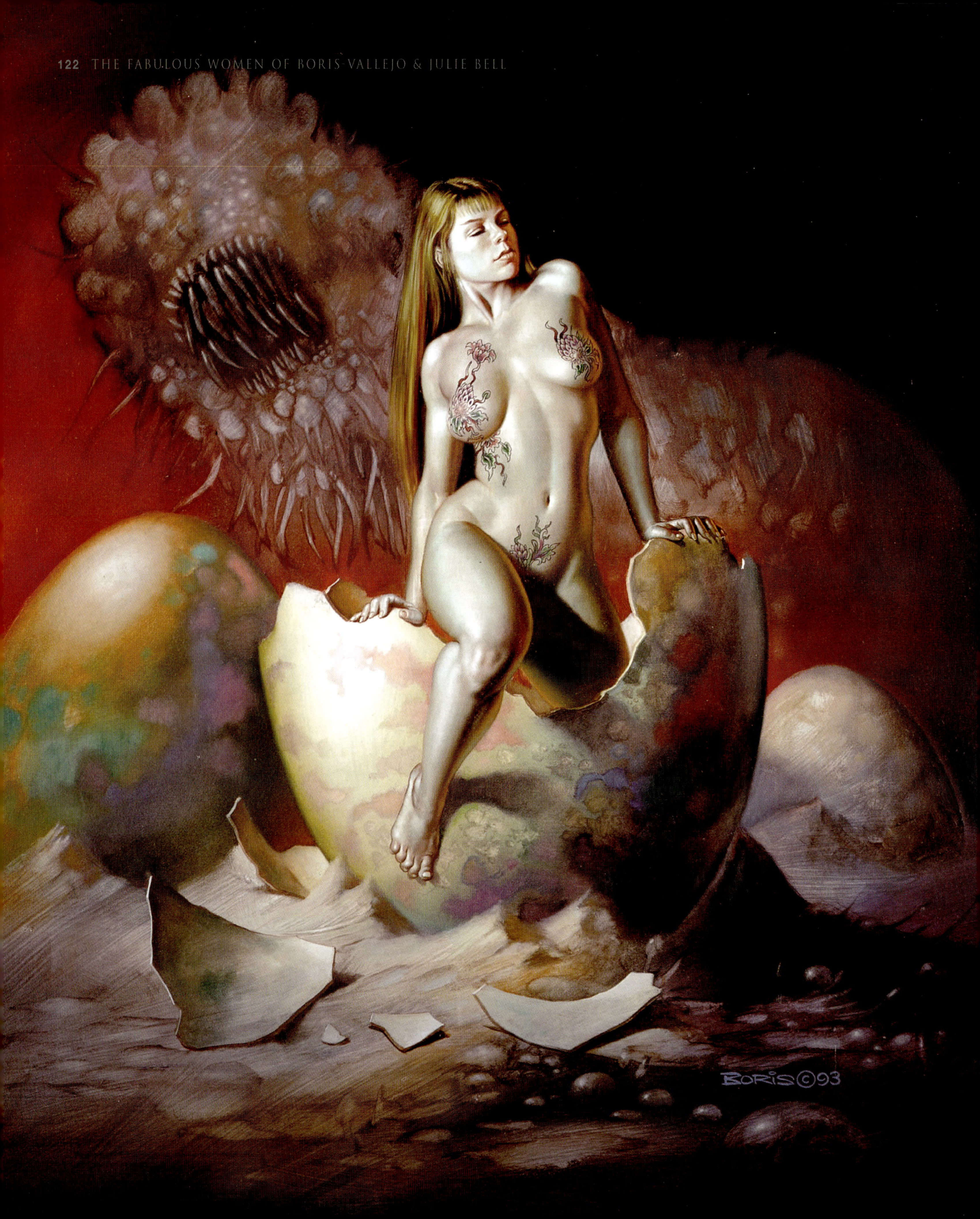
BORIS©93

Hatching,
Boris Vallejo, *1993, calendar*

Julie's sister Suzanne posed for this painting. "She has such beautiful skin, I wanted to push that with these really pearly colors," says Boris.

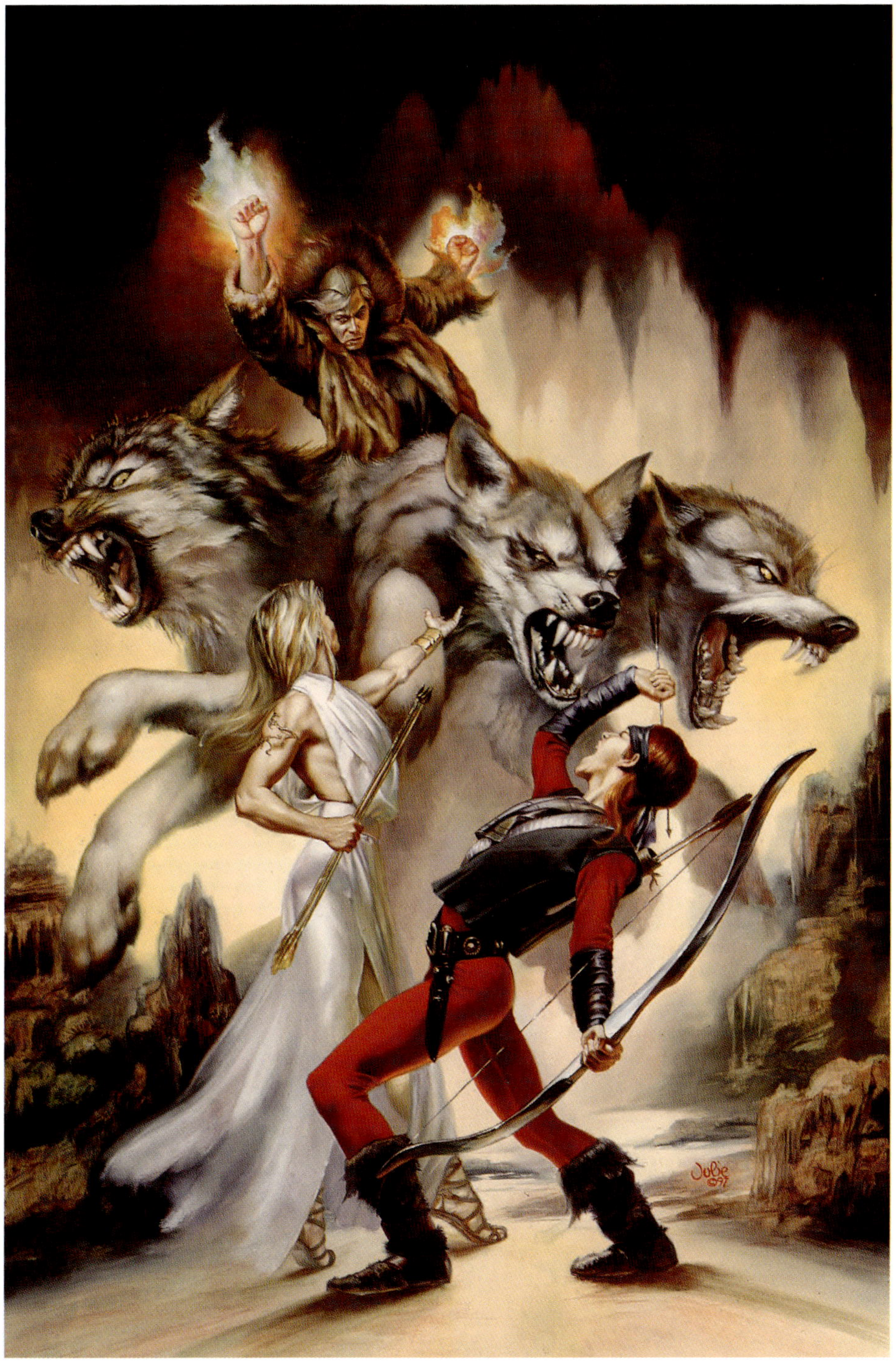

Young Apollo,
Julie Bell, *1997, book cover*

"I like the contrast between the macho imagery of the wolves, and the grace of the woman, like a ballerina." explains Julie. Julie studied ballet as a child. She carried the sense of poise and balance learned in those early lessons with her throughout her bodybuilding days and on into her painting career.

"IT'S HARD TO MAKE THE ANATOMY OF A TWO HEADED ANIMAL LOOK BELIEVABLE, AND HERE JULIE DID IT WITH THREE."

BORIS

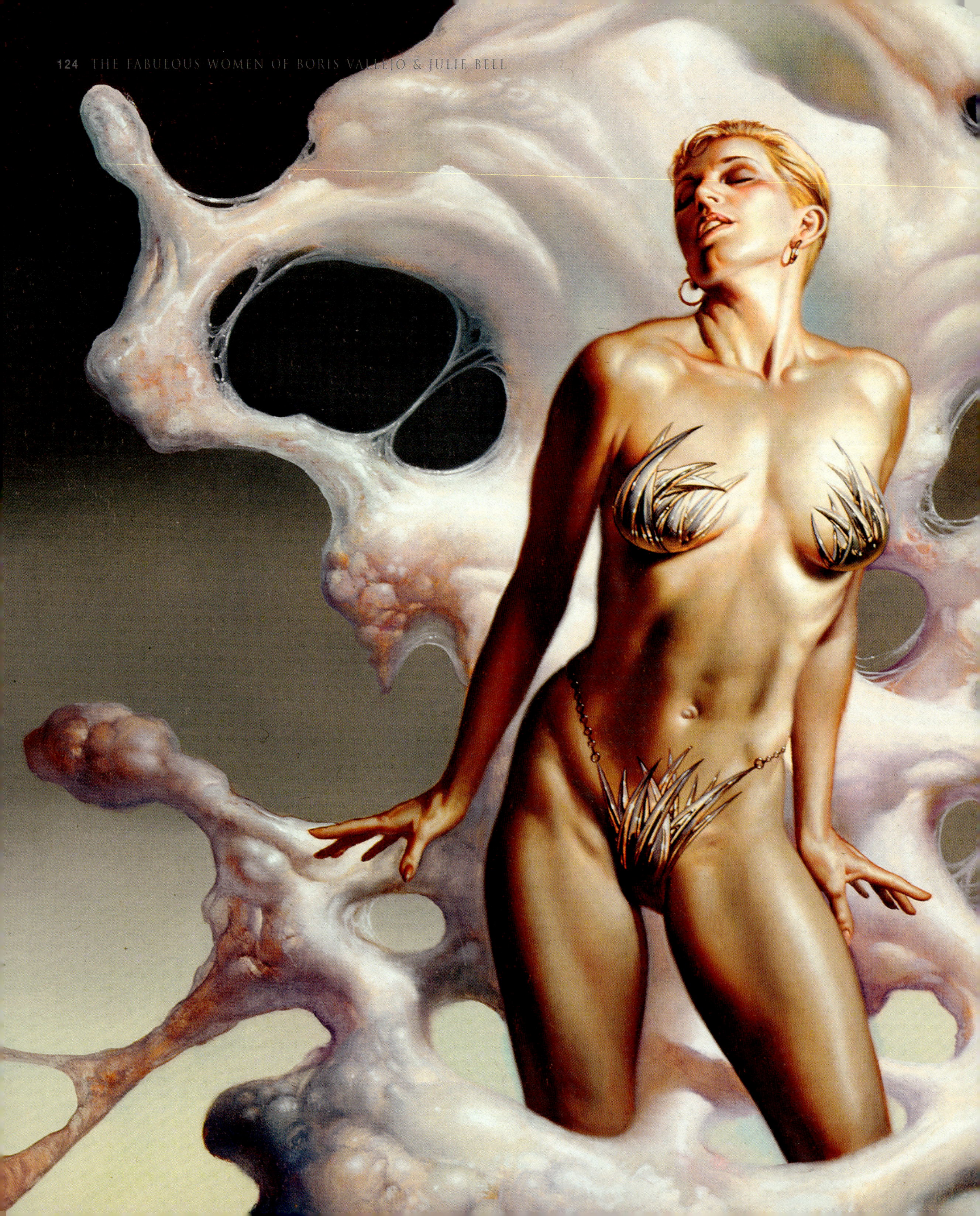

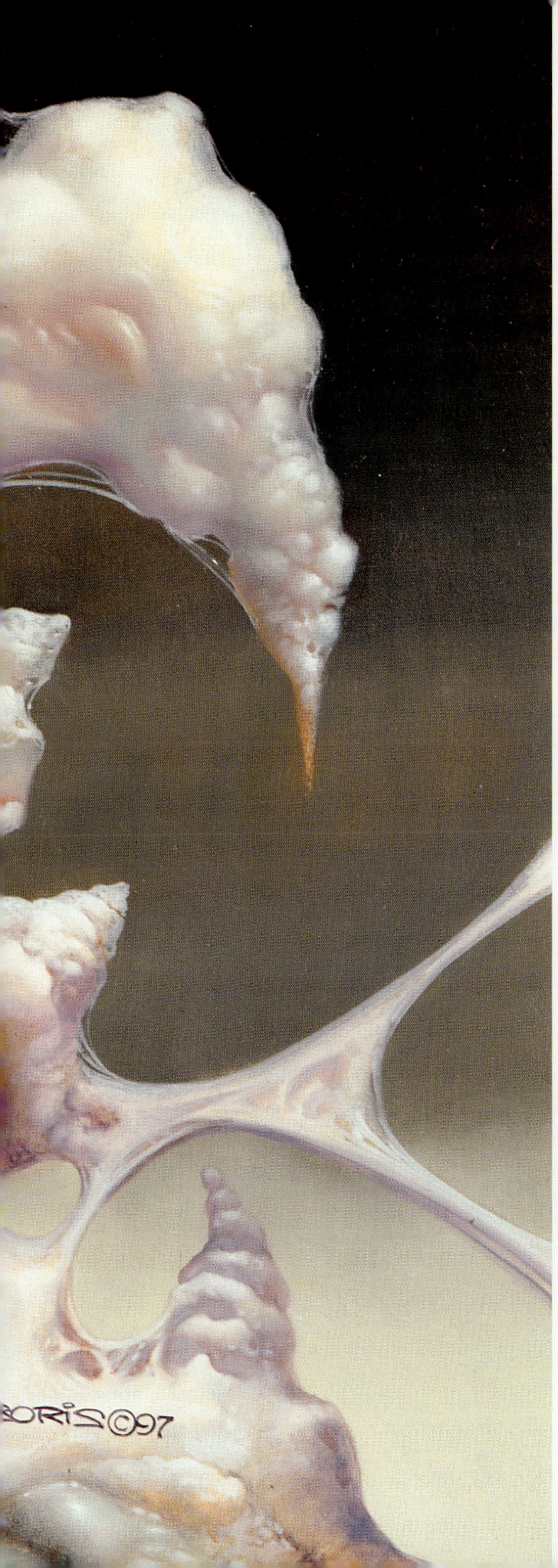

"THIS WHITE STUFF IS JUST ONE OF THOSE THINGS I ENJOY DOING. IT'S A FRAME FOR THE FIGURE, WITH A MYSTERIOUS ORIGIN. YOU CAN'T TELL IF IT'S AND ANIMAL, VEGETABLE, OR MINERAL. I JUST LET IT HAPPEN."

BORIS

◂◂ **Emerging,** Boris Vallejo, *1997, calendar*

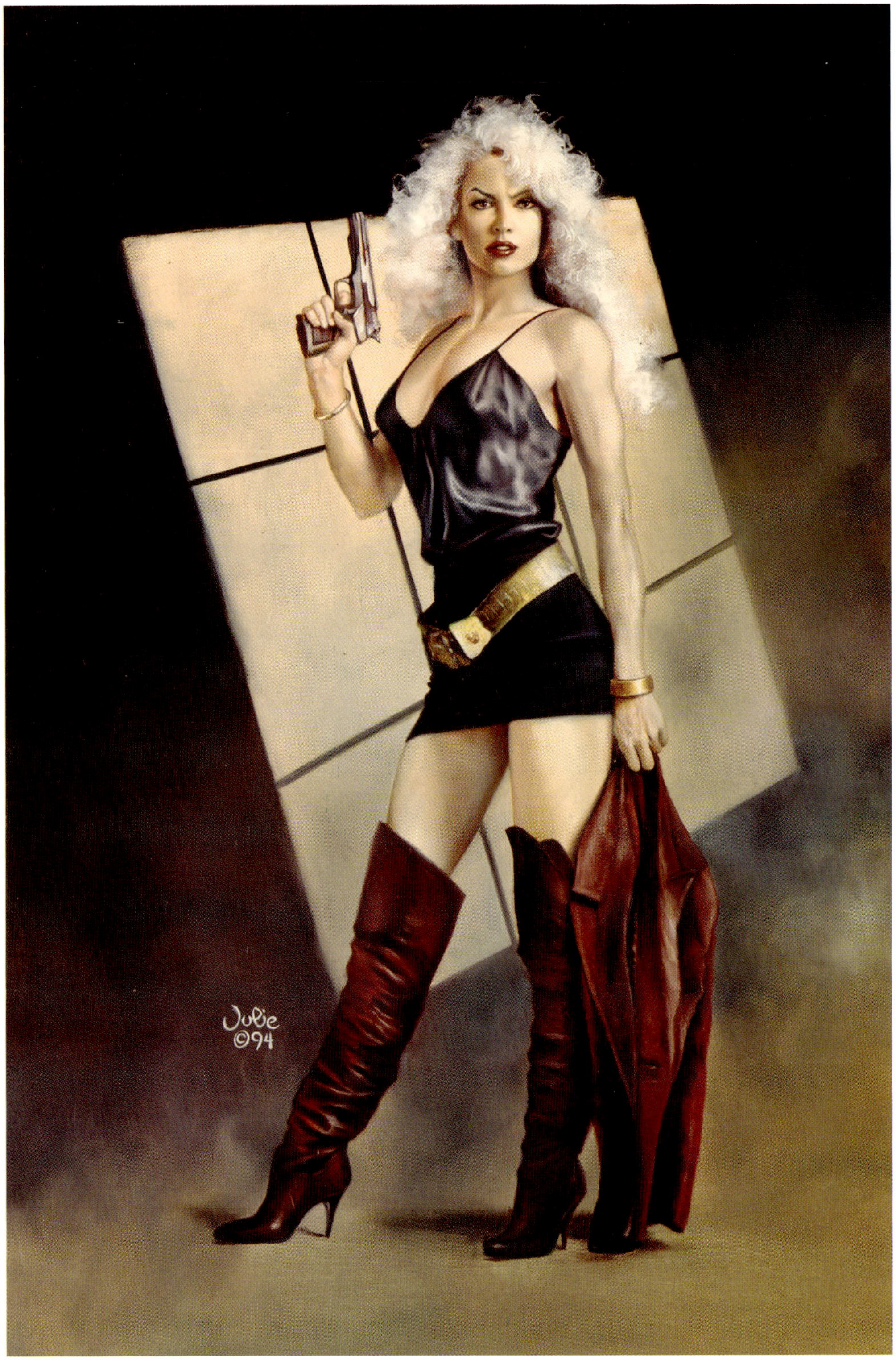

Chicago, Julie Bell, *1994, trading card*

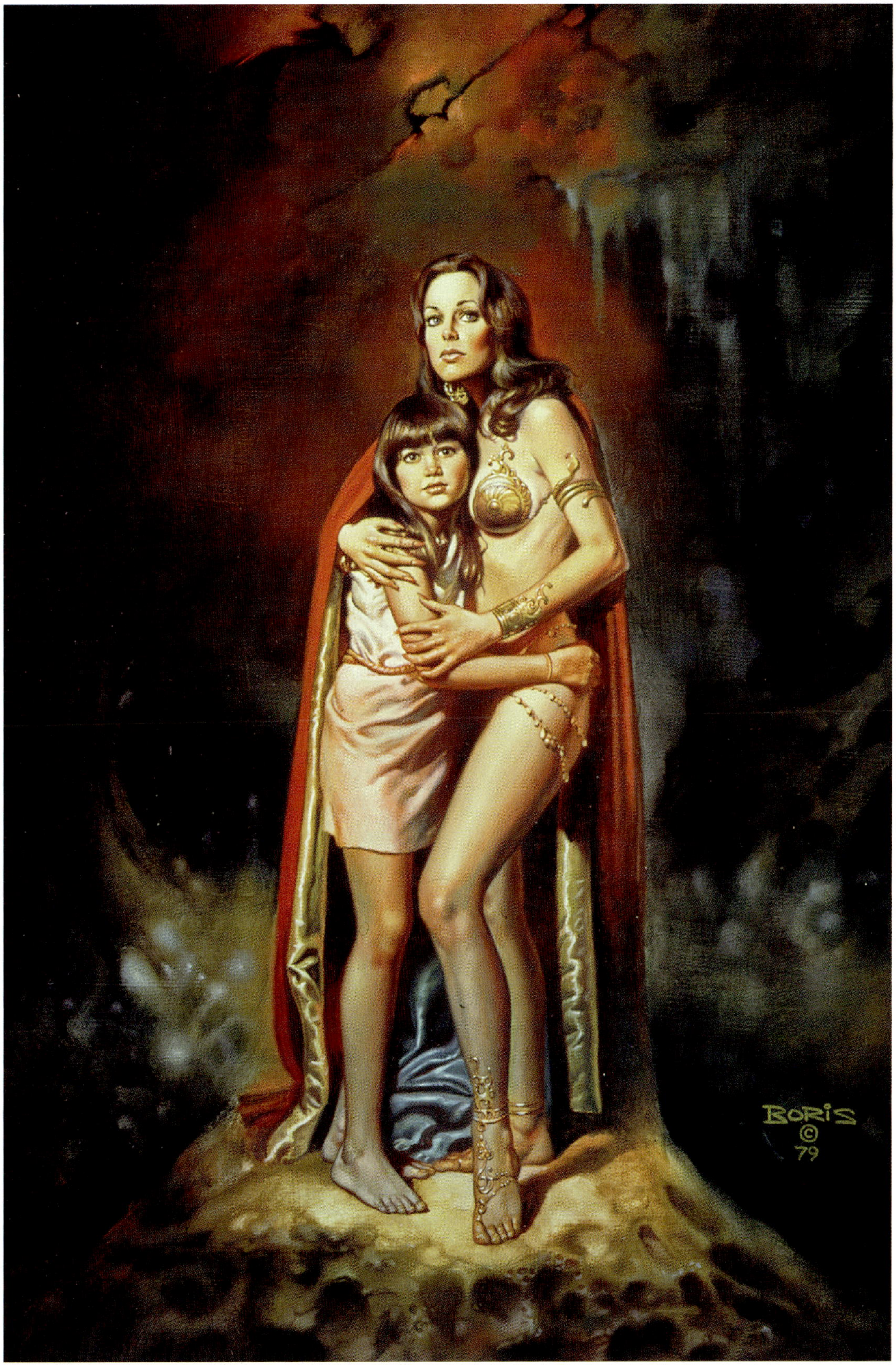

Never Fear, Boris Vallejo, *1979, book jacket*

Boris' daughter, Maya was the model for the young child in this painting done for a book cover. Maya is now a professional photographer.

INDEX OF PICTURES